D0931472

THE POET'S TRUTH

THE POET'S TRUTH

A STUDY OF THE POET IN
VIRGIL'S *GEORGICS*

CHRISTINE G. PERKELL

University of California Press
Berkeley• Los Angeles• London

University of California Press
Berkeley and Los Angeles, California

University of California Press, Ltd.
London, England

Library of Congress Cataloging-in-Publication Data

Perkell, Christine.
    The poet's truth : a study of the poet in Virgil's Georgics/
Christine Perkell.
        p.   cm.
    Bibliography: p.
    Includes index.
    ISBN 0-520-06323-6 (alk. paper)
    1. Virgil, Georgica.   2. Poets in literature.   3. Community
in literature.   I. Title.
PA6804.G4P47   1989
873'.01—dc 19   89-4782
                                                                  CIP

Printed in the United States of America

1   2   3   4   5   6   7   8   9

To my mother and the memory of my father

Contents

Acknowledgments

Now that I have worked on the *Georgics* longer than, as it is said, Virgil did, I have the great pleasure of acknowledging the help of many supportive friends and colleagues.

Professors Jonathan Goldberg, Ralph Johnson, Gary Miles, Michael Putnam, James Tatum, and Christian Wolff read versions of this manuscript, either in whole or in part, and made valuable suggestions. Above all, I wish to thank Professor Zeph Stewart. He initially interested me in the *Georgics* as a dissertation topic, and he read this study as well with his characteristic acumen. His objections have made this a less imperfect work.

Professor Richard Thomas kindly allowed me to profit from his splendid commentary on the *Georgics* while it was still in galley proofs. Gail Vernazza typed this manuscript with professionalism and good spirit. I am grateful also to Richard Holway, Mary Lamprech, and Marion Shotwell at the University of California Press for their constructive attention at every stage of review and production. Dale Sweeney helped greatly with checking references and indexing. My department and the deans at Dartmouth College allowed me time to revise this manuscript and demonstrated thereby their true collegiality, as they have in other ways throughout the years. To my husband, Marco, who has learned more about ancient science than he really needs to know, special thanks are due. My greatest and most abiding debt is expressed elsewhere.

Note on Sources and Translations

Sources are documented in full at first appearance in the notes; subsequent citations are shortened. Abbreviations of classical references follow the *Oxford Classical Dictionary;* a key to abbreviated periodical titles can be found in *L'année philologique.*

Except where noted, translations of the *Georgics* are from C. Day Lewis's translation of the poem (*The* Georgics *of Virgil* [London, 1940]). As the presence of the poet's voice is an essential concept for this study, it seemed necessary to use a poet's translation of the poem. C. Day Lewis's translation has both charm and faithfulness to the original. I have occasionally modified his verses with the more literal rendition by H. R. Fairclough in the Loeb Classical Library (London and Cambridge, Mass., 1916; reprint, 1965) or with one of my own. The Latin text is that of R. A. B. Mynors (*P. Vergili Maronis Opera* [Oxford, 1969]), although I have changed consonantal *u* to *v.*

Except where noted, translations of the *Aeneid* are by Allen Mandelbaum (New York, 1961); of Hesiod by R. M. Frazer, *The Poems of Hesiod* (Norman, Okla., 1983; reprint, 1985); and of Lucretius by Frank O. Copley, *Lucretius: "The Nature of Things"* (New York and London, 1977). Here again I chose verse translations in order to give the reader, as much as possible, a sense of the poetry of these texts.

I have, throughout, taken the liberty of modifying slightly the translations of others in order to clarify their relationship to my argument. Translations from secondary literature are mine.

Introduction

The following couplet, said to have been inscribed on Virgil's tombstone, conveys the substance of what we know about his life:

> Mantua me genuit, Calabri rapuere, tenet nunc
> Parthenope: cecini pascua, rura, duces.

> Mantua gave me birth, Calabri snatched me away,
> Naples now holds me. I sang pastures, fields,
> heroes.

This is to say that Virgil was born in Mantua, died in Brindisi, and was buried in Naples. He was the poet of the *Eclogues,* the *Georgics,* and the *Aeneid.*[1]

Born in 70 B.C. in Mantua, then part of a Roman province, he did not become a Roman citizen until his twentieth year, when all of Transpadane Gaul was admitted to citizenship. He died in 19 B.C. at Brindisi, in southern Italy, on his return from Greece in the company of Augustus. From Virgil's humble birth (*Vita Donati* 1) to his ultimate intimacy with the world's most powerful men, we may infer something of the drama of his life. He became a famous man within his own lifetime, and his poems were received immediately as classics and set for study in schools (Juv. 7.226). Virgil took much joy in time spent in Naples (Parthenope), to which he fondly alludes at the close of the *Georgics* (4.564), the only reference to himself by name in all his works. Naples, founded centuries earlier by Greeks, retained still in Virgil's day its peculiarly Greek ethos and spiritual distance from

---

1. Most scholars now reject the authenticity of the poems collected in the *Appendix Vergiliana,* once held to be compositions of the youthful Virgil. See *OCD,* s.v. "Appendix Vergiliana."

Rome, itself the one city strikingly absent from his epitaph as it never was from his poetry.

The most ancient and best *Life* of Virgil, that of the grammarian Aelius Donatus, dates from the fourth century A.D.,[2] thus long after Virgil's lifetime, and is unreliable in many respects. Its retailing of, for example, prophetic signs at Virgil's birth and its tendency to interpret incidents in Virgil's poetry as references to real events of his life suggest its credulity and naiveté. Some of its account is, nevertheless, plausible: that Virgil had his early schooling in Cremona, Milan, and then Rome; that he spent three years composing the *Eclogues,* seven the *Georgics,* and eleven the *Aeneid,* which his death prevented him from revising fully. At some point, already an accomplished young poet, he made the acquaintance of C. Asinius Pollio, then governor of Cisalpine Gaul and a powerful adherent of Antony's. To Pollio he dedicated the fourth and eighth *Eclogues.* Subsequently he became acquainted also with Maecenas, Octavian's close ally and a cultivated patron of the arts. Ultimately he came also to know Octavian himself. In the *Georgics* he addresses directly both Maecenas and Octavian (whom he calls Caesar in his poetry) with assurance and grace. He was, in his way, a peer of these powerful men, and they accorded him comfortable support for his poetry, both completed and promising.

Of the larger conditions of Virgil's life, which determined his historical and political experience and shaped his thought, we can say more. The rivalries of the first and second triumvirates, dominating the political scene of Virgil's adolescence and early adulthood, erupted in civil wars over such an extended period of time that Roman poets voiced the fear that some, perhaps fratricidal, curse had hung over Rome from its inception (e.g., G. 1.501–502; cf. 2.533). Julius Caesar crossed the Rubicon when Virgil was twenty. His triumph over Pompey was soon followed by his own assassination in 44 B.C., setting off another round of civil dissension, this time between Caesar's assassins,

2. Donatus is thought, however, to have taken much of his material from a *Life* of Virgil, now lost, by Suetonius (fl. second century A.D.). See, for example, W. A. Camps, *An Introduction to Virgil's* Aeneid (Oxford, 1969), 114.

the republicans Brutus and Cassius, and Caesar's would-be heirs, Octavian and Antony. These last engaged in wholesale proscriptions of their enemies (including Cicero), emerged triumphant from the battle of Philippi in 42 (see *G.* 1.490), and then turned to deadly rivalry with each other. An era of stability began with Antony's defeat at Actium in 31. In 29 the doors of the Temple of Janus were closed, signifying that Rome was at peace throughout the empire for the first time in over two hundred years. The year 29[3] saw publication of the *Georgics,* which Virgil is said to have read to Octavian on his triumphant return from the East, his position as the most powerful man in the Roman world unarguably secured.

One might well suppose that experience of such unstable times and bloody events would result in a deeply pessimistic vision, in fear of loss, and in anxiety for the future. David Ross admits to reading Virgil as a poet of deep pessimism, for, as he says, he cannot see how it could be otherwise.[4] Nevertheless, throughout the centuries since Virgil's death, his poems have consistently been read as affirmations of faith in Octavian and in the values and achievements of imperial Rome. Particularly the fourth and fifth *Eclogues,* the second and fourth *Georgics,* and the *Aeneid* as a whole, with its stirring prophecy by Jupiter in Book 1 and its patriotic pageant in Book 6, have been seen as powerful expressions of hope in a redeemed future under Octavian. L. P. Wilkinson, for example, wholly contrary to Ross, can speak of Virgil's "temperament, always sanguine, and his tendency to hero-worship."[5] These views of Ross and Wilkinson well exemplify the current poles of critical discussion about the nature of Virgil's work as a whole and, consequently, of the *Georgics* in particular.

3. This traditional date, though disputed, has recently been accepted as probable by Richard Thomas, ed., *Virgil:* Georgics (Cambridge, 1988), 1:1.

4. David Ross, *Virgil's Elements: Physics and Poetry in the* Georgics (Princeton, 1987), 5. It is also true, however, that people can emerge even from the most harrowing experiences, such as the Holocaust, with life-affirming sentiments. Dan Vittorio Segre, for example, concludes his turbulent *Memoirs of a Fortunate Jew: An Italian Story* (New York, 1987) with someone saying, "Don't be afraid, little soldier; life is stronger than evil" (274).

5. L. P. Wilkinson, *The* Georgics *of Virgil* (Cambridge, 1969), 38.

The controversy over Virgil's work is most familiarly epitomized in the critical history of the *Aeneid,* which may be briefly
summarized. As R. D. Williams points out, the most famous line
of the *Aeneid* during this century has been

> sunt lacrimae rerum et mentem mortalia tangunt
> *(Aen.* 1.462)

> and there are tears for passing things: here, too,
> things mortal touch the mind.

In previous periods it was

> tantae molis erat Romanam condere gentem
> *(Aen.* 1.33)

> So hard it was to found the race of Rome.[6]

The first of these verses looks to the melancholy and sense of loss
that many modern critics, especially American, see in the poem,
to the costs of victory, and to the emotional and moral failures of
Aeneas. The second points to the awesome achievement that
Rome represents, and seems to endorse the discipline and dedica-
tion that brought it about.

Clearly the critical challenge for readers of the *Aeneid* must be
to incorporate both of these verses and what they suggest about
the poem into a truer vision of what the poem does. Since Virgil
wrote both these verses, to privilege one to the exclusion of the
other is surely to falsify the poem. A valid reading of the *Aeneid,*
and of Virgil's other works, must reflect the tensions of his
composition and maintain as vitally present in mind the entire
ambiguity of the whole. A useful reading cannot focus exclusively on the light (or "optimistic") or dark (or "pessimistic")
passages. Indeed, these terms, "optimistic" and "pessimistic,"
long current in criticism of Virgil, now risk seeming facile and
irrelevant. We must move to a reading that accommodates diver-
gent experiences of the poem, for views held by cultivated readers of this or of past centuries cannot reasonably be disregarded

6. R. D. Williams, "Changing Attitudes to Virgil," in *Virgil,* ed. D. R.
Dudley (London, 1969), 134.

as wrong,[7] but must be understood in a larger, more complex and subtle vision of the poem's effects and of the poet's purposes. Certain insights of reader-response criticism, because it eschews the search for a single correct reading to the exclusion of others, can help us with the interpretive problems posed by Virgil's texts. Such criticism emphasizes a reader's progressive revision of the sense of a text over the course of a single or of many readings. Wolfgang Iser speaks of a reader's continuous attempts at "acts of constitution" from the different perspectives present in a text, pointing out that "no single textual perspective may be equated with the meaning of the whole."[8] He further observes, even more importantly, that readers conventionally assume that a text's meaning must ultimately resolve its tensions and conflicts. Readers expect "a meaning that will remove illogicalities, conflicts, and, indeed, the whole contingency of the world in the literary work."[9] Iser considers such an expectation to be particularly inappropriate to many modern texts. My contention is that it is inappropriate to Virgil's as well. Scholars' traditional assumption that Virgil must be consistent and also positive has been the greatest obstacle to a fully appreciative reading of his work. I suggest that Virgil's texts tend to ambiguity and irony, those "evasions of committed speech,"[10] and that, therefore, consistency and unity—at least as conventionally conceived—are not features of his texts. Stanley Fish has demonstrated with certain texts of Milton that, within units as small as a verse or two, two different and even opposed readings may be equally plausible. This may result from the ambiguity of a single term (as *spare* in Milton, *Sonnets* 20.13) or from conflicting claims as to where to locate closure—at verse end, for example,

7. See Thomas, 1:16, for this assumption. I think especially of Dryden, an "optimistic" reader of the poem. See R. D. Williams, "Changing Attitudes," 124–25.
8. Wolfgang Iser, *The Act of Reading: A Theory of Esthetic Response* (Baltimore, 1978), 197; see especially 107–34 ("Grasping a Text").
9. Iser, 223.
10. Barbara Herrnstein Smith, *Poetic Closure: A Study of How Poems End* (Chicago, 1968), 254.

or with the end of a phrase or other sense unit.[11] Of this latter
problem the *Georgics* provides an important example with its
famous and enigmatic verse

> labor omnia vicit
> improbus et duris urgens in rebus egestas.
>   (1.145–46)
> labor conquered all things,
> unremitting labor and need pressing in harsh circumstances.

Some readers, making closure (perhaps even unconsciously) after
vicit, interpret the verse as signifying the triumph of technology
over a hostile world: labor made all things tractable. Reading of
the following verse, with its unexpected qualification of *labor* as
improbus, compels the reader to entertain a different meaning,
even a meaning opposite from that initially envisaged. In this
second case, the verse would have the sense

> Relentless toil and pressing need dominate mortal experience.[12]

In the view of Fish, however, one need not and indeed must not
prefer one reading to another. Rather this very ambiguity and the
questions that it raises for the reader make the meaning of the
verse. One must allow unresolved tensions to stand, both within
verses and between passages. To attempt to "normalize" an ambiguous text, to exclude one sense and privilege another, is to
distort the text by ignoring its resonance and complexity.

Such views are not new to critics of the *Eclogues* or of the
Aeneid. Charles Segal, in attempting to interpret apparent con-

---

11. See Stanley E. Fish, "Literature in the Reader: Affective Stylistics," *New
Literary History* 2 (1970): 123–62, and "Interpreting the Variorum," *Critical
Inquiry* 2 (1976): 465–85. Both are reprinted in Jane P. Tompkins, ed., *Reader-
Response Criticism from Formalism to Post-Structuralism* (Baltimore and Lon-
don, 1980). (Milton *Sonnets* 20.13 reads

> He who of those delights can judge, and spare
> To interpose them oft, is not unwise.)

12. For a fuller treatment of these verses see C. G. Perkell, "Vergil's Theodicy
Reconsidered," in *Vergil at 2000: Commemorative Essays on the Poet and His
Influence,* ed. John D. Bernard (New York, 1986), 67–83.

tradictions in the *Eclogues,* wrote of "tensions . . . unresolved," "suspension amid contraries,"[13] "suspension" in which
"antitheses" are framed.[14] All these phrases reflect the existence
of unresolved oppositions within a single text. More recently
Paul Alpers, in his study of the *Eclogues,* makes much of the
concept of "suspension," deeming the very essence of pastoral to
be "that it holds potential conflicts in suspension."[15] Again, the
poet's mode is "to render and acknowledge truths and relations,
but not to claim the power to resolve them."[16]

The introductory chapter of W. R. Johnson's study of the
Aeneid is a particularly fine demonstration of the degree to which
the *Aeneid* is an "uncommitted meditation on man's nature and
on the possibilities and impossibilities of his fate."[17] He would
avoid the error of imposing a "false and reductive unity" on the
poem or of applying "monochromatic solutions" to it.[18] There is,
in fact, no "solution" to the *Aeneid,* for there is no resolution of
its conflicts. The *Aeneid* is not, in that sense, a unity. Much the
same, I would argue, can be said of the *Georgics.*

The *Georgics* is, in the first instance, the georgic and didactic
poem that it declares itself to be:

> Quid faciat laetas segetes, quo sidere terram
> vertere, Maecenas, ulmisque adiungere vites
> conveniat, quae cura boum, qui cultus habendo
> sit pecori, apibus quanta experientia parcis,
> hinc canere incipiam.
>
> (1.1–5)

13. C. P. Segal, *"Tamen Cantabitis, Arcades:* Exile and Arcadia in *Eclogues*
One and Nine," *Arion* 4 (1965): 243–44.
14. C. P. Segal, "Vergil's *Caelatum Opus:* An Interpretation of the Third
Eclogue," AJP 88 (1967): 302. For the comparable phrase "meaningful ambiguity," aiming at the same tension, see C. P. Segal, "Ancient Texts and Modern
Literary Criticism," *Arethusa* 1 (1968): 9; for "implicit comment" see Kenneth
Quinn, *Virgil's* Aeneid: *A Critical Description* (London, 1968), 339–49.
15. Paul Alpers, *The Singer of the* Eclogues: *A Study of Virgilian Pastoral*
(Berkeley, 1979), 65. For his main exposition of "suspension" see 96ff; for some
references to Segal and others see 97nn. 4, 5, and 6.
16. Alpers, 245.
17. W. R. Johnson, *Darkness Visible: A Study of Virgil's* Aeneid (Berkeley,
1976), 22; see 1–22 for the introductory chapter.
18. Johnson, 19 and 18; see also 158–59 n. 17.

> What makes the cornfields joyous, under what constellation
> It's best to turn the soil, Maecenas, and join the vine
> To the elm; what care suits cattle, and what tending suits flocks,
> What knowledge you need for keeping frugal bees—all this
> I'll now begin to sing.

It does deal with such topics as the planting of grain and the care of vines, livestock, and bees. It deals with much else as well, touching on a variety of issues critical to contemporary Rome. Among these are the character of Iron Age civilization and its technology, Italian patriotism and war, passion and death, religion and the gods. It has, therefore, long been recognized that the poem is not truly an agricultural manual, for which purpose it would, in fact, be both incomplete and inaccurate,[19] but a meditation on urgent political and moral questions.[20]

The *Georgics,* composed probably between 36 and 29, takes its title from a poem (now mostly lost) by Nicander (second century B.C.). For its technical passages the *Historia plantarum* of Theophrastus (370–288 B.C.) and the *De re rustica* of Varro (116–26 B.C.) are the primary sources; but other technical texts (of which there were many) used by Virgil include, for example, Aristotle's *Historia animalium,* the *Phaenomena* of the poet/ metaphrast Aratus (315–240 B.C.), and the *Hermes* of Eratosthenes (275–194 B.C.).[21] In its treatment of moral, ethical, and political issues, the poem finds its closest parallels in the *Works and Days* of Hesiod (seventh century B.C.), like the *Georgics* largely agronomic in focus, and in the *De rerum natura* of Lucretius (94–55? B.C.), an exposition of the atomic theory of matter and a parallel exhortation to the values of Epicurean philosophy, alone suited, as Lucretius represents it, to spiritual peace in a morally random, material world.

---

19. Sen. *Ep.* 86.15: "nec agricolas docere voluit." See Wilkinson, Georgics, 339 n. 8, for bibliography on Pliny's objections to Virgil's errors and omissions.

20. See, for example, George E. Duckworth, "Vergil's *Georgics* and the Laudes Galli," *AJP* 80 (1959): 229: "The poem is thus an epic of man's relation to the world about him and presents a comprehensive picture of nature, country life, Italy, Octavian, and Roman destiny."

21. For fuller treatments of Virgil's sources, both technical and literary, see Wilkinson, Georgics, 56–68, 223–69; and Thomas, 1:1–11.

The *Works and Days* shares substantive concerns with the *Georgics*. In this regard one might adduce Hesiod's sense of man as fallen, as separated from the gods, as well as his anxious reflections on the problematic behavior of Zeus, on the limitations of human knowledge of the true and the false and of the good and the evil, and on the potential of poetry for solace and clarification. The question of the justice of Zeus or the moral quality of human experience and the ambivalence with which it is treated is common to the *Works and Days* and the *Georgics*. While Hesiod sometimes asserts that Zeus is just (e.g., 239, 247, 281) or sometimes merely hopes that he is so (268, 273), the reality and real impetus of his poem is that brothers quarrel and judges take bribes (37–39; cf. 184). Zeus gave men justice, since men do not eat each other as fish and beasts do (276–79). The implication of this observation is that surely then Zeus himself will treat men with justice. Why should men be led to conceive of justice if there is none? Yet Zeus is inscrutable (483–84), and the question of his justice is ultimately unresolved in the poem. The fable of the hawk and the nightingale (202–12), unconcluded as it is, reflects this lack of resolution. The hawk speaks for power and injustice; the nightingale, powerless in the world, does not respond. The conclusion to their encounter seems—yet not conclusively—foregone and unpalatable. Another example of a motif that is central to both poems and equally unresolved is that of moral and cognitive ambiguity. To discriminate clearly between good and evil is not possible in Hesiod's world because evils are either invisible (Zeus gave them no voice 104) or delusive (Pandora, apparently good, is truly evil 57–58). Yet even here the ambiguity intensifies as Pandora/woman, bringer of evil, brings also good (62–89, 702). The enigmatic, haunting incident of Pandora letting loose evils from the jar, yet just retaining hope within it, suggests in another way the ambiguity of the human condition (94–99). In our harrowing condition of being mortal and knowing it, we both have and have not hope, which either is or is not an evil, and makes it possible to live with the knowledge of death. In sum, we live an ambiguous existence, unable to discriminate between good and evil, true and false, unable to know the larger circumstances—Zeus' purposes—that determine our lives. Of these several perceptions of the ambiguities of human life there are correlates in Virgil's text.[22]

Parallels and coincidences between Virgil and Lucretius have been amply demonstrated.[23] Beyond imitation of Lucretius' didactic phrases or similarities between particular passages, however, we can see Virgil deeply engaged with issues treated by Lucretius throughout the *De rerum natura*. Here one might adduce such questions as the possibility and nature of truth, the relative value of science and poetry in this regard, the moral and spiritual potential of human life. From the seductive and patriotic, if ultimately delusive, opening of this poem to its concluding, unlovely truth of the indifference of the whole to human concerns and of the irrelevance of religion and convention to spiritual peace, Lucretius seeks to lead his reader to truth through science, that is, through knowledge and understanding of the physical universe. Virgil explores the possibility of truth in science in the *Georgics* but, as I will argue, finds his deepest truths in poetry.

Lucretius seeks to answer through science the most profound spiritual questions. However, even in Lucretius' poem, a major text in the long dispute between science and poetry, we see that poetry is a necessary completion or suppletion of *ratio,* which is seen to leave much unexplained—attachment to life or to one's own; the swerve of atoms; the power of Venus (the only indisputably divine power, as set forth in Books 1 and 4); and Lucretius' own personal vitality, commitment, and awe. In the final scene of the poem an event of historical truth, the plague at Athens, is transmuted through poetry into something resembling a mythic image. Extracted from history and the contingent conditions of

22. On the other hand, however, Hesiod's notion that the just city will prosper (225ff.) and in a sense recreate the Golden Age is, it will be argued, implicitly rejected in the *Georgics*. In addition, Hesiod's emphasis on prosperity and his tendency to represent various aspects of good and evil in terms of sexual polarities between male and female are absent from the *Georgics*.

23. In (among others) W. A. Merrill, "Parallels and Coincidences in Lucretius and Virgil," *University of California Publications in Classical Philology* 3 (1918): 137–264; and Herta Klepl, *Lucrez und Virgil in ihren Lehrgedichten: vergleichende Interpretationen* (Darmstadt, 1967).

war, the plague assumes the significance of a timeless symbol of death and suggests perhaps a vision of the end of the world.[24] Lucretius renders the event less historically real in order to make it more significantly, deeply true. Virgil exploits a comparable paradoxical relationship between the real and the true at the conclusion of the *Georgics,* as I will attempt to demonstrate. Therefore, in Lucretius as well as in Virgil, all truth is not in science. The symbolic language of poetry can go beyond science in intuiting and expressing the unseen.

In its formal perfection, that is to say, in the finish of its verses, in its attention to structure and balance, in its dense and polemical allusiveness, in its obscure and wide learning, the *Georgics* shows its dependence on Alexandrian esthetics. Richard Thomas discerns the influence of the Alexandrian poet Callimachus (c. 300–240 B.C.) in the division of the poem into four books, in the programmatic openings of *Georgics* 1 and 3, as well as in various more subtle references throughout the text. It is difficult to assess with real certainty the influence of Callimachus and of such Latin Neoteric poets as Cinna, Calvus, and Gallus on the *Georgics,* as their work is either lost or fragmentary. Even the Aristaeus-Orpheus narrative of *Georgic* 4, which is clearly influenced by the sixty-fourth poem of Catullus (84–54 B.C.), itself an exemplar of the epyllion favored by Neoterics, reflects as well certain features of the *Odyssey* of Homer (seventh century B.C.). Certainly, Virgil had read widely in both Greek and Latin, in both prose and poetry, and his poem bears witness to this learning. Yet it would seem, despite the loss to us of many texts that surely influenced the composition of the *Georgics,* that in its formal perfection, in its particular fusion of science and poetry, in its moral urgency and haunting pathos, it has no real predecessor. In form Alexandrian, in substance intensely Roman and contemporary, the *Georgics* is a unique achievement.

---

24. Leo Strauss, *Liberalism Ancient and Modern* (New York and London, 1968), 81. Such an interpretation seems preferable to C. R. Bailey's assumption (*Titi Lucreti Cari* De Rerum Natura *Libri Sex,* 3 vols. [Oxford, 1947; reissued, 1986] ad loc.) that Lucretius is mistranslating Thucydides.

The *Georgics,* as the poet tells us, is a difficult and original poem:[25]

> cetera quae vacuas tenuissent carmine mentes,
> omnia iam vulgata: quis aut Eurysthea durum
> aut inlaudati nescit Busiridis aras?
>
> (3.3−5)
>
> Other themes, which might have pleasured idle minds
> Are hackneyed, all of them: who does not know of cruel
> Eurystheus and the awful altar Busiris built?

The poet disdains idle minds (*vacuas mentes*) and the obvious and familiar (*omnia iam vulgata*). We cannot, consequently, be surprised by the interpretive problems that this challenging and elusive poem has always posed for readers. The variety of critical responses that the poem has occasioned, so disparate as to be termed contradictory, illuminates precisely its points of ambiguity and discrepancy. These instances of ambiguity or discrepancy, which exist both between different passages as well as within individual passages, characterize the poet's procedure in the *Georgics* and consequently pose problems of method and of genre.

In the poem's opening verses the poet states that the intention of his poem is georgic and didactic, but we have suggested that the poem deals most significantly with moral and political questions central to Roman—and, indeed, much of modern—life. There is not, however, critical consensus of even the most general sort concerning the poet's attitude in the poem towards such fundamental issues as the political future of Rome, the role of Caesar therein, the nature of divinity—in sum, the moral quality and potential of human experience. Among the many passages that could be cited as sources of critical controversy we may consider the climax of the poem, the *bougonia,* which tells of the sacrifice of a calf to generate a swarm of bees. This episode has

---

25. The vexed state of the question of whether the poetic temple projected in 3.13−36 refers to the *Georgics* itself or to the *Aeneid* need not prevent us from seeing that the poet is rejecting material that he deems trite, surely in the case of the *Georgics,* as well as in whatever future endeavors he may have envisioned at this time. See Wilkinson, Georgics, 323−24; and Thomas ad loc.

been seen by most critics as a miraculous rebirth or resurrection, which resolves the tensions of the poem and portends a positive future.[26] Others have argued that this image and its accompanying narrative of Aristaeus and Orpheus speak as powerfully of death and irreparable loss as they do of resolution or resurrection.[27] Whether, then, the poem overall expresses a comic or a tragic vision of life is an unresolved issue. Critical disagreement on such central questions suggests that the poem's ambiguity is pervasive and deep.

Since E. Burck's important work in 1929 it has been generally agreed that the poem is an "organic whole."[28] Burck's particular interest was to establish that the poem's mythological "digressions," as they were termed, were not in fact digressive but were functionally related to the text, giving enhanced meaning to the didactic passages that they introduced. The larger critical assumption was that the poem had a transcendent unity subserved by all its parts, a coherence that readers could ultimately and correctly discern.

This view constituted a substantive advance over the views of previous scholars who had little vision of the poem as a composition. The controlling artistic principle was felt to be *variatio,* that is, alternation between light and dark, or, more accurately, between tedium and relief.[29] The mythological digressions and

26. See, for example, J. Perret, *Virgile* (Paris, 1965), 86; F. Klingner, *Virgil: Bucolica, Georgica, Aeneis* (Zurich, 1967), 194; Brooks Otis, *Virgil: A Study in Civilized Poetry* (Oxford, 1964), 154–55; Adam Parry, "The Idea of Art in Virgil's Georgics," *Arethusa* 5 (1972): 46.

27. M. C. J. Putnam, *Virgil's Poem of the Earth: Studies in the Georgics* (Princeton, 1979), and Gary B. Miles, *Virgil's Georgics: A New Interpretation* (Berkeley, 1980), having paid insistent attention to undertone and ambiguity, have a more muted reading of the poem's conclusion than Otis and Klingner. While they, unlike A. J. Boyle, "*In Medio Caesar:* Paradox and Politics in Virgil's *Georgics*" *Ramus* 8 (1979): 77, do not see the conclusion of the poem as a tragedy, they nevertheless perceive in it overall something more melancholy and reflective than the morally edifying and patriotic tract that it is often taken to be. Cf. Jasper Griffin, "The Fourth *Georgic*, Virgil, and Rome," *G&R* 26 (1979): 71, 73; C. G. Perkell, "A Reading of Virgil's Fourth *Georgic,*" *Phoenix* 32 (1978): 211–21; Ross, *Virgil's Elements,* 215–18; and Thomas, 1:21–24.

28. E. Burck, "Die Komposition von Vergils *Georgica,*" *Hermes* 64 (1929): 280.

29. See Wilkinson, Georgics, 72, on *variatio (poikilia)*; and Perret, 66, on tedium and relief.

such set pieces as the so-called praises of Italy and praises of country life were extracted from the poem's larger context and then interpreted as uncomplicated endorsements of Augustan values or as exhortations to (urban, sophisticated) Romans to return to the farm to live with rural simplicity and such traditional Roman values as austerity, discipline, and patriotic self-sacrifice. "In the *Georgics* men responded easily to the underlying moral intention, the ethical precepts, the great sermon on rural and natural virtues, the noble patriotic passages interspersed with the interpretation of nature herself."[30]

Burck's conviction of the poem's unity made possible a more synthetic and substantive evaluation of the *Georgics*. K. Büchner,[31] F. Klingner, and Brooks Otis all study the poem's symbolism, its relation to Roman themes, and the interrelationship of various parts with the whole. Klingner's reading of the poem is deeply sentimental, while Otis's is quite Christian in its attribution of great significance to the image (as he sees it) of resurrection at the poem's conclusion. (Wilkinson's book is different from these in that it is essentially not an interpretive study, but rather a most useful collection of information prerequisite to interpretation.) All these scholars seek unity in the poem despite the fact that they characterize Books 1 and 3 as pessimistic and Books 2 and 4 as optimistic. That is, despite their perception of significant discrepancies in tone between books, they nevertheless see the poet as resolving the tensions of the poem in Book 4, with the miraculous rebirth of the bees portending a positive future and reflecting Virgil's faith in the political and moral renewal of Rome under Octavian.

Within the past ten years, the major works of M. C. J. Putnam and Gary B. Miles changed the tone and altered the direction of discussion of the *Georgics*. Both are what I would term "revisionist" readings of the poem, for both are especially sensitive to ambiguity and to tragic undertone; both apprehend the poem's sympathy for victims, its sensitivity to loss and to the cost of

---

30. R. D. Williams, "Changing Attitudes," 128.
31. K. Büchner, "P. Vergilius Maro," *RE* 8 A 1 (1955): 1021–1264; *RE* 8 A 2 (1958): 1265–1486.

survival. Both do, however, see Aristaeus as the hero of the poem, as a figure who learns, who comes ultimately into a right relation with man and nature, and who in some sense embodies a resolution to the poem's conflicts.[32]

The two most recent major works on the poem are the study by David Ross (*Virgil's Elements: Physics and Poetry in the Georgics* [Princeton, 1987]) and the commentary by Richard Thomas (Cambridge, 1988). These studies, in their decidedly pessimistic readings, mark a complete reversal in interpretation of the poem from antiquity to the present, thus giving the lie to R. D. Williams's assertion that one must take the poem in eighteenth-century terms or not at all.[33]

Ross's book, a contribution in its gathering of scientific sources,[34] proposes to interpret the poem on the basis of the poet's perception (as he sees it) of the world as composed of opposing elements (earth, air, fire, and water) and of opposing qualities (hot, cold, wet, and dry). It is the achievement of science, of agriculture specifically, to resolve elemental oppositions in nature and thus to create civilization. The *pinguis arista,* or "ripe ear of corn," in its synthesis of moist and dry, exemplifies man's skill.[35] Although Ross sees oppositions between elements as capable of resolution, he nevertheless does not see resolution in the poem as a whole, but rather asserts a thoroughgoing pessimism. The brutality, as he reads it, of science and the

32. For bibliographical notes in which each discusses his predecessors and places his work in the context of scholarship on the *Georgics,* see Putnam, *Poem of the Earth,* IX–XI; and Miles, 59–63 and 295–97.

Putnam has the concept of "georgic artist," thus conflating two categories that I see as importantly opposed.

While Gian Biagio Conte, *The Rhetoric of Imitation: Genre and Poetic Memory in Virgil and Other Latin Poets,* ed. Charles Segal (Ithaca, N.Y., 1986), sees complexity, contradiction, and subversion of epic ideology in the *Aeneid,* he has a resolved and optimistic reading of the *Georgics,* wherein Aristaeus is the hero and model of the perfect farmer, whose "existential choice" bears witness to the possibility of happiness based on the "labor of a life governed by simple, sacred rules" (138–40). He neglects to consider many of the poem's significant contradictions, among them the farmer's ignorance of his happiness.

33. R. D. Williams, "Changing Attitudes," 128.

34. Wilkinson is very good on technical sources, although different in focus from Ross. See note 21 above.

35. Ross, *Virgil's Elements,* 37–38.

inevitable mortality of all creatures result for him in a tragic view of the whole. He concludes that "knowledge, science, the *artes:* all are won by violence and lead inevitably to death."[36]

Because it will become the standard reference text for students of the poem, Thomas's commentary will surely have a profound impact on conventional views of the *Georgics*. His is a careful and sensitive work, critically audacious, polemical in many ways (thus rather resembling the Alexandrian poets in whom he is so interested). Thomas downplays the influence of Hesiod and Lucretius on the poem. More than any other commentator he attributes the poem's artistic care, density, learning, and allusiveness not only to Alexandrian esthetics in general but above all to the work of Callimachus in particular. This influence he discerns in major programmatic passages, like the openings of Books 1 and 3, as well as in other discrete references.

In interpretive matters Thomas is negative or pessimistic, although perhaps not quite so negative as Ross. In his reading he sees success and failure as the central motifs of the poem, success being always qualified and failure inevitable. In support of this reading he adduces not only the explicitly pessimistic passages of Books 1 and 3, but dwells attentively on the "subtle denigration" of Roman values (to use his phrase broadly) in the putatively positive passages of Books 2 and 4. His concluding observation is of the "complexity, ambivalence, and ultimate darkness of the Virgilian world view."[37] While, then, much previous criticism entirely dismisses the dark side of the poem, Ross and Thomas (despite the latter's reference to "ambivalence") seem to focus wholly on it.

I propose that we need to move towards a more balanced, inclusive view of the poem, not because balance is inherently admirable or virtuous but because, as I believe, it is truer to the poem and, not incidentally, to life. As life has joy and grief, so this poem reflects the real tensions of most human experience. The concept of suspension (discussed above in its relation to criticism of the *Eclogues* and *Aeneid*), the acknowledgment of

36. Ross, *Virgil's Elements*, 233.
37. Thomas, 1:24. For "subtle denigration" see 20.

unresolved and, perhaps, unresolvable oppositions or tensions within a text, suggests, I argue, an interpretive strategy for reading the *Georgics* as well, since the poem will not ultimately sustain a single interpretation (e.g., optimistic or pessimistic) without complexity or ambiguity.[38] The concept of tension or suspension allows us to see in the *Georgics'* central and unresolved oppositions not just inconsistencies to be normalized or problems to be overcome, but rather an expression or reflection of the poem's deepest vision of the nature of experience. In Plato's *Symposium* (187A) Eryximachus alludes to Heraclitus' description of "a unity which agrees with itself by being at variance, as in the stringing of a bow or a lyre."[39] This image of the tense balance of opposing forces in a strung bow well illustrates the dynamics of the *Georgics* as I see them.

It is the presumption of this study, then, that the *Georgics* is a deliberately ambiguous poem. By making opposing views present in dynamic tension the poet establishes poles of debate and engages readers' imagination and critical thoughtfulness (not *vacuas mentes*) in the issues of the poem. This ambiguity, which leads ultimately to greater awareness of questions that the text centrally and problematically poses, is, I suggest, the poet's characteristic mode in this poem. We can, therefore, say that the ambiguities that readers have always recognized are not problems to be solved, but rather may be perceived as the poem's deepest meaning.

The fact of the poem's ambiguity, of its leaving the reader in a state of suspension between different perspectives, leads us into the question of the poem's genre. As was indicated above, this poem cannot be described adequately as didactic, most obviously because of its incompleteness and inaccuracy in the treatment of agricultural issues. No less important to note, however, is that truly didactic poetry is not, like the *Georgics,* characterized by

38. On unresolved contradictions and dissonances in the *Georgics* see C. P. Segal, "Orpheus and the Fourth *Georgic:* Vergil on Nature and Civilization," *AJP* 87 (1966): 321; Griffin, "Fourth *Georgic,*" 69; and A. J. Boyle's introduction to *Ramus Essays on the* Georgics (*Ramus* 8 [1979]: 4–5).

39. W. Hamilton, trans., *Plato: The* Symposium (Harmondsworth and New York, 1951; reprint, 1974).

ambiguity.[40] Didactic writing requires a reliable narrator, that is, a text in which the response of the reader and the view of the narrator are consistently congruent. At the opening of the *Georgics* the poet states his georgic and didactic purpose with such elegance and grace as to suggest competence and confidence and, hence, to invite the reader's trust. The poem modulates rapidly, however, into an acknowledgment of an order of problems other than georgic, namely, political, religious, philosophical, moral— questions for which the poet claims no answers. For example, political and religious questions are raised in 1.24–39, in which the poet reveals that he is ignorant of the nature of Caesar's future sphere of power, of what kind of a god he will be. In this way the poet represents himself as an unreliable guide for questions that his text raises. As another example, the poem concludes with a myth (that of Aristaeus, Orpheus, and *bougonia*).[41] By concluding with a myth the poem exceeds the bounds of strictly didactic writing, thus calling into question the premises of the genre (i.e., the value and possibility of the materially knowable) and even the stability of the knowable world that the genre implies. By concluding with this particular myth the poet privileges metaphysical and moral questions that agricultural *praecepta,* or precepts, do not address. Through incompleteness, therefore, through inaccuracy, ambiguity, and discrepancy, through the ultimate privileging of mystery and divine revelation over experiment and practice, the poem shows itself to be other than typically didactic.

In the image of *bougonia* that concludes the poem are embodied, it will be argued, such unresolvable oppositions in Roman society as humane value vs. material progress, art vs. profit, myth vs. *praeceptum,* beauty vs. power. This representation of unresolvable oppositions is a feature of the genre of tragedy more

40. Iser, 189.
41. I term *bougonia* "myth" because it is literally false, that is, without georgic truth, yet metaphorically true and significant. Klingner, *Virgil,* 324, observes that *bougonia* had never been given such a climactic position in other didactic works. Cf. G. E. R. Lloyd, *The Revolutions of Wisdom: Studies in the Claims and Practice of Ancient Greek Science* (Berkeley, 1987), 5: "The intelligibility provided by myth is metaphorical, both in the sense that it is of the nature of metaphor and in the sense that it is a qualified intelligibility."

than of the genre of didactic poetry, for it is tragedy that finds beauty and value in the perfect statement of what in real life is intolerable conflict. Tragedy makes exalting the revelation of certain dilemmas as universal, inevitable, and unresolvable.[42] The *Georgics*, then, moves from an explicit opening statement of knowing to an implicit closing statement of not knowing. It moves from didactic, which presumes to know, to tragic, which does not.[43]

The guiding presumption of this study, then, is that the purpose of the poem is not to propagandize in favor of Octavian's political reforms or to prescribe directly to readers remedies for political, social, or moral problems; rather it is to "enlarge the reader's sensibility,"[44] the poet having no real intention or hope of changing what he depicts as eternal relations between man and nature, man and man.[45] In support of this contention, we may note the impotence of the poets in this poem. Orpheus' beautiful song is ultimately useless in achieving his goal; the *Georgic* poet acknowledges his lack of real power in the world (4.559–66).

The subject of this study, as its title indicates, is the figure of the speaker in the poem, whom I call the *Georgic* poet, and his

42. This formulation of the nature of tragedy is taken from the discussion by James M. Redfield, *Nature and Culture in the* Iliad: *The Tragedy of Hektor* (Chicago, 1975), 219ff. Jean Cocteau prefaces his *Orphée* similarly:

> Qu'il est laid le bonheur qu'on veut
> Qu'il est beau le malheur qu'on a.

43. Cf. Stanley Cavell, " 'Who does the wolf love?': *Coriolanus* and the Interpretations of Politics," in *Shakespeare and the Question of Theory*, ed., P. Parker and G. Hartman (New York, 1985), 245: "taking tragedy as an epistemological problem, a refusal to know or to be known, an avoidance of acknowledgment, an expression (or imitation) of skepticism."

44. The phrase is taken from E. R. Dodds, "On Misunderstanding the *Oedipus Rex*," *G&R* 13 (1966): 49; (Dodd's article is reprinted in Michael J. O'Brien, ed., *Twentieth Century Views of* Oedipus Rex [Englewood Cliffs, N.J., 1968], 17–29).

45. William Empson, *Some Versions of Pastoral* (London, 1935; reprint, New York, 1974), 3, concludes, in fact, that the "dreamy, impersonal, universal melancholy [of the *Aeneid*] was a calculated support for Augustus." Similarly he notes that Gray's *Elegy* has "latent political" content, for it represents the British class system as "pathetic" and "inevitable," thus putting the reader "into a mood in which one would not try to alter it" (4).

characteristic vision and values. My approach differs from the most recent major works of Putnam and Miles (and of Otis and Klingner, for example, before them) in not being a book-by-book treatment of the poem. I have chosen rather the single focus of the poet, a subject that has the interest of spanning all four books of the poem and of being central to it, yet not altogether on its surface. My thesis, briefly, is that the poet, like the farmer (the normative figure of a georgic poem), is an Iron Age figure, flawed in his relation to other men and to nature. While the farmer is menaced by nature and the city, the poet is menaced by passion and irrelevance. He has a particular sensibility, distinct from the farmer's, that inclines him to pity (1.41) and to a sense of mission to the Roman community (2.176). While the farmer seeks to restore Golden Age plenty through his labor, the poet seeks to restore Golden Age community through pity. Pity, according to Aristotle, comes from the sense of being liable to suffer the same evil as another.[46] It requires, therefore, identification with the experience of the other and thus generates a moral community, what Pietro Pucci calls a "community of pain."[47] Again, according to Aristotle, only the weak and the wise pity.[48] The poet appeals to Caesar, as if he were a god, to pity the farmers (1.41). As a superior being he cannot pity through weakness but only, if at all, through wisdom. The poem as a whole aims to make its readers feel pity for loss and hence to identify with the weak and to be, in this sense, wise. Caesar and all responsive readers (evidently not those with *vacuas mentes*) will come to pity initially through a sense of superior wisdom but ultimately through a sensed community of the vulnerability and weakness of all human enterprise. Thus the social disparities implicit in the poem's opening are transcended through pity into a moral community that recalls the poet's Golden Age (1.125–28). This hu-

46. Arist. *Rh.* 2.8.2, cited by Pietro Pucci, *The Violence of Pity in Euripides' Medea* (Ithaca, N.Y., 1980), 170.

47. For "community of pain" see Pucci, *Violence of Pity,* 24.

48. Arist. *Rh.* 2.8.3. Those likely to feel pity are "those who have already suffered and escaped evil, old men, because of wisdom and experience, the weak and those who are too timid and the educated" (cited and translated by Pucci, *Violence of Pity,* 231 n. 11).

manizing pity is not pity for the self, such as Aristaeus and Orpheus experience, but pity for the other, which requires identification and thus results in felt community. This lesson of pity, wherein the poet manipulates the reader's sympathy and elicits sorrow for loss, is the poet's mission in the poem.

The subject of chapter 2 is the poet's various representations of the Golden Age, here termed the poet's "vision." Virgil's Golden Age has a quality of community between man and nature and man and man. I argue that it is the poet's special mission to preserve the humane value of pity, thereby creating a moral community. Discrete communal Golden Age features do exist in the communities of the farmers, bees, and plague victims, for example; but they do not thereby constitute a renewed Golden Age. Community remains morally inert without enlightened, willed moral value, which is the poet's special contribution.

In chapter 3, "The Poet's Truth," I study in particular the image of *bougonia,* which illuminates central oppositions between power and beauty, profit and art, material and spiritual in Roman society. Consequently, I also consider the poet's privileging of myth over *praeceptum,* of divine revelation over experiment and practice, of mystery over solution. My contention is that the very presumptions of the farmer's mode, of the materially knowable, of Iron Age value, and of the didactic genre are called into question by the poem's conclusion. I suggest, not without precedent,[49] that we are to see Aristaeus not as a resolution but as a pole of an unresolvable opposition with Orpheus and the *Georgic* poet. The conflicts of georgic and poetic values remain unresolved. As a basis for this contention I attempt to demonstrate that the image of *bougonia* itself offers not resolution of tensions but rather a powerful image of their unresolvability. Miles, in particular, sees the poet's ultimate emphasis to be on the search for solutions, whereas I see it rather on complexity, ambiguity, and mystery. As a correlate of this, my treatment of the Golden Age differs from those of Patricia A. Johnston and

49. See, for instance, Segal, "Orpheus and the Fourth *Georgic*," 307–25; and A. Bradley, "Augustan Culture and a Radical Alternative: Virgil's *Georgics*," *Arion* 8 (1969): 347–58. Segal asks, "How should the poet, after all, resolve what life does not?" (321).

(earlier) H. Altevogt, for example,[50] who see it as a blueprint for the future, to be implemented by Augustus. I treat the Golden Age rather as symbol of the humane value of community for which the poet proselytizes.

The specific topics of poet and community, both central to my study, have been previously treated by others, most notably by Vinzenz Buchheit in *Der Anspruch des Dichters in Vergils* Georgika: *Dichtertum und Heilsweg* (Darmstadt, 1972), Edward W. Spofford in *The Social Poetry of the* Georgics (Salem, N.H., 1981), and, for the *Eclogues,* by Paul Alpers in *The Singer of the* Eclogues: *A Study of Virgilian Pastoral* (Berkeley, 1979).

Buchheit's study is important in attributing significance and coherence to the poet's voice in the *Georgics,* taking his poetic self-consciousness seriously, and seeing the role of the poet as critical to an interpretation of the poem as a whole. His central thesis is that the *Georgics* envisions a new political Golden Age in Italy, secured both by the poet's song (conceived as a priestly act) and by Caesar's military victories. The victorious poet and the victorious Caesar, with their parallel contributions, belong together ultimately in a recreated paradisiacal and musical Italian world. Poet and general are, then, analogous figures in the birth of a new Golden Age. As summary may suggest, this study, despite many strengths, lacks a sense of ambiguity and complexity, tending as it does to disregard passages incompatible with its thesis.[51]

In the view of Spofford's subtle study the poet's mission is to enable farmers/readers to "enrich [their] environment by imagination"[52] and specifically to derive comfort from an imagined world in which rural, urban, and military are pleasantly connected, a world that, through its myths and divinities, demonstrates concern and affection for farmers. The persona of the poet is perceived as genial, affirmative, and witty, both urbane

---

50. Patricia A. Johnston, *Vergil's Agricultural Golden Age: A Study of the* Georgics (Leiden, 1980); H. Altevogt, *Labor Improbus: Eine Vergilstudie* (Münster, 1952).

51. See M. C. J. Putnam's review, *CP* 71 (1976): 279–82.

52. Edward W. Spofford, *The Social Poetry of the* Georgics (Salem, N. H., 1981), IX.

and of generous sensibility. The poet addresses both Maecenas and farmers, thus suggesting his own wide-ranging interests and imagination, which he invites readers to share. Community is an important motif in Spofford's book, for, in his view, the *Georgics* implies that the whole cosmos is an interrelated community, as is shown by, for example, the portents at Caesar's death, the pervasive effects of plague, or, more positively, the willingness of gods to respond when summoned. Thus the poet would both create community between himself and readers and also invite readers to acknowledge the larger community of the world, which they share with others.

This original and valuable study gives pause only, if at all, in its perception of tone. Spofford reads the poet as genial and amused, no matter how apparently grim (to this reader) is the passage under discussion.[53] Consequently he makes nothing of the poet's implicit self-criticism, sense of limitation, or characteristic melancholy and haunting pathos. While Spofford perceives the poet as attempting to make farmers happy in a refuge of imagination, the argument of this study is rather that the poem memorializes sorrow and finds a certain painful beauty precisely in tragedy, not in forgetfulness of or distance from it.

Alpers sees community as the very essence of Virgilian pastoral, noting that shepherds/poets come together to sing and that their song relies for its vitality on a responsive natural and human audience. He argues that no one sings a song purely his own, but that each speaker, while seeking self-expression, "reaches out to, speaks and sings for, the other."[54] Indeed the "central myth" of the *Eclogues* is that poetry "is produced by and exists for" the community.[55] In the *Eclogues,* then, Alpers

---

53. See, for example, Spofford, 28, 34, 46. Compare Jasper Griffin, " *Haec super arvorum cultu,*" *CR* 31 (1981): 33, who finds much wit in the poem and assails Putnam for reading it as if it were devoid of humor and "portentous in its solemnity." Griffin wonders in addition "whether some parts [of the poem] are less than wholly relevant or excellent" (32). The thesis of the present study, although challenged by Griffin, is that the *Georgics* is indeed "one uniformly elevated and uniformly complex work" (33). Not surprisingly Thomas, 2:148, also declines to see humor in the poem.

54. Alpers, 91.

55. Alpers, 221.

sees community as created by shared song, shared tradition, and mutuality of concern. This concept of poets in community illuminates by contrast the position of the poet in the *Georgics,* where, as an isolated figure, he sings his song alone, for no one else shares his sensibility. Learning, sophistication, and moral perspective separate him from the farmer, as do power and social status from Maecenas and Octavian. His mission, precisely, is to create community where none as yet exists.

The subject of my final chapter, the privileging of myth and mystery over material *praecepta,* with its consequent questioning of the presumptions of Iron Age materialism and of the georgic genre as a whole, has not (to my knowledge) been observed or dealt with by others. In treating this topic I hope to contribute to and advance earlier readings of the *Georgics* by suggesting how its unresolved contradictions may be meaningfully comprehended in a larger, more complex view of the whole.

I

The Figure of the Poet

The subject of this chapter is the figure of the poet in the *Georgics,* the poet being represented by both the *Georgic* poet, that is, the first-person speaker in the poem, and also by the singer Orpheus, as he is portrayed in *Georgic* 4.[1] Both the poet and Orpheus have been the subjects of previous studies. Buchheit's study of the poet, although it arrives at conclusions different from those to be drawn here, makes a great contribution to critical understanding of the first-person speaker in the poem in its focus on the significance and coherence of the poet's voice in the *Georgics.* Orpheus also, especially in his polar relationship to Aristaeus, has been carefully studied by other scholars.[2] The particular effort of this chapter, then, will be to study the figures of the *Georgic* poet and of Orpheus together, as significant embodiments of poetic sensibility and achievement. Parallel in some ways, different in others, they exemplify different dimensions of the experience of the poet in the Iron Age world. Features common to both suggest the fundamental nature and aspiration of the poet as Virgil conceives it. Distinctions between them allow us to isolate characteristics unique to the *Georgic* poet, whom we are ultimately invited to identify with Virgil himself (4.559–66).

---

1. On Orpheus as paradigmatic poet see, for instance, Segal, "Orpheus and the Fourth *Georgic,*" 313; P. J. Davis, "Vergil's *Georgics* and the Pastoral Ideal," *Ramus* 8 (1979): 31, who cites *Ecls.* 3.46; 4.55, 57; 6.30; 8.55, 56. Ross's view is unusual. Based on his reading of the *Eclogues,* which he extrapolates to the *Georgics,* he sees Orpheus as the "exemplary poet of science" and of "intellectual understanding" (*Virgil's Elements* 226–29). It appears, however, that in the text of the *Georgics* Orpheus' power derives from charm and magic, not intellectual understanding.

2. For example, Bradley, 355–58; Segal, "Orpheus and the Fourth *Georgic,*" 313–17.

The figure of the poet emerges most clearly in distinction from the farmer, the normative figure of a georgic poem, for they have different aspirations, values, and sensibilities. As the *Georgic* poet and Orpheus are taken in this study to exemplify the idea of the poet, so the farmer (variously termed *agricola, arator, colonus*) in the poem and Aristaeus will be taken to exemplify the idea of the farmer. Oppositions between Aristaeus and Orpheus may be summarized by saying that while Aristaeus is concerned with work and control, Orpheus is concerned with beauty and sympathy; Aristaeus is materially productive, while Orpheus is materially useless; Aristaeus' relationship to nature is agonistic, while Orpheus' is liberating and benign. In this chapter these fundamental observations concerning Aristaeus and Orpheus will be elaborated and extended to the whole concept of farmer and poet throughout the *Georgics* in an effort to isolate and illuminate the characteristic qualities of the poet. We should note further that while the poet emerges primarily in distinction from the farmer, he is carefully distinguished as well from Maecenas, a sophisticated and socially elevated reader and the poet's addressee, and from Caesar, a powerful political figure, evoked above all in his military aspect.[3]

Differences between Aristaeus and Orpheus are reflected and elaborated in the relationship between the farmer and the poet, where we see a different sensibility and relationship to nature and to other men. The farmer, like Aristaeus, values the material and the useful; the poet, like Orpheus, the nonmaterial, useless, and beautiful. One could expand these observations in the poem's terms by noting that, with respect to knowledge, the farmer relies on *experientia* and *usus,* the findings of which may be summarized in *praecepta,* while the poet relies on the Muses and on divine revelation. And while, overall, the farmer's relationship to nature is one of domination and control in which he compels nature to ends that are productive for man, the poet's relationship to nature is characterized by harmony, song, and

---

3. Contrast Buchheit (e.g., 92ff.), who sees the poet as an analogue of Caesar. Spofford, 1ff., is important on the social distinctions implicit in the poem's opening.

play. The poet, therefore, unlike the farmer, embodies a set of values that are tangential to Roman culture, values that constitute in many ways an alternative culture. This contrast between farmer and poet, although not without complexity or exceptions to the description above, is nowhere resolved in the poem, but remains a constitutive polarity of the text and central to its meaning.[4]

THE FARMER

The role of the farmer is paradigmatic in the *Georgics,* as the farmer is certainly the normative figure in a georgic poem. I would suggest also, with Wilkinson, that the farmer represents Man in general. "For the farmer's life is sometimes taken as typical of all human life, and in it man is brought starkly face to face with the facts of nature and the powers that govern the universe."[5] The farmer represents Man in respect to Iron Age experience; he exemplifies also, in certain specific qualities, the traditional values of Roman man.

A number of different considerations lead the reader to perceive the farmer as representative of man in general in his relationship to the larger forces that shape and limit his experience. First, the farmer is the agent of agriculture, which often is represented as the paradigmatic activity of civilized man and therefore, by metonymy, can stand for civilization as a whole.[6] A. Bradley observes that *cultus* of the fields is a metaphor for culture in general, as the etymology of our word makes clear. Since the ostensible purpose of the *Georgics* is to offer instruction to the farmer, the poem is largely centered on the farmer's activities and concerns. He is its main and primary focus. Nevertheless the *Georgic* poet suggests his overall concern not only with agriculture specifically but also with other related forms of skilled endeavor. For example, in the "theodicy" of *Georgic* 1, which describes the development of Iron Age technology, he

4. Contrast Putnam's concept of the georgic artist.
5. Wilkinson, Georgics, 15.
6. T. Haecker, *Vergil: Vater des Abendlandes* (Munich, 1952), 163. Similarly Büchner, *RE* 8 A2 (1958): 1268.

alludes to hunting, trapping, and sailing, among other occupations, which are analogous to farming in skill. Similarly, in metaphors and similes that imply equivalence between various occupations, as in 1.302–4, where he compares farmers and sailors, he suggests a common quality in all human endeavor and thereby facilitates the reader's vision of the paradigmatic status of the farmer's *labor*. (Other examples are 2.279, comparing farmers and soldiers; 3.346, comparing herdsmen and soldiers; 2.541–42 and 4.116–17, comparing the poet himself to charioteers and sailors.)

Another perspective on the symbolic and paradigmatic status of the farmer in the poem comes from the poet's archaizing description of him, wherein the farmer appears as an individual *colonus,* working his land without slaves. Scholars have noted that Virgil's treatment of farming and of the farmer here is different from that of Cato and Varro, whose prose works are aimed at large-scale commercial farming and assume a landowner with many slaves to work his sizeable estate. Such practice was increasingly common in Virgil's time, and according to Wilkinson, "even quite a modest *colonus* would have some slaves,"[7] so that the absence of any mention of slavery in the *Georgics* is striking and provocative. Farming without slavery, as Virgil describes it, had not been common for centuries,[8] as one may infer from references to slaves even in Hesiod's *Works and Days* (e.g., 406). Virgil's poem, however, seems generally to assume an individual farmer working his own land, as is implied by the *tu* form of address or by the scene of the farmer selling his produce in the city in exchange for a millstone or pitch (1.273–75) or sharpening knives by a winter fire while his wife weaves (1.291–96).[9] Since the independent free peasant was a phenomenon of increasing rarity in Virgil's time and had virtually disap-

7. Wilkinson, Georgics, 54.

8. Wilkinson, Georgics, 50–55.

9. Joan M. Frayn, "Subsistence Farming during the Roman Period: A Preliminary Discussion of the Evidence," *G & R* 21 (1974): 16. See also her *Subsistence Farming in Roman Italy* (London, 1979).

peared from Italy's most important farming areas,[10] Virgil creates a picture in this poem that seems calculated to evoke memories of an earlier period. To a contemporary reader it would probably seem regressive and idealized. The idealization is no doubt intensified by the fact that Virgil's farmer is never specifically directed towards *fructus* ("profit"), which the poet never mentions. (A subtle and discreet exception may be argued for 3.306–7.) In attempting to interpret the archaizing descriptions of the farmer we may adduce a useful critical principle of Büchner's, namely, that the less practical a *praeceptum* is, the greater is its symbolic value.[11] This insight will be especially relevant to the discussion of *bougonia,* but for our present purposes we may infer, by analogy or extension of this principle, that the archaizing descriptions of the farmer in this poem, as they are no longer relevant or practical for Virgil's contemporaries, throw the poet's emphasis on the farmer as symbol. Almost as a mythic symbol he exemplifies the experience of the individual confronting, without intermediary, the stark terms of his existence. These include not only the challenges and hardships of nature, with its unpredictability, ungovernability, and overwhelming power; but also inevitable decline, mortality, and the gods (or however we might define those conditions that seem to limit human existence and are greater than man). The effect of the anachronistic representation of the farmer, to the degree that it is of no practical use, is precisely to support the paradigmatic, symbolic value of the farmer as an individual, facing on his own the larger terms and conditions of mortal experience.

Again, the poet opens the poem with the absolutely primal moments of farming: plowing an unknown field and making a plow. According to W. Steidle plowing is the most representative and important activity of the farmer; and with the phrase *ignotum aequor (at prius ignotum ferro quam scindimus aequor,* "Yet before we cleave with iron an unknown plain" 1.50), the

---

10. Wilkinson, Georgics, 50–55; Miles, 26ff; K. D. White, *Roman Farming* (Ithaca, N.Y., 1970), 52.

11. Büchner, *RE* 8 A2 (1958): 1310.

poet places the farmer at the very inception of his efforts ("Ur-situation des Bauern"), extraordinary for the organization of a didactic poem.[12] The instructions for the making of a plow (1.169ff.) are equally primal in substance, since as early as Hesiod's time one bought plows instead of making them. Cato (*Agr.* 135) gives names of the best manufacturers in Italy, and Varro (1.22.1) does not mention the plow as something that could be made even on a large farm.[13] As, therefore, this description of the making of a plow is without practical usefulness, we may infer that it signifies as symbol, illuminating the poet's vision of the individual, lonely, unmediated existence of the farmer in this poem.

Finally, the poet's changing forms of address from "we" to "you" to "he" dissolve boundaries between the groups of farmers and readers and poet and thereby challenge the natural assumption of such readers as Maecenas and Caesar and ourselves that they/we are different from the farmers conceived in the poem. Such verses as

> depresso incipiat iam tum *mihi* taurus aratro
> ingemere
>
> $$(1.45-46)^{14}$$
>
> even then would *I* have my bull groan
> over the deep-driven plough

contrast with

> et segnem *patiere* situ durescere campum
> $$(1.72)^{15}$$
>
> *you* will also let the plain idly stiffen with scurf

---

12. W. Steidle, "Die Anordnung der Arbeiten im ersten Buch von Vergils *Georgica*," *RhM* 109 (1966): 138, asserts that plowing is the most important function on a farm, citing Cato *Agr.* 61.1, Pliny *HN* 18.174, and *Georgics* 1.1, 119, 147; 2.513. On the "Ursituation des Bauern" and the primal significance of the "unknown plain" see 139; on the primal significance of the plow see 157.

13. Wilkinson, Georgics, 58.

14. Cf. 1.50, 204, 351.

15. Cf. 1.155, 156, 157.

and

> aut unde iratus silvam devexit arator
> (2.207)[16]

from which the angry ploughman has carried off the timber.

The fluidity of boundaries between groups reinforces the suggestion of their equivalence. The idea of a bounded or limited community that includes only farmers and excludes, for example, urban sophisticates or victorious generals is hard to sustain. While sometimes, then, poet and reader are explicitly identified with the farmer's experience, at other times they are dissociated from it, thus allowing the poet continually to pose the question of the relative identities of farmers and readers. On occasion, then, throughout the poem, the reader, despite his superior sophistication (a subject to be discussed below), is invited to share the farmer's experience, since he and the farmer, who represents all men, are implicitly identified.

If the farmer is symbolic of Man, he is also a figure of enhanced and special resonance for Romans because he is seen to embody those qualities in themselves that they most admired and to which they attributed their exceptional military successes and consequent political power. Such qualities as endurance, courage, discipline, and simplicity were seen to characterize those who worked the land and were also seen to be responsible for Roman military expansion. Frequently cited in this regard are Cato's words in the preface to his *De agricultura:*

> Et virum bonum quom laudabant, ita laudabant, bonum agricolam bonumque colonum. Amplissime laudari existimabatur qui ita laudabatur. Mercatorem autem strenuum studiosumque rei quaerendae existimo, verum, ut supra dixi, periculosum et calamitosum. At ex agricolis et viri fortissimi et milites strenuissimi gignuntur, maximeque pius quaestus stabilissimusque consequitur minimeque invidiosus, minimeque male cogitantes sunt qui in eo studio occupati sunt.[17]

16. Cf. 2.405, 514–15.
17. For this and other related passages see Miles, 1–15.

And when they would praise a worthy man their praise took this form: "good husbandman," "good farmer"; one so praised was thought to have received the greatest commendation. The trader I consider to be an energetic man, and one bent on making money; but, as I said above, it is a dangerous career and one subject to disaster. On the other hand, it is from the farming class that the bravest men and the sturdiest soldiers come, their calling is most pious, their livelihood is most assured and is looked on with the least hostility, and those who are engaged in that pursuit are least inclined to be disaffected.[18]

From Vegetius' fourth-century *Epitoma rei militaris* (1.3) comes a similar sentiment:

> numquam credo potuisse dubitari aptiorem armis rusticam ple-bem, quae sub divo et in labore nutritur, solis patiens, umbrae neglegens, balnearum nescia, deliciarum ignara.

> I think that there never could have been any doubt that rustic people are better suited to arms [than urban people], since they are nurtured under the open sky and in toil, enduring of sun, indifferent to shade, without experience of baths, ignorant of luxuries.[19]

---

18. W. D. Hooper and H. B. Ash, trans., *Cato and Varro: De re rustica*, Loeb Classical Library (London and Cambridge, Mass., 1934; reprint, 1967).
   19. Author's translation; cited by Frayn, 11. Cf. *Aen.* 9.607–13:

> at patiens operum parvoque adsueta iuventus
> aut rastris terram domat aut quatit oppida bello.
> omne aevum ferro teritur, versaque iuvencum
> terga fatigamus hasta, nec tarda senectus
> debilitat viris animi mutatque vigorem:
> canitiem galea premimus, semperque recentis
> comportare iuvat praedas et vivere rapto.

> As youths
> they learn frugality and patient labor
> and tame the earth with harrows or compel
> towns to tremble. All our life
> is spent with steel; we goad the backs of bullocks
> with our inverted spears, and even slow
> old age can never sap our force of spirit
> or body's vigor. We clamp down gray hairs
> beneath a helmet, always take delight
> in our new plunder, in a violent life.

The farmer then is also and especially Roman man, embodying the characteristic Roman veneration of tradition, discipline, order, and courage.

Finally and most significantly the farmer is also Iron Age man with, in this poem, a technology to which the poet ascribes an aggressive and destructive quality:

> tunc alnos primum fluvii sensere cavatas;
> navita tum stellis numeros et nomina fecit
> Pleiadas, Hyadas, claramque Lycaonis Arcton;
> tum laqueis captare feras et fallere visco
> inventum et magnos canibus circumdare saltus;
> atque alius latum funda iam verberat amnem
> alta petens, pelagoque alius trahit umida lina;
> tum ferri rigor atque argutae lammina serrae
> (nam primi cuneis scindebant fissile lignum),
> tum variae venere artes.
>
> (1.136–45)

Then first did rivers feel the hollowed out alder-trunks;
Then did the mariner group and name the stars—the Pleiades,
Hyades and the bright Bear.
Then was invented the snare for taking game, the tricky
Bird-lime, the casting of hounds about the broad wood-coverts.
One whips now the wide river with casting-net and
Searches deep pools, another trawls his dripping line in the
Sea. Then came the rigid strength of steel and the shrill saw-blade
(For primitive man was wont to split his wood with wedges);
Then came the various arts.

Iron Age technology, as the poet characterizes it in this programmatic passage, is aimed at dominance and control, and its techniques, from the point of view of nature, are violent. As Otis notes, "The items . . . that Virgil selects involve at every point the rending and perversion of natural things (i.e. the discovery of fire, navigation, trapping, hunting and fishing, iron and steel tools)."[20] The verbs *captare* and *fallere* (139), *verberat* (141), and *scindebant* (144) suggest the assault on nature that Iron Age

---

20. Otis, *Virgil,* 157 n. 1. Cf. Perkell, "Virgil's Fourth *Georgic,*" 216–17 and notes, on the violence of agriculture. Ross, *Virgil's Elements,* 78, cites Servius similarly at 1.198.

civilization entails. That agriculture requires the destruction and domination of natural things becomes a leitmotif of the poem, ultimately and most dramatically exemplified, as we shall see, in the *bougonia* that concludes *Georgic* 4.

In this poem the poet attributes to farming a military character, which serves to suggest that the farmer is engaged in a war of sorts with nature. The farmer's mode is to vanquish nature through his technology, the aggressive character of which is implicit in the military terms that the poet applies to agriculture throughout the *Georgics*. For example, following the Golden Age, when nature, unasked, produced all things everywhere in abundance (1.127–28), man has been in mortal combat with his surroundings for his very existence. To cite an example:

> exercetque frequens tellurem atque imperat arvis.
> (1.99)

At his post he disciplines the ground and commands the fields.

Note here especially the term *imperat*. Another example:

> quid dicam iacto qui semine comminus arva
> insequitur
> (1.104–5)

Why tell of him who, throwing the seed, closes upon the field hand to hand?

Frequens (1.99) is used of a soldier at his standards, and *iacto* (1.104) implies that as the legionnaire throws his spear and then runs in to grapple hand to hand with his enemy, so the farmer throws his seed and grapples with the land. Comparable expressions are found in

> ante Iovem nulli subigebant arva coloni
> (1.125)

Before Jove's time, no settlers brought the land under subjection.

> quod nisi et adsiduis herbam insectabere rastris
> (1.155)

Unless you assail the weeds relentlessly with your mattock

Dicendum et quae sint duris agrestibus arma
(1.160)

I'll tell you too the armoury of the tough countryman.

The farmer dominates by tilling (2.114), compels (*cogendae, domandae* 2.60–62), imposes his hard rule (*dura exerce imperia* 2.370).[21] His actions towards nature's creatures are violent:

hic plantas tenero abscindens de corpore matrum
deposuit sulcis

(2.23–24)

One man tears suckers from the tender body of the mother
And plants them in trenches.

Tenero (23), which personifies the plants, and *abscindens* (23) assure that the reader's sympathy is with the plant as helpless victim. Similarly in

aut unde iratus silvam devexit arator
et nemora evertit multos ignava per annos,
antiquasque domos avium cum stirpibus imis
eruit; illae altum nidis petiere relictis,
at rudis enituit impulso vomere campus.
(2.207–11)

Or acres from which the angry ploughman has carted away the
    wood,
Levelling the groves that stood idle for many a year;
He felled them, root and branch he demolished the ancient
    dwellings
Of birds; their nests abandoned, the birds have made for the sky,
But the land that once was wild is gleaming now with furrows.

---

21. Cf. John Conington and Henry Nettleship, eds., *The Works of Virgil* (London, 1898; reprint, Hildesheim, 1963), at 1.99, 104–5, 125, 155, 160; 2.207–11, 277, 367–70; 3.468–69; 4.106–8. Cf. Aya Betensky, "The Farmer's Battles," *Ramus* 8 (1979): 108–19, whose essential thesis is that the positive qualities of war can be put to good use in agriculture. My argument is that such a moral distinction is arbitrary. Cf. Altevogt, 24, on the "military character of agricultural labor." Cf. Bradley, 350, on the order and productivity that come from warfare.

We see that the farmer tears up the birds' ancient homes, and the poet, since he follows the birds' anguished responses, necessarily involves the reader's sympathy with their fate. By making the reader identify with what is destroyed, the poet makes him realize the cost of a field productive for man.

Especially striking since it is without precedent is the use of *arma* for farm tools.[22] Elsewhere, as in Varro 1.17.1, farm tools are termed *instrumenta*. Such an original usage for *arma* ("arms") confirms the poet's pattern of characterizing farming as a military operation against nature. This language, consistent throughout the poem, is not paralleled in earlier writers like Cato, Varro, and Lucretius, who do not characteristically use language that represents farming as a kind of aggression against nature or nature's creatures.

Another significant feature of the poet's description of technology is that the arts that man has been compelled to contrive are all aimed at material survival and therefore lead to visible and quantifiable, but not to moral or esthetic, progress. We may note how this description of the discovery of civilization includes the material and the practical, but omits *fas* ("divine right") and art. In this respect the *Georgic* poet differs significantly from, for example, Lucretius, who includes the fine arts in his description of the discovery of civilization:

> Navigia atque agri culturas moenia leges
> arma vias vestis et cetera de genere horum,
> praemia, delicias quoque vitae funditus omnis,
> carmina picturas, et daedala signa polire,
> usus et impigrae simul experientia mentis
> paulatim docuit pedetemptim progredientis.
> (Lucr. 5.1448–53)

> Navigation, agriculture, cities, law,
> war, travel, clothing, and all such things else,
> money, and life's delights, from top to bottom,
> poetry, painting, the cunning sculptor's art,
> the searching, the trial and error of nimble minds
> have taught us, inching forward, step by step.

22. Wilkinson, Georgics, 80.

If Jove has any concern for spiritual purpose or moral conscience in man, it is not so stated in this passage. Neither is it reflected in Iron Age reality, since a necessary consequence of Jove's intervention in mortal affairs is that man's moral relationships become compromised. Merely for survival man must become aggressive towards nature. In this way both man and technology appear to be instruments of Jove's purposes, which are represented as indifferent to moral qualities or aspirations. Thus Virgil's poetry, as it often does, points to discrepancies between moral values and divine actions.

The military character of agricultural labor in this poem, as outlined above, has been noted by many and is not at issue here. What is at issue is the interpretation of this motif. My thesis is that the military activity of the farmer, analogous as it is to war, suggests the moral ambiguity and tension of the human condition as it is epitomized in the farmer's experience, where material progress is pitted against humane value in man's relationship both to nature and to other men. Further to intensify the ambiguity of man's relationship to nature is the fact that, despite its characteristic military quality, it is also sometimes sustaining. On occasion, instead of being represented as aggressing against nature militarily, man is represented as helping:

> Multum adeo, rastris glaebas qui frangit inertis
> vimineasque trahit crates, iuvat arva
>
> (1.94–95)
>
> He greatly helps his land who takes a mattock
> To break the sluggish clods, and drags bush-harrows.[23]

Another such example is

> sic quoque mutatis requiescunt fetibus arva,
> nec nulla interea est inaratae gratia terrae.
>
> (1.82–83)
>
> So too are the fields rested by a rotation of crops,
> And meanwhile not thankless is the untilled earth.

23. L. P. Wilkinson, trans., *Virgil: The* Georgics (Harmondsworth and New York, 1982).

Similarly, although the farmer is often metaphorically and some-times even literally a soldier (as when he is conscripted into the army [1.506–8]), the farmer is sometimes the antithesis of the soldier, morally distinct from and implicitly superior to him in the moral hierarchy that the poem at times suggests. At the end of *Georgic* 2, for example, the farmer is *procul discordibus armis,* "far from discordant arms" (459). Analogously, at the end of *Georgic* 1 the poet envisions a future moment at Philippi, twice, as he says, the site of Romans dying at Roman hands, when the farmer will upturn with his plow rusted weapons and bare bones (493–97). The farmer will endure, laboring and pro-ductive, although in a declining world, while the soldier, whose anonymous bones he upheaves, once a destroyer, is now himself long destroyed. Here we infer an apparent dichotomy between, on the one hand, the peacefulness of rural life and its distance from war and, on the other, the violence and horror that war entails. And further to intensify the ambiguity even of the war theme, we must note—although it may be perhaps ironic—that Caesar's wars are apparently benign (4.560–62).

The unresolved ambivalence that the poem expresses towards agriculture may be summed up in the tension between the follow-ing two passages, which imply contrasting attitudes towards the effect of agriculture on nature. The first is 2.207–11 (cited on p. 35). Here, despite evident depredation of nature, the field is seen to gleam as a result of the plow's work. At 2.438–39, however, the poet is rapturous at the sight of a field untouched by man:

> iuvat arva videre
> non rastris, hominum non ulli obnoxia curae.

> What a joy it is
> to look on land beholden to no drag-hoes
> nor any human care![24]

Man's developing relationship with nature, characteristically, but not exclusively, aggressive and destructive, parallels in its ambiguity his relationship with other men. As man becomes

24. Wilkinson, trans.

aggressive towards nature, so he becomes competitive with or negligent of others. While pre-Jovian men cared for the common good (1.127), modern man finds himself, envying another's plenty, left to starve alone (1.155–59). Comparable in substance is *condit opes alius defossoque incubat auro* (2.507), where a miser hoards his secret wealth. Some men (perhaps only city men) are worse than merely negligent. They seek actively to harm others, sometimes their own brothers (2.496, 510), inferior in this way even to beasts, which grieve at their brothers' death (3.518). Yet the farmer, on the other hand, sustains his country and his grandchildren through his *labor* (2.514–15), thus serving both his private interests and those of the nation. Indeed, a certain austere morality is attributed to the farmer's life, as in

> casta pudicitiam servat domus
> (2.524)

> a house that preserves the tradition of chastity.

And yet, contrarily, Justice is said to have left even these (relatively) virtuous inhabitants of the country:

> extrema per illos
> Iustitia excedens terris vestigia fecit.
> (2.473–74)

> When justice
> left earth, her latest footprints were stamped on folk like these.

In effect, then, and truly enough, the farmer is represented both as victim (of nature and of the city) and as victimizer (of nature and its creatures). He is nature's victim in such passages as 1.324–27, in which devastating storm dissolves all his achievements. He is necessarily limited by the tendency of all things to deteriorate (1.197–203). He is victim of the city at 1.507, for example, conscripted for wars that overtake his life and ruin his efforts. In these passages the farmer's life is represented as inevitably defeating, an existence that is at best one of poverty and deprivation (2.472).[25]

---

25. The difficulties of farming were known to all. Not even the urban *plebs* wished to return to the land. Cf. Miles, 26–27 and 39–40, for citations.

Sometimes, alternatively, the farmer's life is idealized as one of peace, ease, simplicity, and reverence:

> at secura quies et nescia fallere vita,
> dives opum variarum, at latis otia fundis
> speluncae vivique lacus at frigida tempe
> mugitusque boum mollesque sub arbore somni
> non absunt; illic saltus ac lustra ferarum,
> et patiens operum exiguoque adsueta iuventus,
> sacra deum sanctique patres.
>
> (2.467–73)

> But calm security and a life that will not cheat you,
> Rich in its own rewards, are here: the broad ease of the farmlands,
> Caves, living lakes, and combes that are cool even at midsummer,
> Mooing of herds, and slumber mild in the trees' shade,
> Here are glades game-haunted,
> Lads hardened to labour, inured to simple ways,
> Reverence for God, respect for the family.

At other times the poet implies that readers of the poem may well find the farmer's life distasteful:

> arida tantum
> ne saturare fimo pingui pudeat sola neve
> effetos cinerem immundum iactare per agros.
>
> (1.79–81)

> only be not
> ashamed to feed fat the dried-out soil
> with rich dung, and to scatter grimy
> ashes over the exhausted fields.

> Possum multa tibi veterum praecepta referre,
> ni refugis tenuisque piget cognoscere curas.
>
> (1.176–77)

> I can repeat for you many olden maxims,
> unless you shrink back and are loath
> to learn such trivial cares.

These attitudes are interestingly paralleled in *Eclogue* 2, wherein the shepherd-speaker Corydon invites the urban Alexis to join him in his "humble hut" (*humilis . . . casas* 29) and "country squalor" (*sordida rura* 28), terms expressing the speaker's understanding of an urban person's view, acknowledging his invitation to Alexis as, in some sense, an invitation to join a smaller world.

This judgment is not, of course, Corydon's own, which rather envisions the country as idyllic (45–55).

As Corydon perceives his rustic naiveté (*rusticus es, Corydon* 56), so in the *Georgics* it is evident that the farmer's entertainments are not of the sort to attract the wholehearted participation of such sophisticated readers (e.g., Maecenas and Caesar) as the poem anticipates:

> ipse dies agitat festos fususque per herbam,
> ignis ubi in medio et socii cratera coronant,
> te libans, Lenaee, vocat pecorisque magistris
> velocis iaculi certamina ponit in ulmo,
> corporaque agresti nudant praedura palaestra.
>
> (2.527–31)

The farmer himself keeps holidays when, at ease in a meadow,
A fire in the midst and friends there to crown the flowing bowl,
He drinks the health of the Wine-god and arranges for his
    herdsmen
A darts-match, setting up the target upon an elm tree,
And the labourers bare their sinewy bodies for country wrestling.

As Spofford excellently puts it, the poet is the locus of true taste in the poem, for he can both satirize the corruption of the city and also recognize the naiveté of the country.[26] As is finely suggested here in the distance and difference implied in the adjective *agresti* ("country"), the poet is more sophisticated than the rustics whose lives he praises but nevertheless declines to live.[27]

The poet treats with ambiguity even the presumed moral qualities of simplicity and purity in the farmer's life, as these qualities may result as much from ignorance as from virtue. For example, the concluding passages of *Georgic* 2 certainly suggest a moral superiority of farmers to city dwellers since neither cities

26. Spofford, 47.
27. Cf., analogously, Leo Marx, *The Machine in the Garden: Technology and the Pastoral Ideal in America* (Oxford, 1964; reprint, 1981), 25: "In one way or another, if only by virtue of the unmistakeable sophistication with which they are composed, these works [pastorals] manage to qualify, or call into question, or bring irony to bear against the illusion of peace and harmony in a green pasture. . . . [T]he pastoral design . . . embraces some token of a larger, more complicated order of experience."

nor their inhabitants have much to recommend them in the *Georgics*. At 2.155 cities are heaped-up stones, the result of technology, *labor,* and (implicit) defensive needs. At 1.273–75 the city is a place to sell things. Wars come from cities (1.510), which fight against their neighbors, thus exemplifying the complete loss of Golden Age community. Not only is there no concern for the common good, but brothers plot against brothers. Cities in the *Georgics* are corrupt, their luxuries reflecting depravity more than refinement, esthetic sensibility, or cultural achievement. The following extract, describing urban faults from which the farmer is free, illustrates some of these points:

> si non ingentem foribus domus alta superbis
> mane salutantum totis vomit aedibus undam,
> nec varios inhiant pulchra testudine postis,
> inlusasque auro vestis Ephyreiaque aera,
> alba neque Assyrio fucatur lana veneno,
> nec casia liquidi corrumpitur usus olivi;
>   (2.461–66)

>   What if no lofty
> dwelling vomits forth from haughty gates at
> dawn a flood of callers; what if
> they never gape at doorposts inlaid with
> beautiful tortoise-shell, at garments
> tricked out with gold, or at bronzes of
> Ephyra; what if their white wool is not
> stained with Assyrian dye nor the use
> of their clear olive oil spoiled with cassia?

While urban luxury could have been made to correspond positively with the cultural richness with which the poet characterizes his own work in *Georgic* 3.11–36 and that presumably differentiates his poetry from the *carminibus patriis* (2.394), *versibus incomptis,* and *risu soluto* (2.386) of the Italian farmers, here it is represented as almost wholly negative. It is possible to say "almost wholly" and not "entirely" because the term *pulchra* (2.463) suggests that although the farmer may indeed be free from urban vice, he is also deprived of urban beauty. He lives without art or poetry, never seeing doors inlaid with beautiful shell, clothes embroidered with gold, or bronzes from Corinth (Ephyra). *Pulchra* is the significant term here, for although these

objects may connote decadence, they are also works of acknowledged beauty, expressions of the refinement and depth of the
human spirit. Here the poet touches on the cultural barrenness of
rural life, which, as not infrequently in Roman poetry, characterizes the Roman tradition.[28] One might compare the words of
Anchises in *Aeneid* 6.847–53, when he concedes to peoples other
than Romans the greatest excellence in artistic expression. Because the farmer lives without art, beauty, and poetry such as the
Georgic poet makes, the poet can assert that his mission is to
bring *Ascraeum carmen* ("Hesiodic song") to Italy (2.174–76).
Therefore we must infer that the farmer's virtue is inadvertent,
the result of naiveté or of narrowness of experience, and consequently is not the result of deliberate and willed moral choice.
Since the farmer does not know urban corruption, he cannot be
credited with having declined or resisted it. He is free from envy,
as indeed he is also free from pity (*neque ille/aut doluit miserans
inopem aut invidit habenti* 2.498–99), because he has neither seen
nor experienced anything that would move him to such a state.
To the extent that farmers are virtuous, they are so from ignorance, thus resembling the "prepolitical" men of Book 5 of
Lucretius' *De rerum natura*. These men have the essential Epicurean virtues of freedom from religious fear and from unnecessary
desire. They have family life, simple society, and are bound by
friendship. Yet their lives are not endorsed by Lucretius as a
model to be emulated because "the limitation of men's desires to
what is by nature good did not come from wise choice based on
knowledge of nature, but from ignorance and lack of exposure to
anything else."[29] Since they lacked the enlightenment of Epicurus' truth, they were not able truly to know nature or, consequently, to choose to live the good life. True happiness, which
results from knowledge and, therefore, enlightened choice, is

28. On the narrowness of rural life see Livy 7.4.6–7 and Sall. *Cat.* 4.1.2 (cited
by Miles, 29, 30). Cf. Griffin, "Fourth *Georgic*," 64–65, on the traditional
Roman's indifference to art, citing Hor. *Ars poetica* 323ff. In the article Griffin
discusses the collective, impersonal, unreflective character of traditional Rome (as
exemplified by the bees of *Georgic* 4).

29. For this citation and the term "prepolitical" see James H. Nichols, Jr.,
Epicurean Political Philosophy: The De Rerum Natura *of Lucretius* (Ithaca,
N.Y., 1976), 126ff.

available only to the Epicurean. Analogously in the *Georgics,* true moral virtue would belong only to a person who, having knowledge of the city, deliberately chose an alternative life. Ignorance, however, is a striking feature of farmers in this poem. Farmers are defined by their limited vision and perspective:

> ignarosque viae mecum miseratus agrestis
> (1.41)
>
> pitying with me the farmers who are ignorant
> of the way.

Ignarosque viae is a phrase of broad philosophical import, not to be restricted to farming.[30] Comparable in its implication of ignorance is

> O fortunatos nimium, sua si bona norint,
> agricolas!
> (2.458–59)
>
> O happy, too happy, if they were to know
> their luck, are the farmers!

Thus, farmers, as they represent all men, experience the limited vision and understanding that characterize the mortal condition. Since the poet has knowledge of both city and country, he is less limited than the farmer, whom he virtually patronizes in 2.458. Nevertheless the poet also confesses his own ignorance of, for example, "the ways of the sky and the stars" (*caelique vias et sidera* 2.477). He differs from the farmer, perhaps, in his greater interest in knowing *causas* rather than *praecepta.* Unlike Lucretius, however, the *Georgic* poet does not assume that one can achieve happiness (either by becoming *felix,* a permanent state, or even *fortunatus*)[31] and hence proposes no dogma or system for achieving such a state.

With the term *pulchra* and the observation that, for example, the farmer has no experience of envy or pity, the poet implies that the farmer's virtue results from a kind of naiveté. His life is

30. Cf. Will Richter, *Vergil:* Georgica (Munich, 1957), ad loc.; Klingner, *Virgil,* 259.
31. For the distinction between *felix* and *fortunatus* see J. S. Clay, "The Argument of the End of Virgil's Second *Georgic,*" *Philologus* 2 (1976): 237ff.

without self-conscious, deliberate art (although it is not entirely without music)[32] and without enlightened moral choice.

In sum, the picture of the farmer that emerges in the *Georgics* is a wholly ambiguous one from a moral point of view. The farmer both helps nature and hurts it. He is both aggressive towards nature and its victim. He is a man of peace, but also a man of war—often so metaphorically, sometimes even literally. Although sometimes he is like a soldier, at other times he is the antithesis of a soldier. His life seems both idyllic, inviting, and also sordid, repellent. He has moral virtues, but for inadequate reasons. Thus the farmer exemplifies the moral ambiguity that characterizes the relationship of Iron Age man to nature, to other men, to knowledge, and to moral choice.

Thus far the discussion has been of the farmer, the figure who imposes a form and meaning upon nature and thereby establishes culture. We turn now to the poet, who imposes form and meaning upon culture and thereby creates art. As nature is to the farmer, so the farmer is to the poet.[33]

THE POET

It has been suggested that a tension exists in the *Georgics* between the figures of the farmer and the poet. The farmer is held to represent Man, that is, the common mortal experience of human beings with respect to nature and to other men; he values the material, the useful, and is largely represented as aggressive towards nature. The poet values useless song, is in harmony with nature and even nurtured by it. Despite these oppositions, however, both farmer and poet are Iron Age figures, flawed in their relationships to nature and to other men. While the farmer is

---

32. The farmer's wife solaces herself with song (1.293–94); the last vine-dresser sings his finished rows (2.417); the nightingale has song (4.511–15), but she is more like the poet than the farmer. Hell has no song without Orpheus. The nymphs in 4.345–48 are "taken" or "charmed" (*captae*) by tales of loves of the gods. (Cf. 1.293–94.) Song, therefore, is sometimes for solace (or just distraction), sometimes for the preservation of grief. The *Georgic* poet's song is the most interpretive and sophisticated.

33. See Redfield, 204–23, on the relationship between art, culture, and nature.

menaced by nature, the city, and his limited mortal vision, the poet is menaced by his own passions and his weakness in the world. While the farmer may be seen as seeking to restore Golden Age plenty through his *labor,* the poet seeks to restore Golden Age community through his song of pity (as will be argued below). The poet differs from the farmer most fundamentally in his basic sensibility, which inclines him to gratuitous and selfless pity, a behavior antithetical to the farmer's mode. As pity most significantly characterizes the poet, I will focus on the motifs of the poet's pity and his sense of poetic mission, both of which distinguish his values from the farmer's. I will then proceed to consider how, on the other hand, the poet shares with other men certain characteristic Iron Age flaws, with the result that we shall come to see the poet as simultaneously exalted (as the sole carrier of humane value) and diminished (as an impotent figure in the world of power). Thus the poet, like the farmer, experiences in his work the moral tension that is the lot of all Iron Age men.

For the farmer pity is counterproductive and only costly. Cato and Varro, therefore, throughout their writings, prescribe the elimination of old or sick animals in favor of those that will bring a profit.[34] In the *Georgics* the farmer is exhorted to eschew pity for nature and its creatures (e.g., 3.95–100) except on such occasions as pity will prove ultimately to be advantageous. The beekeeper, for example, is advised to spare and pity his bees (4.239–40) because this will result in greater future productivity. As the farmer cannot pity nature unless his pity will prove productive, so he also lacks pity (if through ignorance) for other men (2.498–99), as we have seen.

It is easy enough, on the other hand, to demonstrate that the poet's sensibility inclines him to pity and that he aims to elicit pity as a response from his readers. At 1.41 the poet explicitly calls upon Caesar to pity with him the farmers who are "ignorant

---

34. See Cato *Agr.* 2.7, for instance: boves vetulos, armenta delicula, oves deliculas, lanam, pelles, plostrum vetus, ferramenta vetera, servum senem, servum morbosum, et siquid aliut supersit, vendat. "Sell worn-out oxen, blemished cattle, blemished sheep, wool, hides, an old wagon, old tools, an old slave, a sickly slave, and whatever else is superfluous" (trans. Hooper and Ash). Cf. Varro 1.17.3. See Richter at 3.95–100 on the difficulties of interpreting *abde domo.*

of the way." There are other examples, less explicit but more moving, of calls to pity, in which the poet elicits the reader's pity by creating a scene of powerful pathos. Numerous passages in the *Georgics* elicit pity from the reader by involving his feelings and empathy, moving him to regret for the losses or sufferings of both man and nature. As an example we may consider 2.207–11, in which significant details manipulate the reader's vision and value judgment of the scene. The *arator* is *iratus* ("angry"), therefore, we may infer, violent and destructive. He *tears up* the *ancient* homes of the birds from their *deepest* roots. *Antiquas, cum stirpibus imis, eruit* are all significant details that focus the reader's attention on the anguished responses of the displaced birds, who suffer loss of their "ancient homes," the farmer thus violating tradition, for which Romans had special reverence.

Another such scene is 3.371–75:

> hos non immissis canibus, non cassibus ullis
> puniceaeve agitant pavidos formidine pennae,
> sed frustra oppositum trudentis pectore montem
> comminus obtruncant ferro graviterque rudentis
> caedunt et magno laeti clamore reportant.

> Men hunt them not with hounds now, nor do they use the nets,
> No scarlet-featured toils are needed to break their nerve;
> But the deer vainly shove at the banked-up snow with their
>   shoulders,
> The men attack them at close quarters, they cut them down
> Belling loud, and cheerfully shout as they bring them home.

Here attention focuses on the careless (*laeti* 375) brutality (*obtruncant* 374) of the killing; sympathy goes to the victims because of the term *frustra* ("in vain" 373). The animals are seen as helpless victims in a doomed contest, while the men, more savage than the beasts whose skins they wear, vulgarly exploit their technological superiority.

Comparable are the death struggles of the calf at 4.299–302:

> tum vitulus bima curvans iam cornua fronte
> quaeritur: huic geminae nares et spiritus oris
> multa reluctanti obstruitur, plagisque perempto
> tunsa per integram solvuntur viscera pellem.

> A two-year-old calf is obtained, whose horns are beginning to
>   curve
> From his forehead. They stopper up, though he struggle wildly,
>   his two
> Nostrils and breathing mouth, and they beat him to death with
>   blows
> That pound his flesh to pulp but leave the hide intact.

The detail of the calf's horns just beginning to grow from his forehead suggests the promise of his future growth and vitality; it allows us to visualize and individualize the animal in our minds. *Multa reluctanti* and *plagisque perempto* (301) emphasize the calf's unwillingness to die, his futile fight for life, his helpless victimization, and the brutality of such sacrifice.[35]

The scenes considered thus far are expressed by the voice of the *Georgic* poet. The tale of Orpheus, which is told by Proteus, is famous for its resonant pathos and its engaging of the reader's sympathy and pity for Eurydice and for Orpheus, the victim of Aristaeus' and his own passion. Otis, in his important discussion of Virgil's "subjective style,"[36] points to such details as the rhetorical questions at 4.504ff.:

> quid faceret? quo se rapta bis coniuge ferret?
> quo fletu Manis, quae numina voce moveret?
>
> What could he do, where go, his wife twice taken from him?
> What lament would move death now? What deities hear his song?

These questions deeply involve readers with Orpheus' experience and loss, while leaving them emotionally indifferent to Aristaeus' success.

An analogous example is that of the nightingale:

> qualis populea maerens philomela sub umbra
> amissos queritur fetus, quos durus arator
> observans nido implumis detraxit; at illa
> flet noctem, ramoque sedens miserabile carmen
> integrat, et maestis late loca questibus implet.
>
> (4.511–15)

---

35. See Büchner, *RE* 8 A2 (1958): 1310, on the repellent "brutality of the sacrifice, which discourages imitation and bespeaks the barbarism of a foreign land."

36. Otis, *Virgil,* 200–208 particularly.

> As a nightingale he sang that sorrowing under a poplar's
> Shade laments the young she has lost, whom a heartless
>   ploughman
> Has noticed and dragged from the nest unfledged; and the
>   nightingale
> Weeps all night, on a branch repeating the piteous song,
> Loading the acres around with the burden of her lament.

She mourns eternally because the unfeeling (*durus* 512) farmer has plundered her nest and robbed her of her children. *Observans* (513) shows that the crime is deliberate, premeditated; *implumis* (513) that the victims are helpless, young, cannot escape. It is a pitiable (*miserabile* 514) and irremediable loss that the nightingale sings. In sum, then, while Hell never pities (4.470, 489) and farmers pity only when it furthers their interests, the *Georgic* poet's unique contribution, for which the tone is set at 1.41, is his gratuitous pity, empathy, and involvement with the suffering of others.[37]

As we consider this relationship between the poet and pity in the *Georgics,* we may note with interest that the effect of art in *Aeneid* 1.459–62 and also of the *Aeneid* itself as a whole is to

---

37. G. 1.466, in which the sun's eclipse is attributed to its pity for Caesar's death, is the poet's interpretation and does not detract from the unique quality of his sensibility. Proteus, another poet-figure, also feels pity. For all occurrences in the *Georgics:*

miser	2.152, 505
	3.66, 262, 313, 483
	4.494, 526
miserabilis	4.454, 514, 532 (Cyrene speaking here)
miseror	1.41, 466
	2.499
	3.478
	4.240

Jacques Derrida, *Of Grammatology,* trans. G. C. Spivak (Baltimore and London, 1976), 171–91, explicates several of Rousseau's thoughts on pity, which are interesting for the present study. Rousseau sees pity as a prereflexive virtue, awakened by the imagination rather than by reason. If he is correct, it becomes clear why the poet (and not the farmer, general, or philosopher) can best elicit this sentiment. Rousseau sees imagination as the correlate of humanity, passion, speech, liberty, and perfectibility, thus making the poet the likely carrier of humane value.

involve the reader's pity and empathy for loss and suffering. Aeneas understands that the message of the paintings in Dido's temple to Juno is pity for the mortal condition:

> sunt lacrimae rerum et mentem mortalia tangunt
> *Aen.* 1.462

> There are tears for misfortune and mortal sorrows touch the heart.

Aeneas sees in the paintings tears for sorrow, and the mortality of the human condition moves the heart of the beholder. Dido subsequently confirms Aeneas' interpretation of the paintings, explaining that she has compassion for others' suffering because she has suffered herself:

> me quoque per multos similis fortuna labores
> iactatam hac demum voluit consistere terra.
> non ignara mali miseris succurrere disco.
> *Aen.* 1.628–30

> Me, too, has a like fortune driven through many toils, and willed that at last I should find rest in this land. Not ignorant of ill do I learn to befriend the unhappy.

Later it is precisely because Aeneas feels no pity for her, because he appears inhuman and inhumane (4.365–66), that she becomes most enraged at him and bitterly destructive:

> num fletu ingemuit nostro? num lumina flexit?
> num lacrimas victus dedit aut miseratus amantem est?
> *Aen.* 4.369–70

> Did he sigh while I wept? Did he turn on me a glance? Did he yield and shed tears or pity her who loved him?

As a last example we may consider the final simile of the *Aeneid,* in which readers are virtually compelled, through the use of the first-person plural verb, to identify with the terror and weakness of Turnus and to pity him as he is vanquished by Aeneas:

ac uelut in somnis, oculos ubi languida pressit
nocte quies, nequiquam avidos extendere cursus
velle *videmur* et in mediis conatibus aegri
succidimus; non lingua valet, non corpore notae
sufficiunt vires nec vox aut verba sequuntur:
sic Turno, quacumque viam virtute petivit,
successum dea dira negat.

Aen. 12.908–14

Just as in dreams of night, when languid rest
has closed our eyes, we seem in vain to wish
to press on down a path, but as we strain,
we falter, weak; our tongues can say nothing,
the body loses its familiar force,
no voice, no word can follow; so whatever
courage he calls upon to find a way,
the cursed goddess keeps success from Turnus.

Readers are here made to identify with Turnus' nightmare of
helpless victimization, to see it both as their own and as universal,
thus necessarily are invited to become members of a moral
community that pities loss and grieves at the costs of victory.
This motif, though climactically placed at the poem's conclusion,
occurs throughout the *Aeneid* and contributes to the haunting
melancholy of the whole.[38]

The *Georgic* poet's inclination to pity moves him to bring a
"lesson of poetry" (in Adam Parry's fine phrase)[39] to Roman
towns (2.176) and similarly to bring the Muses from Greece to
Italy (3.10–15). The poet has just described Italian peoples as
characteristically and distinctively fierce and military:

haec genus acre virum, Marsos pubemque Sabellam
adsuetumque malo Ligurem Volscosque verutos

38. M. P.-H. Schrijvers, "La valeur de la pitié chez Virgile dans l'Enéide et
chez quelques-uns de ses interprètes," in *Présence de Virgile,* ed. R. Chevalier
(Paris, 1978), 483–95, cites references that suggest that the conventional Roman's
conception of pity was narrower than that of Homer, for example, and was
directed towards family, friends, and country, not strangers or enemies. Therefore
he argues that the *Aeneid* legitimizes the final vindictiveness of Aeneas. He
ignores the possibility, observed by Iser, 3, 77, 146, that great texts may challenge
problematic convention, not merely endorse it.
39. Parry, 51.

extulit, haec Decios, Marios magnosque Camillos,
Scipiadas duros bello, et te, maxime Caesar,
qui nunc extremis Asiae iam victor in oris
imbellem avertis Romanis arcibus Indum.

(2.167–72)

Her breed of men—the Marsians and Sabellians,
Ligurians used to hardship, Volscian javelin-throwers;
Mother she is of the Decii, Marii, great Camilli,
The Scipios relentless in war; and of you, most royal Caesar,
Who now triumphant along the furthest Asian frontiers
Keep the war-worthless Indians away from the towers of Rome.

It is not implausible that such militaristic peoples might lack or fail to express artistic sensibility. The Muses apparently live in Greece (3.10–15), and the poet does not include them in his praise of Italy (2.136ff.) although they are the supreme object of his reverence (2.475–76). Cicero (*Tusc.* 1.2.3) had noted (*Sero igitur a nostris poetae vel cogniti vel recepti*) and Horace (*Ars poet.* 323ff.) had lamented that traditional Romans were unfitted for poetry.[40] Here the poet perceives himself as on a mission to bring poetry to his people. In particular he refers to his poetry as Ascraean (i.e., Hesiodic) song, which shall be taken here to denote didactic poetry that, like Hesiod's, describes a fallen world, our Iron Age world, morally inferior to the Golden Age;[41] a world that, through the poet's song, maintains a vision of

40. See remarks in note 28 on Griffin's view.
41. J. P. Vernant, "Le mythe hésiodique des races: Essai d'analyse structurale," *RHR* 157 (1960): 21–54, has shown that the succession and opposition of races (golden, silver, bronze, heroic, and iron) in Hesiod are based not on continuous decline but on the major conflict of *hubris* and *dike*. Hubris and *dike* do not seem to be equally available options for human beings in the *Georgics;* rather the oppositions of the Iron Age seem unnegotiable. Virgil eliminates from his account in the *Georgics* Hesiod's stories of Prometheus and Pandora and the possibility of cycling ages (cf. *Works and Days* 175, where Hesiod wishes he had been born earlier *or later*). Thus in the *Georgics* guilt for the human condition is less attributable to any particular party, and no resolution to Iron Age conflicts can be expected in time.
    The question of how to interpret "Ascraean" song is a surprisingly vexed one. For Putnam, *Poem of the Earth,* 107, for example, it is an allusion to Hesiod's "pessimistic spirit." For Ross, *Virgil's Elements,* 119, it is an allusion to the unreliability of Hesiod's Muses with respect to truth. For Thomas ad loc. the

something better, more just, more harmonious, more humane. The poet thus emerges as a moral teacher, seeking in particular to remedy dissension between brothers (a conflict of special resonance for Romans plagued by civil wars). The expressed intent of the *Georgic* poet (2.176) is to bring this message to his people, to turn them into readers of sensibility, who have an apprehension and appreciation of noncompetitive peace, harmony, and community. He would make readers who could see the moral value of such Golden Age visions.

Pity arises from identification with the suffering of another, from the sense or knowledge that this suffering or something like it could become one's own. Through the pathos of many passages in the *Georgics,* we readers are made to share others' sorrow, to identify with their suffering, to experience it as potentially our own, and hence to feel bonds of common pain that unite us with others. Pity, then, makes of readers a community, because pity requires identification with the pain of another. The essential thing to note here, in terms of the poet's conception of his mission, is the fact that he imagines the Golden Age precisely as a community—a community among all men and between men and nature:

> ante Iovem nulli subigebant arva coloni,
> ne signare quidem aut partiri limite campum
> fas erat: in medium quaerebant, ipsaque tellus
> omnia liberius nullo poscente ferebat.
>
> (1.125–28)

> Before Jove's time no settlers subdued the land; it was not right even to mark the fields or to divide them with boundary lines. All sought the common gain; and earth of her own accord brought forth all things more freely, when no one was asking.[42]

---

allusion is, in the first instance, to Hesiod as a favored model of Alexandrian poets. Secondly, he says, as the adjective (as applied to Hesiod) is first attested in Hellenistic literature (in Nicander), it may have been used by Callimachus and therefore may, in the *Georgics* passage, allude most significantly to Callimachus himself.

42. Author's translation.

These few verses suggest the traditional Golden Age, with its characteristic abundance of food, freedom from war, toil, and unhappiness. Most significant for this account, however, are harmony between man and nature (nature, unasked, gives all things more freely 127–28) and harmony among all men equally (they look to the common good 127). We note also the deeply solemn moral quality of *fas* (127), "right" of absolute or divine, as opposed to human, origin. Plowing the earth, represented as a kind of aggression against nature by man, is not allowed (125); neither is the possession of earth by man (127) nor, consequently, the pursuit of private interest.

The moral effect of Virgil's poetry is precisely to create community, especially Golden Age community as he represents it. His poetry, since it embodies the ideal of harmony over conquest, of compassion for loss over pride in victory, teaches a sense of victory's cost. Through its preservation of a moral ideal and through its appreciation of sentiment, this poetry seeks to expand the sensibility of readers and to fashion them into a humane community. In instituting the Iron Age, Jove (1.121ff.) allowed the dissolution of moral quality (*fas* 127; cf. 1.505) in men's relations with nature and with each other. For his own purposes he allowed these relations to become exploitive and aggressive (e.g., 1.139–45) instead of harmonious. The poet, therefore, in seeking to create through pity a moral community and in representing as positive the values of nonexploitive peace and harmony, attempts to redress the omission of Jove. In this way the poet establishes an alternative set of values and creates a moral ideal. Thus he becomes the essential carrier of humane value, the bearer of the vision of noncompetitive peace and harmony; he becomes the carrier of what we must call, in terms of this poem, Golden Age values. Community is restored through pity; in particular, moral or Golden Age community is restored through the poet's poetry. He hopes, through his song, to restore the bonds between man and nature, now broken by technology, as well as those between man and man, now broken by civil and foreign war. The boldness of such aspirations well deserves the term *audax* that the poet applies to it at 1.40, with echoes at 2.175 and 4.565.

Since the feeling of pity is an ennobling one, the conviction of moral mission and superior moral sensibility might lead to complacency, even arrogance, in both poet and readers. Yet the *Georgic* poet does not assume an unambiguous superiority, nor is he represented as content in his separate values. Neither uncritical nor lacking in perspective on himself and his aspirations, he suggests in the emergent self-portrait in this poem certain limitations and inconsistencies that confirm his identity as an Iron Age figure.

The major flaw that the poet perceives in his work is what he represents as its futility because the value of pity is negligible in the political world. Events and motifs in the *Georgics* (as well as in the *Aeneid*) suggest that pity is an inadequate, if humane, response to the moral and political dilemmas of the world of power. One could argue also, even more sadly, that the gratification that pity provides to the pitier is cheap and easy, almost a kind of play, as the poet may be suggesting with the verb *ludere* in 4.565 to describe his own song. Euripides had made Orestes say

> Uneducated men are pitiless,
> but we who are educated pity much. And we pay
> a high price for being intelligent. Wisdom hurts.
> (*El.* 294–96)[43]

There is clearly here a self-congratulating element to pity. Pitiers esteem themselves for their superior sensibility and intellectuality, even while they see (with their fine intelligence) the limitations of pity and superiority. As Augustine much later observed, people like to feel pity as long as it is for the suffering of others:

> quid est, quod ibi homo vult dolere luctuosa et tragica, quae tamen pati ipse nollet? et tamen pati vult ex eis dolorem spectator, et dolor ipse est voluptas eius . . . quamquam, cum ipse patitur, miseria, cum aliis compatitur, misericordia dici solet . . . non enim ad subveniendum provocatur auditor, sed tantum ad dolendum invitatur . . . lacrimae ergo amantur et dolores.
> (*Confessions* 3.2.2–3)

---

43. Emily Townsend Vermeule, trans., *Euripides:* Electra, in *Euripides,* vol. 5, ed. David Grene and Richmond Lattimore (Chicago and London, 1959; reprint, 1968).

> Why is it that a man likes to grieve over death and tragic events which he would not want to happen to himself? The spectator likes to experience grief at such scenes, and this very sorrow is a pleasure to him. . . . However, when he himself suffers it, it is usually called misery; when he suffers it with regard to others it is called pity. The auditor is not aroused to help others; he is only asked to grieve over them. . . . Tears and sorrow, therefore, are objects of love.[44]

Pity is perhaps a kind of play, a self-indulgence, that translates into no effective action in a world where power and choice have only serious consequence.

Such thoughts on the limitations and self-gratification of pity as are expressed by Euripides, Aristotle (see p. 20), and Augustine are implicit in the *Georgics* in the experiences of the poet-figures, who are the carriers of the value of pity in the poem. Not only the *Georgic* poet but also Orpheus, Proteus, and the nightingale fulfill poetic functions in the *Georgics* and reveal aspects of the poet's experience. All are represented variously as weak or failed in the world;[45] all are shown as having a certain regressive focus and pleasure in sorrow and loss, which they turn into beautiful, if ineffective, song.

The story of Orpheus and Eurydice, the most moving and haunting passage in the *Georgics,* is attributed to Proteus. The *Georgic* poet is the singer of the Orpheus tale only indirectly or at second hand. Proteus' performance, although not described as musical (4.452), is nevertheless the most beautiful and moving poetry of the poem. Orpheus' song, apparently beyond human powers to describe, is never heard by readers. Therefore Proteus'

44. John K. Ryan, trans., *The* Confessions *of St. Augustine* (Garden City, N.Y., 1958).

45. For this theme in the *Eclogues,* see J. B. Solodow, "*Poeta Impotens:* The Last Three *Eclogues,*" *Latomus* 36 (1977): 757–71. In a valuable article, "Daedalus, Virgil, and the End of Art," *AJP* 108 (1987): 173–89, M. C. J. Putnam notes that Daedalus creates his art because of pity (*Aen.* 6.28) for Ariadne. The artist becomes creative through pity. For our purposes here we should observe further that Daedalus, when it comes to depicting his *own* failure and loss (i.e., the death of Icarus), is incapable of completing the work (*Aen.* 6.30–31). This suggests, it seems, a distinction between the ease of pity that one can feel for others and then turn to artistic ends and the incapacity one feels at one's own grief and failure. Pity appears more likely than grief to come to artistic expression.

song is the most beautiful within our world of experience; he is the best poet we hear. And again, in him, we find a failure or loser in the world of power, for he is violated, compelled, and outmaneuvered (*vim duram et vincula capto/tende* 4.399–400; cf. *victus,* "vanquished" 443) by a power (Cyrene's knowledge, Aristaeus' force) more determined and aggressive than his own capacity to escape it. In addition to being vanquished and victimized himself, he also feels sympathy for Orpheus, the loser in his own drama with Aristaeus. Proteus and Orpheus are both, at least in part, victims of Aristaeus and the real power he represents.

We see, of course, a similar dynamic in the vignette of the nightingale (4.511–15), to which Orpheus is likened. Again there is the victimization of the beautiful singer by the stronger agent of the real world. As in the above examples, the beauty of the nightingale's song lies in its pathos (her children are lost, they are *implumis* 512–13) and in its eternal voicing of irremediable tragedy (514–15). The key for this discussion is that the nightingale's song is perceived by listeners as beautiful and as tragic. The hypothetical explanation of the melancholy of the nightingale's song (that she mourns her lost children, that the loss is eternal) illuminates the intimate and necessary relationship between tragedy and beauty and powerlessness, which has been the entire subject of this discussion.

This simile of the nightingale and the farmer recalls not only *Odyssey* 19.518–23 and 16.216–18 but also the fable of the nightingale and the hawk in Hesiod's *Works and Days* (202–12):

Now I shall tell a fable to the perceptive kings.
Thus spoke the hawk to the nightingale, the speckle-necked bird,
As he was carrying her gripped in his talons high in the clouds,
And she was piteously crying, for she was pierced by the grip of his
Bent talons; thus he spoke and strongly advised her:
"Foolish thing, why are you shrieking? Your captor is much stronger than you.
There shall you go wherever I take you though you're a singer,
And, as I wish, I shall eat you for dinner or let you go free.
Foolish the man who wishes to fight against those who are stronger;

He loses the victory and suffers pain in addition to shame."
Thus spoke the swift-flying hawk, the long-winged bird.

The ostensible moral of this fable, as the hawk speaks it, is that
might makes right, arbitrarily (209) and regardless of justice. Yet
the unpalatable characterization of the hawk and the pathos
(205) of the nightingale's circumstance assure both that the
reader's sympathy is with the nightingale and that the reader,
despite the hawk's apparent present superiority, hears his moral
with a certain irony, believing or hoping that Zeus will ultimately
destroy the immoral hawk. The emotional dynamic of the fable
is that Hesiod identifies with the nightingale, the singer (208),
weak and victimized, and similarly involves the reader's sympathy. In this the fable is parallel to the simile in the *Georgics*. The
significant difference is that in Hesiod the fable is unconcluded;
there is hope that justice, in the end, will triumph and that the
singer will go free. The reader's hope is of a piece with Hesiod's
exhortation to justice. In the *Georgics* passage, on the contrary,
the tragic outcome (the nightingale's loss of her young) has
already occurred. The substance of the simile is to express the
inevitable victimization of the weak by the strong and the related
intimate connection between tragedy and beauty and powerlessness.

It is the *Georgic* poet, above all, who composes beautiful and
tragic poetry, for his poem contains not only the pathos of the
tale of Orpheus but a grand vision of the ambiguity of human
experience as a whole, as will be discussed in the third chapter.
He is, consequently, the poem's greatest poet and its most daring
figure (1.40; 2.174; 4.565; and cf. 4.469 of Orpheus). Yet he
acknowledges with graceful and only partial irony that he has no
power in the world when compared to Caesar (4.559–66). Despite the real courage, if not audacity, of his efforts, he is of
negligible significance in the world of politics and conquest. The
poet values and even proselytizes on behalf of pity. He conceives
of his poetic mission as the bringing of pity, of a "lesson of
poetry," to his people. Yet the poet also has the perception that
poets lose in the real world and that, consequently, pity itself is a
kind of self-indulgent play (4.563–66). One might see in the word

ludere (4.565) not only a technical term but also Virgil's derogation of his own poetry, simultaneously ironic and serious. For,
futile as it may be, pity is nevertheless the most humane value,
necessary to the development of society (cf. Lucr. 5.1023: *imbe-
cillorum esse aecum misererier omnis,* "that it was right for all to
pity the weak") and to the maintenance of a humane order.
Therefore the *Georgics* performs the highest moral function in
making readers sensitive to loss and sympathetic to sorrow.
Responsive readers must come to sense and to acknowledge the
community and vulnerability of all mortal enterprise. Although
the poet realizes the particular vulnerability of poets and of pity,
he nevertheless consistently engages the reader's sympathy with
these variously failed figures.

We see, then, that the poet, as represented in the figures of the
Georgic poet, Orpheus, Proteus, and even the nightingale, is
simultaneously exalted and disparaged. He is exalted for the
beauty and emotional power of his song, for the humane value of
pity that it voices and preserves. He is disparaged for his impotence in the world, for the inadequacy of his song as a response
to the world's troubles, for his inclination to make of tragedy and
loss a beautiful thing. This last propensity is of deeply ambiguous
value, for it makes the poet ever backward-looking and hence
ineffective. Yet it also makes him the only carrier of humane
value in a material world that esteems profit and success above
all, regardless of cost. These contrasting perspectives on the poet
remain unresolved through the poem's final verses and constitute
one of its essential tensions.

In addition to the weaknesses of a poetic method that relies on
and appeals to pity, the poet reveals in himself other flaws or,
better, inconsistencies that cause him dissatisfaction and identify
him as an Iron Age figure. Among these are his pursuit of glory,
his domination by irrational *amor* (both of which he deplores in
others), and, finally, a certain alienation that he feels in his own
time and place, since he repeatedly idealizes an irretrievable past
and aspires to knowledge he cannot have.

The poet experiences ambition for glory and longs for victory
and to be first (4.6;3.8–10, 17). While he sings for the community,
he represents himself as happiest when seeking his individual

goal of poetic victory and primacy (3.291–92). His victory will be one of song, hence without exploitation of nature or violence towards other men. Nevertheless, since pursuit of *honor* and *gloria* is explicitly condemned in Book 2 (e.g., 2.503ff.), we must infer the poet's awareness within himself of contradictory, Iron Age drives. Although acknowledging the moral inferiority of urban to rural life, he nevertheless distances himself from the latter by declaring his own passion for poetry. His desire to write poetry is not willed, but stems from love (*amor*) for the Muses (2.476), by which he is struck. The poet has desires for *honor* and *gloria* because of his own particular *amor*, of which he cannot fail to recognize the irrational source (2.476, 3.285).[46] His poetry originates in *amor:*

> quarum sacra fero ingenti percussus amore
> (2.476)
>
> whose sacred emblems I bear, struck by a mighty love
>
> singula dum capti circumvectamur amore
> (3.285)
>
> while we, seized by love, tarry at each separate detail
>
> sed me Parnasi deserta per ardua dulcis
> raptat amor
> (3.291–92)
>
> But over these lonely heights of Parnassus
> I'm driven by sweet love.

When the poet terms his *amor dulcis* ("sweet" 3.291) and Leander's *durus* ("harsh" 3.259), one senses the ironic awareness of self-delusion. The juxtaposition of *ardua* ("steep") and *dulcis*

---

46. Richter ad loc., who notes the significant recurrence of the term *amor* here, is unclear about whether Virgil sees a parallel between his own feelings and those of the animals and human beings he has just described. Virgil, however, as is reflected in his choice of terms, sees *amor* as leading to passion and conflict as well as to poetry. Miles, 186, points out that "the explicit assertion that men, no less than animals, are vulnerable to *amor*'s disruptive influence argues for the inescapable ambiguity of human potential as well." In discussing 3.285 and 3.292, however, he detects no ironic self-awareness on the poet's part.

(3.291) suggests the effortful pleasure that the poet takes in his irrational passions and Iron Age strivings. *Percussus* ("struck" 2.476), *capti* ("caught" 3.285), and *raptat* ("seizes," "drives" 3.292) reveal the compelling nature of his passion. Like the charioteers straining for victory (3.103ff), like the stallion longing for challenge and combat (3.77ff), like the city dwellers condemned in Book 2, the poet experiences a passion that can know no permanent satisfaction. There is irony, subtlety, and acuity in the poet's portrait of himself. Certainly the poet's victory will come without violence or exploitation. Since, however, there is no competition (or art, apparently) in the Golden Age, we must see the poet's art and the competitive, irrational urges that sustain it as an Iron Age phenomenon.

The substance of the poet's victory will be its originality and seriousness of purpose (3.4–8). The Muses do not live in Italy, but must be brought there from Greece (3.11–12). Should the poet succeed in his mission of bringing the Muses (and all that they signify) to his own country, he would construe this as a victory for himself. To express meaningfully the magnitude of his accomplishment in terms valued by Roman tradition, he calls himself *victor* (3.9–17) and proceeds to describe his victory in such a way as to suggest simultaneously a Roman triumph and an Olympic victory:

> in medio mihi Caesar erit templumque tenebit.
> illi victor ego et Tyrio conspectus in ostro
> centum quadriiugos agitabo ad flumina currus.
> cuncta mihi Alpheum linquens locosque Molorchi
> cursibus et crudo decernet Graecia caestu.
> ipse caput tonsae foliis ornatus olivae
> dona feram.
>
> (3.16–22)

Caesar's image shall stand there in the midst, commanding my
    temple,
While I, a victor, conspicuous in crimson robes, shall drive
A hundred four-horse chariots up and down by the river.
All Greece will leave Alpheus and the Peloponnesian groves
To take part in the races and boxing-bouts I've arranged.
I myself, wearing a chaplet of trimmed olive,
Will present the prizes.

By juxtaposing his name to that of Caesar and by attributing the epithet *victor* as well as the nominative case to himself, he implies that his victory compares favorably with Caesar's. In 3.26–33 he imagines his creation:

> in foribus pugnam ex auro solidoque elephanto
> Gangaridum faciam victorisque arma Quirini,
> atque hic undantem bello magnumque fluentem
> Nilum ac navali surgentis aere columnas.
> addam urbes Asiae domitas pulsumque Niphaten
> fidentemque fuga Parthum versisque sagittis
> et duo rapta manu diverso ex hoste tropaea
> bisque triumphatas utroque ab litore gentes.

> On the doors of my temple I'll have engraved in gold and solid
> Ivory the battle of the Ganges and the arms of victorious Quirinus
> And here the enormous stream of Nile a-surge with a naval
> Battle, and columns rising cast from the bronze of warships.
> I'll add the cities of Asia we've mastered, Armenians routed,
> Parthians whose strength is flight and shooting over their
>   shoulder;
> Two trophies taken in battle from distant foes, a double
> Triumph from either shore.

He reveals that the significant feature of his victory in contrast to Caesar's is that it is achieved through song (3.1, 3.3; cf. 4.471), hence without aggression—unlike the farmer's or soldier's. And though the poet triumphs peacefully, he is not passive but emphatically active: *deducam* (11), *referam* (12), *ponam* (13), *agitabo* (18), *feram* (22), *addam* (30). The monument to Caesar's glory is dependent upon the poet, a function of his song.[47]

Primacy is an important aspect of the poet's victory, although the claim to being first is familiar for poets. Commentators, for example, find parallels for these lines in Lucretius:

---

47. Cf. Thomas at 3.1–48, one of the most impressive passages of his commentary. Based on inferences from texts extant and otherwise, he is able to discern in this proem a thoroughgoing allusion to Callimachus in which Virgil simultaneously rejects Neoteric/Callimachean themes and genres (in envisioning the *Aeneid*) and yet also manifests commitment to a Callimachean esthetic. As Thomas puts it (at 3.28), it is "a proem which rejects the Callimachean rejection of epic."

avia Pieridum peragro loca nullius ante
trita solo. iuvat integros accedere fontis
atque haurire, iuvatque novos decerpere flores
insignemque meo capiti petere inde coronam
unde prius nulli velarint tempora Musae.

(Lucr. 1.926–30)

I travel the Muses' pathless places; none
Before has walked where I walk. I love to find
New founts and drink, to gather fresh, new flowers
And seek the laureate's crown whence Muses never
Till now have veiled the brow of any man.

(Lucr. 1.117–18, concerning Ennius, is similar. Horace refers to his own original achievement in *Odes* 3.30.13: *princeps.*) What is not paralleled in these passages, namely, the claim to be *victor,* establishes that the military-athletic parallel is not mere convention but expresses significantly the context in which the poet wishes to place his achievement. (*Vincere* similarly describes his accomplishment in 3.289.) *Victor* is an emphatic addition to the traditional claim of primacy, and it makes clear the competitive, Iron Age drive of the poet.

The opulence of the temple's artistry, glorious with bronze, ivory, gold, and Parian marble, involves the poet in another inconsistency. The beauty of the poet's conceptions and aspirations, represented in the temple's precious metals and skilled artwork, is at variance with the ethic of utility and material austerity apparently endorsed in the *laudes ruris* of Book 2.458ff.[48] From the point of view of this ethic, the poet's temple of poetry would have to be condemned as extravagant and decadent. Neither beauty nor ornament serves a useful function or is appropriate to the previously idealized rural values of simplicity, naturalness, discipline, and rigorous restraint. Rather than affirming rural values, the poet's temple tends instead to identify him with city dwellers, who are competitive, ambitious, and eager for luxury.

---

48. Putnam, *Poem of the Earth,* 169 (also Miles, 175–77), notes the inconsistency of the poet's aspirations here with those values presumably scorned in 2.458ff. Cf. Boyle, 78–79.

These inconsistencies are points of moral tension for the poet, in which he reveals himself as very much an Iron Age figure. These drives set him apart from Golden Age ideals as he represents them in *Georgic* 1 and identify him rather with charioteers, soldiers, and city dwellers. Although the poet's goal is humane and sustaining of culture and of the spirit, although his chosen "weapon" of combat is song, his drives are irrational (*amor*) and competitive. It is, therefore, difficult for readers to maintain a deep distinction between him and the other flawed Iron Age figures who people this poem.

The poet is also identified as an Iron Age figure by the discontent that he experiences in seeking a knowledge he cannot have, a time (the Golden Age) that is past, and a place (Greek poetic sources) that is unavailable.

The poet desires unattainable knowledge:

> Me vero primum dulces ante omnia Musae,
> quarum sacra fero ingenti percussus amore,
> accipiant caelique vias et sidera monstrent,
> defectus solis varios lunaeque labores;
> unde tremor terris, qua vi maria alta tumescant
> obicibus ruptis rursusque in se ipsa residant,
> quid tantum Oceano properent se tinguere soles
> hiberni, vel quae tardis mora noctibus obstet.
> (2.475–82)

> But as for me—may the Muses, sweet above all,
> Whose holy emblems, I, struck by a mighty passion, bear,
> Take me to themselves and reveal heaven's pathways, the stars,
> The several eclipses of the sun and the moon's travails,
> The cause of earthquakes and the force that compels the deep sea
> To swell, to break all bounds, to fall back on itself again;
> The reason why winter suns race on to dip in Ocean,
> And what delays the long nights.

While the farmer does not *know* his blessings, the poet aspires precisely to knowledge, but not of *praecepta* ("precepts", "maxims"), practical and productive. Rather he aspires to knowledge of *causae* ("causes") of ultimate truths, which he represents as the gift of the Muses, for whom he experiences a religious awe. The possibility of failing in this aspiration (483ff.) is very real to the poet. Thus he confronts openly the reality of a poetic quest forever unfulfilled.

As a second choice he wishes for a kind of rural retreat (486–89), but not to the Italian countryside, although he has just praised it (2.136–76). Rather he desires explicitly to be transported to the countryside of Greek poetry,[49] his spiritual homeland, dwelling place of the Muses, where he hopes to become intimate somehow with the sources of his poetic passion. The ungrammatical effusion in which he expresses his desire suggests the abandon, the sense of rapture and communion with something beyond the material that the poet seeks.[50] In his longing for Greece the poet expresses cultural ideals different from traditionally conceived Roman ones, which do not entirely satisfy his passions nor match his feelings of religious or poetic fervor. His prayer for knowledge shows his aspirations to be different from the farmer's since it expresses spiritual and intellectual goals not encompassed by the farmer's concerns. His prayer for ecstatic experience in Greece suggests the deep bonds that he feels to a tradition outside his own.

The poet's recurrent absorption with the motif of the Golden Age also implies a dissatisfaction with the present and a sense of continuing decline in the moral quality of human experience. He expresses a powerful nostalgia for what he represents as a lost and more perfect past in such passages as 1.125–35 and 2.336–42, 532–40, the myth of the Golden Age embodying a standard by which the present is implicitly measured and found wanting. The present is experienced as a time of tension with the Golden Age, with a certain unrecoverable moral quality that not even the poet fully embodies.

49. Putnam, *Poem of the Earth,* 148, comments: "What startles here is not only the ardent immediacy of this double supplication, but the precise location away from Italy in a completely Hellenic setting. In spite of the *laudes Italiae,* it is to Greece, not to his homeland, that Virgil turns when his mind is bent on charting its inspiration."

50. T. C. Page, ed., *P. Vergili Maronis:* Bucolica *et* Georgica (London, 1898; reprint, 1965), remarks ad loc.: "It is difficult to say what is the exact grammar of this rapturous outburst."

Simultaneously the poet is deeply bound to the present and to Italy by patriotic pride and deep commitment. Among many examples, the prayers that bracket Book 1 (5ff. and 498ff.) reveal the poet's concern with Italy's fate, with his contemporary Romans in desperate confrontation with the consequences of their political life. These prayers suggest the urgency of the poet's mission to Italy, which he has not abandoned, despite his desires for Greece. Surely and deeply immured in his world, he feels the responsibility to sing of and for it. His mission to Italy is expressed in grave, exalted tones of religious fervor (2.174–76) and includes the entire complex of attitudes that he embodies, such as capacity for sentiment, aspiration to mystery and to the Muses' truth, and pity, which makes humane community.

His sense of mission is implicit also in his treatment of the Corycian gardener (a subject to be discussed more fully in Chapter 2). In this passage (4.116–48) the poet describes himself as wishing to pursue his vision of the gardener but as prevented, by limitations of time and space, from doing so (4.116–19, 147–48). Like the Golden Age the Corycian gardener is an ideal unavailable to the poet. Isolated in the genre of georgic poetry (which does not ordinarily treat gardens), in time past, and in distance from Rome, the gardener is an irretrievable dream. In his growing of flowers and in the esthetic disposition of his garden, the gardener embodies an ideal of superfluous beauty or art for its own sake and without political content, which the *Georgic* poet conceives as unavailable to himself.

In his portrait of the gardener there is a fine expression of the poet's awareness of his unalterable discontent. He is prevented from pursuing his desire, the ideal of the gardener, as he would wish, since he feels the constraints of time and mission. Unlike the gardener he is not free to pursue an isolated and apolitical ideal of beauty. The *Georgic* poet, deeply committed to his world and sensitive to its suffering, sings the urgency of its troubles.

Throughout the *Georgics* the *Georgic* poet is represented in ways that both exalt and depreciate him. He is the sole carrier of the humane value of pity, for we do not find pity characteristic of farmers, city dwellers, or Hell. It is the poet's mission of high courage and daring to bring Ascraean song to Italian peoples. As Hesiod is a moral teacher to Perses, so the *Georgic* poet would be a moral teacher to his addressees and to all readers. The beauty of his song has the power to move the spirit and to forge moral values, for he finds even in tragedy a source of beautiful despair that is sustaining to the spirit. On the other hand, the poet is backward-looking, self-indulgent in pursuing his tragic visions, and committed to a song of pity that is impotent in the world of military power and politics. These contrasting perspectives on the poet remain unresolved through the poem's final verses and constitute one of its central tensions.

ARISTAEUS AND ORPHEUS

In the myth and tradition outside the *Georgics* both Orpheus and Aristaeus are culture heroes—Aristaeus for agriculture and Orpheus for religious rites, mysteries, and poetry. In this way they exemplify a range of human cultural activity. While exemplary in tradition prior to this poem, both are represented in the *Georgics* as passionate and, ultimately, destructive, for both destroy Eurydice, who dies once because of each of them.[51]

51. It will be obvious to the reader of this study that I believe the Aristaeus epyllion to be integral to the *Georgics*, summarizing, as it does in so many ways, the central themes of the poem. Servius' allegation that this passage was inserted, at the request of Augustus, in place of an original passage concerning Gallus has not had the support of scholarly consensus since 1933, when W. B. Anderson published his refutation of the story ("Gallus and the Fourth *Georgic*," *CQ* 27 [1933]: 36–45). Thomas, 13–16, accepts the primacy and authenticity of the passage, with a good discussion of the issues involved. See also Wilkinson, *Georgics,* 325–26. A recent attack on the primacy of the piece is seen in H. Jacobsen, "Aristaeus, Orpheus, and the *Laudes Galli,*" *AJP* 105 (1984): 271–300. This is a genuinely astonishing piece of work, as Jacobsen implicitly accuses Virgil of carelessness, imperfect poetic imagination, and faulty revision. He then proposes revisions by which, according to his own taste, Virgil could have improved the *Georgics.* I am reminded of an apposite remark by Page, XXXVIII: "[Virgil's] place indeed is assured by the verdict of eighteen centuries, and for an ordinary man to criticize his poetic power is almost an impertinence."

In any case, Virgil left us the present poem. Whether it represents an early or a late draft, it reflects the poet's last intention. Therefore it is legitimate for us to interpret what we have.

Much scholarly effort has been devoted to reconstructing the history and treatment of the Orpheus myth before Virgil.[52] The consensus of this work is that Virgil is probably the first to have represented Orpheus as losing Eurydice, despite the beauty of his music and the daring of his descent to Hades to retrieve her. The fact that Virgil's telling of Aristaeus' story is equally unparalleled has not received similar attention.[53] Nevertheless, the association of Aristaeus with the process of *bougonia* and with Eurydice, and through her with Orpheus, is unprecedented in previous accounts as well as unimitated in subsequent ones. Virgil is original in his treatment of both figures, and we see, therefore, that in his role as *Georgic* poet he is creating new myths from old myths in order to tell his own truth. Here, in powerful and significant innovation, the poet makes the stories of Aristaeus and Orpheus cross in the figure of Eurydice, thus bringing together these two figures, polar in the scope of human culture, in such a way as to suggest their significant similarities and oppositions and to comment, through these, on the character of Iron Age culture.

Each, in his feelings towards Eurydice, reveals a significant aspect of his character. Aristaeus yields to transient and destructive passion; Orpheus' passion is consuming, until death and

---

52. Important studies are Jacques Heurgon, "Orphée et Eurydice avant Virgile," *MEFR* 49 (1932): 6–60; E. Norden, "Orpheus und Eurydice," *S. Ak. Berlin phil.-hist. Kl.* 22(1934): 626–83. (= *Kleine Schriften* [Berlin, 1966], 468–532); K. Ziegler, "Orpheus," *RE* 17.1 (1939): 1200–1316. Prior to Virgil the only known (serious) versions of Orpheus' descent to Hades for Eurydice (i.e., Eur. *Alc.* 357–62; Isoc. *Bus.* [11] 7ff.; Hermesianax *Leontion* B3; [Moschus] *Lament for Bion* 123–25) tell of his success. Even some versions subsequent to Virgil (e.g., Manilius *Astronomica* 5.326–28; Lucian *Dial. mort.* 23.3 Jacobitz) have happy endings, showing that that tradition was still viable. It has been supposed by some (Bowra ["Orpheus and Eurydice," *CQ* n.s. 2 (1952): 113–26], Heurgon, Richter) that a now lost Hellenistic poem, which described Orpheus' loss of Eurydice, was imitated here by Virgil. Brooks Otis, "A New Study of the *Georgics*," *Phoenix* 26 (1972): 58, sums up: "The important point is that Virgil either invented or selected a very unusual variation of the myth for an obvious purpose, i.e. to depict an attempt at resurrection that was frustrated by passion." Cf. Thomas at 4.453–527.

53. An exception is W. S. Anderson, "The Orpheus of Virgil and Ovid: *flebile nescio quid*," in *Orpheus: The Metamorphoses of a Myth*, ed. John Warden (Toronto, 1982), 27.

even after. This passionate quality of Aristaeus and Orpheus stands out when we compare them to the first individual treated in Book 4, the Corycian gardener, since they are represented as young where he is old, sexual and driven where he is asexual and without longings. In Aristaeus' case, his passion threatened to destroy all his accomplishments; so it eventually happens with Orpheus. Similarly the structural feature of *katabasis* (descent) links the stories of Aristaeus and Orpheus in that both descend to another world. Here, though, their stories begin to diverge. While Orpheus goes to Hades, where he sees tragic visions that seem to reflect his own predilection for sorrow (4.471–77), Aristaeus descends to a world that is different from himself—a purely feminine world, both peaceful and nurturant. Again, both Aristaeus and Orpheus participate in attempts at regeneration of life. Aristaeus' attempt to acquire new bees succeeds (although it is essential to note that these bees are not reborn, as they are not identical to those that had perished), while Orpheus' attempt to resurrect Eurydice ultimately fails. Aristaeus, content with substitution or exchange, succeeds on earth and in heaven, becoming a god in the Iron Age world. Orpheus, rejecting any substitution, preserves through song the memory of the ideal that he has lost, thus becoming increasingly isolated from any human community or relationship. As a consequence, he is eventually destroyed. Although there is a sterility to Orpheus' grief (as suggested in his frozen wanderings), there is—very importantly—a sterility to Aristaeus' success as well, for the impersonal, inhuman bees are emotionally inadequate as recompense for the loss of Orpheus and Eurydice.

From this summary alone we see that the stories of Aristaeus and Orpheus are elaborately parallel as well as significantly different in details and in outcome. Our task will be to probe this myth as the poet tells it, for it crystallizes certain oppositions or tensions central to the *Georgics*. Aristaeus is aggressive and successful without regard to cost; he is not inclined to retrospect (he does not look back), nor is he reflective. The figure of Aristaeus stands in the same relation to Orpheus as does the farmer to the *Georgic* poet. In brief, as critics have noted, Aristaeus in this poem stands for "productivity" and for "control" of nature, thus epitomizing Iron Age man, while Orpheus stands for "creativity" and "sympathy" with nature. From this we see that Aristaeus' relationship with nature typifies the Iron Age, while Orpheus' recalls the Golden Age. Aristaeus is productive of material goods, while Orpheus is productive of nonmaterial song. In distinction from the material, military mode of the farmer, Orpheus typifies the artist. In the Iron Age world, then, he is set apart, ineffective, becoming the chance victim of Aristaeus' violence and also of his own tragic sensibility.

ARISTAEUS

In myth and tradition outside the *Georgics,* as far as can be ascertained, Aristaeus is an exemplary figure, a culture hero, a true benefactor of mankind through his teaching of agriculture, cattle breeding, hunting, and beekeeping.[54] The *Georgic* poet makes Aristaeus representative of all Iron Age men in that the glory of his mortal life, as he himself declares, is his productive labor:

> en etiam hunc ipsum vitae mortalis honorem,
> quem mihi vix frugum et pecudum custodia sollers
> omnia temptanti extuderat, te matre relinquo.
> (4.326–28)

> Look, even this mere honor of mortal life, which I won
> So hardly by craft and much resourcefulness from the care of
> Harvest and herd—though you are my mother—I abandon.

The phrase *vitae mortalis honorem* ("honor of mortal life" 326) suggests that Aristaeus represents the continuing aspirations of all mortals as he strives to achieve his greatest ambitions, in his case the hope of divinity:

> quid me caelum sperare iubebas?
> (4.325)

> Why tell me to hope for heaven?

54. For sources on Aristaeus see W. H. Roscher, *Ausführliches Lexikon der griechischen und römischen Mythologie* (Leipzig, 1884–90), s.v. "Aristaeus"; Friedrich Hiller v. Gaertringen, "Aristaios," *RE* 2 (1896): 852–59; Miles, 258 n. 14; Johnston, 111; Wilkinson, Georgics, 108 n. 1.

In his relationship to nature as well he epitomizes Iron Age man, for he seeks through his labor to dominate nature, to make it productive for himself, and consequently to achieve *gloria* and *honor*. In this poem, then, he is suitably guilty of the rape of Eurydice, for she is a figure of nature,[55] and as we have seen, it is a thematic leitmotif of the *Georgics* that agricultural productivity or progress absolutely requires the domination of natural things. If one sees rape as an act of domination, it becomes clear that rape is the paradigmatic gesture of productive man to nature. Therefore, by making Aristaeus, the tutelary god of agriculture, guilty of rape and, inadvertently, of the death of Eurydice—not at all a goal in itself but rather an instance of accidental destruction[56]—the *Georgic* poet makes him represent the Iron Age experience in relation to nature as a whole. It is suggestive that in this instance Aristaeus wishes merely to rape, not to kill; thus he does not succeed where he wishes and is more destructive than he intends. As he needs to control nature's creatures for his glory, so it is consistent that he acts violently, exploitively, and without sentiment towards Eurydice.

Violence and struggle are again required, as Cyrene reveals, for Aristaeus to learn the cause of his suffering and its cure:

> nam sine vi non ulla dabit praecepta, neque illum
> orando flectes; vim duram et vincula capto
> tende
>
> (4.398–400)

Except to violence he yields not one word of advice; entreaties
Have no effect: you must seize him, offer him force and fetters

> ad haec vates vi denique multa
> ardentis oculos intorsit lumine glauco,
> et graviter frendens sic fatis ora resolvit.
>
> (4.450–52)

---

55. On Eurydice as a figure of nature see, for example, André Oltramare, *Étude sur l'épisode d'Aristée dans les Géorgiques de Virgile* (Geneva, 1892), 158. Cf. Dorothea S. Wender, "Resurrection in the Fourth *Georgic*," *AJP* 90 (1969): 431; Johnston, 113 and 113n. 11; Segal, "Orpheus and the Fourth *Georgic*," 317.
56. Cf. *Aen.* 4.68–73.

> At this the seer, yielding at last to mighty force,
> Rolled his glaring eyes so they shone with a glassy light,
> Harshly ground his teeth, and thus gave tongue to fate.

Aristaeus is successful in his quest because this necessary violence is not uncongenial to him. Proteus, having endured his assault, addresses him as *iuvenum confidentissime* ("boldest of youths" 4.445). Yet his aggression is not represented as daring or courageous, for Eurydice is an undefended female, and Proteus, another figure of nature,[57] an exhausted old man:

> vix *defessa* senem passus componere membra
> cum clamore ruit magno, manicisque iacentem
> occupat.
>
> (4.438–40)

> Scarcely letting the old man lay down his weary limbs,
> He rushed him with a great shout and shackled him where he lay.

This scene parallels the sacrifice of the calf in the *bougonia* (4.299–302), also defenseless, whose sufferings and terror are narrated in some detail.

Like the Romans in 1.501–2, Aristaeus is, according to Proteus, in the position of having to atone for his guilt:

> non te nullius exercent numinis irae;
> magna luis commissa: tibi has miserabilis Orpheus
> haudquaquam ob meritum poenas, ni fata resistant,
> suscitat, et rapta graviter pro coniuge saevit.
>
> (4.453–56)

> Not without sanction divine is the anger that hunts you down.
> Great is the crime you pay for. Piteous Orpheus calls
> This vengeance against you—if fate did not interpose—far short
> Of your deserts; bitter his anguish for the wife taken from him.

Further, he is like the farmers (*ignaros . . . viae* 1.41) in his ignorance of the causes of his suffering. An unreflective character, he fails to put the blame for his actions on himself, where, as the reader ultimately learns, it would seem to belong,[58] but

---

57. Cf. Putnam, *Poem of the Earth*, 284.
58. See Miles, 261, 270, on Aristaeus' refusal to accept responsibility and his attribution of the blame to his mother. Richter, 388, is more kindly: "Aristaeus is

instead attributes the blame to his mother, whom he charges with cruelty (4.321–32).

Most significant, when we recall that the stated purpose of the *Georgic* poet's poem is pity (1.41), is that—in contrast to Orpheus—Aristaeus, though guilty of attempted rape and indirectly responsible for Eurydice's death, voices no acknowledgment or understanding of guilt nor regret for his action once its consequences have been revealed to him.[59] He expresses no awareness of loss, no pity for his victims. Except when directed towards himself (cf. 4.321–32), the quality of pity is lacking in him. With respect to his bees, he cares for them only as they subserve the ultimate purpose of his glory. Certainly he is not bound to them by sentiment, and, consequently, he is satisfied with a replacement. This is not an unreasonable position for him, given that he cannot perceive his bees as individuals. His hope for future divinity is what drives him—not sentiment, appreciation of the unique, regret for the past, or compassion.[60]

In his *labor,* then, in his striving for *honor,* in his aggression against natural forces, in his need to atone, in his ignorance of the causes of his suffering, Aristaeus epitomizes Roman and Iron Age experience. The poet would seem to imply that it is precisely this vitality and aggression, when deliberately channeled, that allow him to survive. Thus Aristaeus, though guilty, survives crime and punishment, while the bees, the sacrificed cattle, Orpheus, and Eurydice perish. Aristaeus' success is bought at a high price, for his passion—misdirected—destroys Eurydice and, more importantly to him, his bees, and thus nearly dooms his entire *labor* and hope for *honor.* This portrait, as we see, differs strikingly

---

not without energy and power." Ross, *Virgil's Elements,* 226, downplays the significance of Aristaeus' guilt, suggesting that it was merely a way of linking the stories of Aristaeus and Orpheus. Yet surely Virgil could have thought of another link, had he wished to. Finally, Proteus certainly attributes great significance to Aristaeus' guilt (4.453–56).

59. See Miles, 270–71; and Putnam, *Poem of the Earth,* 314 n. 61, for different interpretations of Aristaeus' silence.

60. John Van Sickle, *The Design of Virgil's* Bucolics (Rome, 1978), 227, puts it another way: Aristaeus is "concerned above all about property."

from tradition and thereby emphasizes, to the extent that Aristaeus is a culture hero, the aggressive and destructive quality of culture as it relates to nature in this poem.

A very revealing, indeed critical, dimension of the quality of Aristaeus' success is that it is achieved through the *bougonia*. Whereas in other accounts Aristaeus is associated with the discovery of real and practical improvements in agricultural techniques, here alone is he credited with the fantastical process of *bougonia*. In order to estimate accurately the quality of Aristaeus' achievement and the symbolic value of the poem's conclusion, we must consider, for a moment, the specific significance of *bougonia* for the ancients.

Because of the fact that the carcass of a calf or an ox, no matter how treated, will not yield bees, we must assume—for this reason alone—that *bougonia* was for the ancients (as well as for moderns) a procedure of uncertain or suspect truth and value. At the least we are constrained to say that it could not have had for them the familiar truth of routine reality, since it never happened. Sure knowledge the ancients did not and could not have had. Possibly they believed in *bougonia* as if it were something on the order of religious faith. Possibly they doubted it. In fact, agricultural writers of antiquity evidence a certain diffidence in writing about *bougonia*. Varro, for example, does not authenticate it in his own voice at all, but rather cites another source (Merula), who in his turn cites another source:

> Merula, ut cetera fecit, historicos quae sequi melitturgoe soleant demonstrabit. Primum apes nascuntur partim ex apibus, partim ex bubulo corpore putrefacto. Itaque Archelaus in epigrammate ait eas esse βοὸς φθιμένης πεπλανημένα τέκνα.
>
> *(Rust.* 3.16.3–4)

> Our well-versed Merula, as he has done in other cases, will tell you of the practice followed by bee-keepers.
> "In the first place, bees are produced partly from bees, and partly from the rotted carcass of a bullock. And so Archelaus, in an epigram, says that they are 'the roaming children of a dead cow.' "[61]

---

61. Hooper and Ash, trans.

Varro omits *bougonia* altogether at 3.16.37–38, where he discusses treatment of ailing bees. Columella is equally diffident in declining to discuss it:

> quam rationem diligentius prosequi supervacuam puto, consentiens Celso, qui prudentissime ait, non tanto interitu pecus istud amitti, ut sic requirendum sit.
>
> *(Rust.* 9.14.6)

> I think it unnecessary to pursue this method further, agreeing as I do with Celsus, who most reasonably says that the hive is never so annihilated that this cure must be sought.[62]

Since *bougonia* is not a precept of verified and routine value (contrast *ut varias usus meditando extunderet artis/paulatim* 1.133–34), we may wonder why the poet attributes it to Aristaeus, elsewhere a true culture hero, and makes of it his crowning discovery in this poem. He may be suggesting that there is an illusory quality to *ars* or to cultural achievement overall. Consistent with this interpretation is the fact that *bougonia* merely regains for Aristaeus what he had lost through his own violence. As a consequence of the deaths of Orpheus, Eurydice, and the sacrificed cattle, he is not materially advanced but rather, in fact, restored to his previous condition. In this way he resembles the rower at 1.201–3, whose ceaseless striving succeeds only in preventing his headlong rush downstream. Another, less questionable, view (invoking the Büchner rule that the less the practical value of a *praeceptum,* the greater is its symbolic value) is that Virgil has chosen to epitomize or crown Iron Age technology with the *bougonia* because of its symbolic value, which, as will be argued here, is that of a dynamic or economy of exchange.

Although, as Büchner says,[63] it would be difficult to prove

62. Author's translation.
63. Büchner, *RE* 8 A2 (1958): 1309. I first argued (in "Virgil's Fourth *Georgic*") that Virgil was fully aware of the literal untruth of *bougonia* and that this untruth was a significant feature of the metaphorical meaning of *bougonia* for the *Georgics* as a whole. Ross, *Virgil's Elements,* 215–18, argues, for reasons largely, but not exclusively, different from those presented there, that *bougonia* is not necessarily to be believed. "A *thaumasion* is worthy of wonder, but not intended to be believed" (216). On *thaumasion* see Thomas at 3.281–314 and his *Lands and Peoples in Roman Poetry: The Ethnographical Tradition* (Cambridge, 1982), 85.

that Virgil did *not* believe in *bougonia*, it is nevertheless true that many features of his narrative suggest that he viewed *bougonia* as fantastical or mythical. Both Klingner and Büchner observe the change in narrative style at this point in the poem.[64] It becomes impersonal instead of direct: "a place is chosen," "they enclose it" (4.295ff.). Said to originate in Egypt, the *bougonia* is made literally and emotionally distant from the reader's reality. It is not described as something that the reader knows, but rather as something unfamiliar and alien, occurring in a distant land from which there may be only hearsay.

To summarize, *bougonia* is not a practical precept for generating bees; it was not part of routine reality, regularly practiced and/or observed by the peoples of the ancient world. Therefore it seems prudent to assume, as is implicit in the ancient writers cited above, that the ancients were in varying degrees diffident in their approach to it as a *praeceptum*. Such reality as they may have accorded to it must have had a different quality from that of daily experience and must have resembled a matter of faith rather than a matter of knowledge.

If we may adopt for a moment and for purposes of discussion the hypothesis that Virgil and his contemporaries either doubted the value of *bougonia* or attributed to it a kind of reality different from observable routine, we will then see that the conclusion of the poem, the character of Aristaeus, and the value of his achievement assume a significance different from that usually attributed to them. The prevailing view is that *bougonia* portends resurrection and a positive resolution to the conflicts of the poem.[65] Such a positive view of *bougonia* does not seem to be supported by the dynamics or economy of *bougonia* as understood by the ancients. For them *bougonia* apparently signified an exchange of death for life rather than rebirth or resurrection. While new bees clearly are born, they are not *re*born, as there is no regeneration of the bees that had previously died and that

64. Klingner, *Virgil,* 324; Büchner, *RE* 8 A2 (1958): 1309–10; similarly Putnam, *Poem of the Earth,* 273.
65. See, for example, Otis, *Virgil,* 213; Segal, "Orpheus and the Fourth Georgic," 325; Putnam, *Poem of the Earth,* 318–20.

remain irretrievable. Most telling, this process requires the destruction of a calf, whose body and soul are needed to generate
new bees, for the soul of the dead calf was perceived as animating
the newly emergent bees. "The main idea seems to be that the life
of the bull passes into that of the bees; the closing of the ears and
nostrils, as well as the insistence on death by slow contusion,
seem to aim at preservation of the soul within the carcass."[66] As
an image, then, *bougonia* signifies not resurrection but rather
sacrifice or the exchange of death for life. Let us look at the
passage now:

> exiguus primum atque ipsos contractus in usus
> eligitur locus; hunc angustique imbrice tecti
> parietibusque premunt artis, et quattuor addunt,
> quattuor a ventis obliqua luce fenestras.
> tum vitulus bima curvans iam cornua fronte
> quaeritur; huic geminae nares et spiritus oris
> multa reluctanti obstruitur, plagisque perempto
> tunsa per integram solvuntur viscera pellem.
> sic positum in clauso linquunt, et ramea costis
> subiciunt fragmenta, thymum casiasque recentis.
> hoc geritur Zephyris primum impellentibus undas,
> ante novis rubeant quam prata coloribus, ante
> garrula quam tignis nidum suspendat hirundo.
> interea teneris tepefactus in ossibus umor
> aestuat, et visenda modis animalia miris,
> trunca pedum primo, mox et stridentia pennis,
> miscentur, tenuemque magis magis aëra carpunt,

66. B. G. Whitfield, "Virgil and the Bees: A Study in Ancient Apicultural
Lore," *G & R* 3 (1956): 117. Cf. D. E. W. Wormell, "*Apibus quanta experientia
parcis:* Virgil, *Georgics* 4.1–227," in *Vergiliana: Recherches sur Virgile,* ed. H.
Bardon and R. Verdière (Leiden, 1971), 432. This procedure has very little in
common with religious sacrifice, as is evident from Walter Burkert, *Homo
Necans: The Anthropology of Ancient Greek Sacrificial Ritual and Myth,* trans.
Peter Bing (Berkeley, 1983). There is in the *bougonia* no shedding of the victim's
blood, no sacrificial meal. Note also that the victim resists, struggles against death
(4.302). Contrast Burkert, 3–4: "Legends often tell of animals that offered
themselves up for sacrifice, apparent evidence of a higher will that commands
assent." This utilitarian ritual of *bougonia* takes on a more specifically Roman
and religious character in Aristaeus' atonement. Cyrene, in her instructions to
Aristaeus, seems to turn the Egyptian *bougonia* into something resembling
Roman sacrifice to the dead. See Miles, 284f. Aristaeus' *bougonia* is, then, more
religious than "scientific."

donec ut aestivis effusus nubibus imber
erupere, aut ut nervo pulsante sagittae,
prima leves ineunt si quando proelia Parthi.
(4.295-314)

First a small place is chosen, a site that is narrowed further
For this same purpose: they close it in with a pantile roof
And prisoning walls: they add
Four windows with slanting lights that face towards the four
winds.
A two-year old calf is obtained, whose horns are beginning to
curve
From his forehead. They stopper up, though he struggle wildly,
his two
Nostrils and breathing mouth, and they beat him to death with
blows
That pound his flesh to pulp but leave the hide intact.
Battened down in that narrow room they leave him, under his
ribs
Laying fresh cassia and thyme and broken branches.
This is done as soon as a west wind ruffles the water,
Before the meadows are flushed with vernal color, before
The talkative martin hangs her nest under the rafters.
Meanwhile, within the marrowy bones of the calf, the humors
Grow warm, ferment, till appear creatures miraculous—
Limbless at first, but soon they fidget, their wings vibrate,
And more, more they sip, they take the delicate air:
At last they come pouring out, like a shower from summer
clouds,
Or thick and fast as arrows
When Parthian archers, their bowstrings throbbing, advance to
battle.

As a symbol of exchange the *bougonia* exemplifies perfectly the
central vision of the poem: the moral ambiguity and cost of Iron
Age culture, the tense apprehension of an enduring opposition
between certain kinds of material progress and humane value.
The poet does not allow the reader to remain unaware of the cost
of progress,[67] for in describing the calf's death he arouses the

67. Statements comparable to this are found in Putnam, *Poem of the Earth*
(e.g., 265-71) and Miles (e.g., 253ff.). The difference is that, in their case, these
observations are marshalled ultimately in defense of the thesis that the dynamics
of *bougonia* ("a hopeful possibility of radical renewal" [Miles, 254], an "act of
renewal" [Putnam, *Poem of the Earth*, 273]) and the success of Aristaeus'

reader's sympathy for the calf's terrified struggle (4.299–302).
We may compare also

> hic vero subitum ac dictu mirabile monstrum
> aspiciunt, liquefacta boum per viscera toto
> stridere apes utero et ruptis effervere costis,
> immensasque trahi nubes, iamque arbore summa
> confluere et lentis uvam demittere ramis.
>
> (4.554–57)

> Here, to be sure, a portent sudden and miraculous to tell
> They behold: from the oxen's bellies all over their rotting flesh
> Creatures are humming, swarming through the wreckage of their
> ribs—
> Huge and trailing clouds of bees, that now in the treetops
> Unite and hang like a bunch of grapes from the pliant branches.

Any revulsion that a modern reader may experience cannot be
merely an aberration of modern sensibility, for other similes used
to describe the bees' birth also have negative connotations (e.g.,
4.312–14). This birth is simultaneously miraculous and monstrous (*dictu mirabile monstrum* 4.554).

In sum, the emphasis here seems to be on the notion of death
and destruction as the basis of new life rather than on resurrection and the uncomplicated joy of success. The poet evokes pity
for the suffering victim and thus does not allow the reader to
overlook the costs of progress. *Bougonia,* therefore, symbolizes
exchange and unresolvable tensions; it illuminates the ambivalence of compromise and the pathos of loss.

To place *bougonia* in the context of the *Georgics,* then, and in
the context of Aristaeus' whole experience, we may observe that
while Aristaeus is indeed represented as a culture hero, he represents a culture or technology of a particular sort. Aristaeus'
technology or contribution, symbolic rather than practical, is
aggressive towards nature, even destructive of it. His technology
is aimed at success as he sees it, according to his needs, and is

---

atonement constitute in some sense a positive resolution of the poem's conflicts.
The argument of this study is that *bougonia,* rather than illuminating the positive
truth that life comes from death, the pure from the corrupt, and so forth, suggests
most powerfully the continuing suspension or unresolvability of opposing claims.

negligent of cost. It relies on a dynamic of exchange, here, of death for life, and thus embodies the moral ambiguity of the Iron Age towards nature and other men, a motif already familiar to readers of the *Georgics*.

Let us now move on to the portrait of Orpheus, the paradigmatic poet, in order to consider how Virgil represents him in relationship to the poem's major issues, as they have so far been set forth.

ORPHEUS

For the most part Virgil's representation of Orpheus accords with traditional accounts. He was a minstrel; with his lyre he played and sang; the son and servant of the Muses, he was the father of song, an ancestor of Homer and Hesiod. He did not believe in killing, and he taught other men to abstain from bloodshed. Thus the legend portrays a gentle man who, through music and magic, could accomplish feats impossible for others. Diodorus' account of Orpheus (4.25) is particularly valuable to us because he is contemporary with Virgil. From him we learn that Orpheus was Thracian, son of Oeagrus, distinguished for learning, song, and poetry; he could charm beasts and trees, was associated with theology and ritual, and participated in the Argonautic expedition. Finally, of greatest importance for us, he was permitted by Persephone to retrieve his wife from the lower world. Diodorus makes no mention of a second disappearance of Eurydice or of a passionate flaw in Orpheus.[68]

It is crucial to a correct understanding of this myth in the *Georgics* to realize that the traditional version before Virgil included Orpheus' success in bringing Eurydice back to life. That Orpheus, traditionally a gentle, civilizing musician (poet), should lose his wife through *dementia* and *furor* is antithetical to the tradition as we know it, both in Orpheus' failure and in the emotions that the poet attributes to him. Every reader of the Orpheus story experiences its haunting and melancholy beauty. Its sadness overshadows the fourth book, dominating the read-

68. Heurgon, 27, comments that Diodorus had collected almost all the fables that Alexandrian mythographers had transcribed. Diodorus' work informs us, therefore, about the state of the Orpheus-Eurydice legend in all Hellenistic circles.

er's memory and his response to the poem as a whole. The tale as told in the *Georgics* is tragic; in the context of the reader's expectations, it is emphatically so. Either by inventing this version or by choosing an obscure variant on a traditionally happy story, the poet emphasizes the tragedy of Orpheus' loss, invests tragedy with a certain pleasure and beauty, and gives expression to his own inclination to sing sad songs.

Orpheus' failure to retrieve Eurydice is the major example of the failure of art in the poem. Orpheus is exceptionally gifted, his song of such unimaginable beauty and power that we do not hear it directly but only hear of its effects. Spirits long dead and otherwise insensitive to pity or human feeling are moved (*commotae* 4.471):

> quin ipsae stupuere domus atque intima Leti
> Tartara caeruleosque implexae crinibus anguis
> Eumenides, tenuitque inhians tria Cerberus ora,
> atque Ixionii vento rota constitit orbis.
> (4.481–84)

> Why, Death's very home and holy of holies was shaken
> To hear that song, and the Furies with steel-blue snakes entwined
> In their tresses; the watch-dog Cerberus gaped open his triple
>   mouth;
> Ixion's wheel stopped dead from whirling in the wind.

> et caligantem nigra formidine lucum
> ingressus, Manisque adiit regemque tremendum
> nesciaque humanis precibus mansuescere corda.
> at cantu commotae Erebi de sedibus imis
> umbrae ibant tenues simulcraque luce carentum.
> (4.469–72)

> The gorge of Taenarus even, deep gate of the underworld,
> He entered, and that grove where fear hangs like a black fog:
> Approached the ghostly people, approached the King of Terrors
> And the hearts that know not how to be touched by human
>   prayer.
> But, by his song aroused from Hell's nethermost realms,
> There came the bodiless shades, the phantoms lost to light.

The power of his music moves the dead and enables him to gain from Persephone permission for Eurydice to return from the dead. This would constitute a true resurrection, that is, the restoration of a deceased individual to life, and would thus be significantly different from and superior to the *bougonia* of Aristaeus, which is an *exchange* of death for life and which involves permanent loss of the creatures that die. This miraculous possibility is achieved entirely through song and without sacrifice and loss. The power of song then, its ability to move the spirit, is greater than the power of legions or plows or religious rituals, for example. Thus song is powerfully beautiful; and yet it is ultimately useless, since Orpheus fails to achieve his goal. The suggestion, both (as here) literal and also metaphorical, is that Orpheus fails of his goal because he is backward-looking (490–93).[69] Eurydice terms his backward glance at her *furor* (495). We can define it perhaps more precisely as part of the characteristic pattern of his absorption with and idealization of the past, as when he obsessively mourns Eurydice's loss, both after her first death (464–66) and after the second (507–20), calling her even beyond the moment of his own death (523–29). It is in the past that he finds perfection and beauty. He seems to cultivate and nurture in himself sensations of pathos and loss, and therefore he makes beautiful songs out of tragic visions. He likes to sing songs of his loss and the pathetic groupings that he sees in Hades (475–77) reflect his own vision, which tends to focus on sorrow. Hades contains all the dead, yet Orpheus sees in particular youths and girls unwedded, those having missed therefore the crown and purpose of their lives (476; cf. *implumis* 513). There is further pathos in the detail of children buried before their parents. (The too-early loss of the young is a powerful motif also in the *Aeneid*.) Both Orpheus and the *Georgic* poet, who makes poetry of Orpheus' experience, find in tragedy a thing of beauty. At Eurydice's death Orpheus cannot accept this necessary and inevitable loss in order to proceed with life; rather he looks back incessantly, sees his ideal in the past, and seeks to restore it/her through song. In this way he parallels the *Georgic* poet, who also places his ideal—the Golden Age—in the past. This metaphorical looking back becomes literal when Orpheus turns to glance at

69. See Harold Bloom, *A Map of Misreading* (New York, 1975), 11ff., on the regressive goal of the poet. Conte, 130–40 (esp. 134–37), conceives the significance of Orpheus more narrowly than is argued here. For him Orpheus is exclusively a poet of tragic love rather than of suffering and loss more generally.

Eurydice. The backward glance is, then, a physical expression of his characteristic tragic and regressive inclination. The wintery, isolated landscape (508–10) that forms the background for his subsequent laments suggests the sterility of his backward quest. Yet again his song has power beyond human imagination. Where previously he had charmed the dead, here he soothes tigers and moves oak trees (510). Thus the constraints of both fate and nature are subject to his song, so skilled is he at the manipulation of pity (for he moves Hades to grant his prayer) and beauty (for he moves the dead, the wild, and the inanimate). Yet all this power is of no avail because Orpheus' own determination and vision of his goal, the regaining of Eurydice, are inadequately sustained. Perhaps his *dementia* ("madness" 488) is that he takes more pleasure in sorrow than in success. The continuing and cold beauty of his song has nature as its witness (527), not Eurydice or any other human being. Virgil has taken the figure of Orpheus, the paradigmatic poet, and made it a portrait of the failure of the artist, despite all the emotional power and beauty of his art, to affect or effect action in the real world. (We may compare Aeneas' emotion before the *pictura . . . inani,* "vain picture," in *Aen.* 1.464.) Orpheus' endeavor, as we have seen, fails through his uncompromising—in some sense, sterile—nostalgia for Eurydice, that is, his longing for an irretrievable ideal. The triumph of love or of song over death is, therefore, surely not the message here.[70] Rather the poet is defeated by regressive passion, isolation, and death. As an inhabitant of the Iron Age world, Orpheus, just like Aristaeus, has flaws that menace his achievements.

The parallels between Orpheus and the *Georgic* poet are suggestive of the poet's view of the value of poets and of poetry in this poem. For example, while Orpheus is ultimately the loser in the struggle for survival, he appears nevertheless to have greater courage than Aristaeus. Orpheus, whose initial cause for lament is surely as great as Aristaeus', takes the more courageous approach to his loss in relying on his own songs to charm the dead. He dares to descend alone to Hades to face the "king of

---

70. Contrast Büchner, *RE* 8 A2 (1958): 1313–14.

terrors" (4.467–70). These verses suggest the fearfulness of the hell to which Orpheus descends alone, with a courage or audacity that recalls the *Georgic* poet's (1.40, 2.175, 4.565). While Aristaeus whines to his mother, Orpheus acts, sings (466, 471), has the courage to face death. Neither Orpheus nor Aristaeus, however, has the courage to face life with any compromise.

Orpheus' vision seeks out sorrow, and he sees in Hades particularly pathetic groupings that reflect his own inclinations. His vision of hell parallels his own emotional experience and esthetic sensibility:

> at cantu commotae Erebi de sedibus imis
> umbrae ibant tenues simulacraque luce carentum,
> quam multa in foliis avium se milia condunt,
> vesper ubi aut hibernus agit de montibus imber,
> matres atque viri defunctaque corpora vita
> magnanimum heroum, pueri innuptaeque puellae,
> impositique rogis iuvenes ante ora parentum.
>
> (4.471–77)

> But, by his song aroused from Hell's nethermost realms
> There came the flimsy shades, the phantoms lost to light,
> In number like to the millions of birds that hide in the leaves
> When evening or winter rain from the hills has driven them—
> Mothers and men, the dead
> Bodies of great-hearted heroes, boys and unmarried maidens,
> Young men laid on the pyre before their parents' eyes.

The melancholy character of these apparitions—unwedded girls and parents burying their children—reflects Orpheus' own sensibility to loss and his own capacity for suffering. He sees a reflection of what he is, and the sadness of his vision fixes on premature loss. The pathetic focus of this grouping suits Orpheus' capacity for sentiment, which quality, lacking in Aristaeus, he has in the extreme. Time of darkness and season of death are powerfully suggested by the simile of 473–74, an image of dashed hopes and lost glory.

Like the *Georgic* poet, Orpheus is passionate, dissatisfied, and nostalgic. *Dementia* (Proteus' term 488) and *furor* (Eurydice's term 495) precipitate his loss of Eurydice, but, significantly, the *Georgic* poet presents his actions with sympathy (489):

iamque pedem referens casus evaserat omnis,
redditaque Eurydice superas veniebat ad auras
pone sequens (namque hanc dederat Proserpina legem),
cum subita incautum dementia cepit amantem,
ignoscenda quidem, scirent si ignoscere Manes:
restitit, Eurydicenque suam iam luce sub ipsa
immemor heu! victusque animi respexit. ibi omnis
effusus labor atque immitis rupta tyranni
foedera.

(4.485–93)

And now he's avoided every pitfall of the homeward path,
And Eurydice, regained, is nearing the upper air
Close behind him (for this condition has Proserpine made),
When a sudden madness catches her lover off his guard—
Pardonable indeed, if Death knew how to pardon.
He halts. Eurydice, his own, is now on the lip of
Daylight. Forgetful alas! Broken in purpose, he looked back.
His labor was lost, the pact he had made with the merciless king
Annulled.

In his longing for Eurydice, Orpheus is, like the *Georgic* poet, nostalgic for the past, thus making of Eurydice the final embodiment in the poem of the meaning of the Golden Age.

Exclusively absorbed in his passion for Eurydice, refusing compromise or substitution, Orpheus sings only of loss. In this way he resembles the nightingale (4.511–15), who never ceases to sing her mourning song. Orpheus and the nightingale are parallel in the beauty of their song and in their impotence to achieve what they long for.

Orpheus' grief, austere and uncompromising, renders him an isolated and in some sense sterile figure:

septem illum totos perhibent ex ordine mensis
rupe sub aëria deserti ad Strymonis undam
flesse sibi, et gelidis haec evolvisse sub astris[71]
mulcentem tigris et agentem carmine quercus

. . . .

nulla Venus, non ulli animum flexere hymenaei:
solus Hyperboreas glacies Tanaimque nivalem

71. Reading *astris* for Mynors's *antris*.

arvaque Riphaeis numquam viduata pruinis
lustrabat, raptam Eurydicen atque inrita Ditis
dona querens.

(4.507–10, 517–20)

Month after month, they say, for seven months alone
He wept beneath a crag high up by the lonely waters
Of Strymon, and under the ice-cold stars poured out his dirge
That charmed the tigers and made the oak trees follow him

. . . .

No love, no marriage could turn his mind away from grief:
Alone through Arctic ice, through the snows of Tanais, over
Frost-bound Riphaean plateaux
He ranged, bewailing his lost Eurydice and the wasted
Bounty of death.

Deserti (508) recalls *sed me Parnasi deserta per ardua dulcis/ raptat amor* (3.291–92, cited on p. 60) and tends to corroborate the earlier suggestion that the poet feels himself to be, to some degree, isolated from others and embodying separate values. Very interesting in this regard is Raymond Williams's observation, in his discussion of Wordsworth, that the poet who feels alienated can either retreat "into a deep subjectivity" (as Orpheus does here) or attempt "to discover, in some form, community," as has been argued above of the *Georgic* poet.[72]

Through his song Orpheus' grief is continually renewed, not solaced. In his refusal to accept another mate, he reveals his inability to compromise with reality, and consequently he perishes:

spretae Ciconum quo munere matres
inter sacra deum nocturnique orgia Bacchi
discerptum latos iuvenem sparsere per agros.

(4.520–22)

In the end the Ciconian women, scorned
By this devotion, amidst sacred rites and nocturnal orgies of
Bacchus,
Tore him limb from limb and scattered him over the land.

72. Raymond Williams, *The Country and the City* (New York, 1973), 295.

Aristaeus is able to accept a substitute for his lost bees, in some sense to compromise, since he is not concerned with individual human value (except in himself). Orpheus is not viable in the world precisely because of his inability to compromise, to live without the ideal, and to look forward. His final loss of Eurydice and his death at the hands of the Ciconian women are the consequences of his own character. What remains of him is intangible—the pathos of loss, the vulnerability of love and artistic strivings, and the beauty of the poetry that sings of these things:

> tum quoque marmorea caput a cervice revulsum
> gurgite cum medio portans Oeagrius Hebrus
> volveret, Eurydicen vox ipsa et frigida lingua
> a miseram Eurydicen! anima fugiente vocabat.
> Eurydicen toto referebant flumine ripae.
>
> (4.523–27)

> But even then that head, plucked from the marble-pale
> Neck, and rolling down mid-stream on the Oeagrian Hebrus,
> The voice alone and the death-cold tongue cried out "Eurydice!"
> Cried "Poor Eurydice!" as the soul of the singer fled,
> And the banks of the river echoed, re-echoed "Eurydice!"

• • •

By his self-assertion, Aristaeus achieves his desired divinity, moving from unacknowledged and unregretted crime to atonement without sentiment and, finally, to success and satisfaction in a substitution for his lost past. One could reasonably argue on Aristaeus' behalf, as have Putnam and Miles,[73] that he is somehow morally or cognitively improved by his descent to the source of waters, where he sees a world different from himself—feminine, nurturant, peaceful. Additionally to his credit one could argue that Aristaeus succeeds because he is bonded to someone, his mother, who wishes to help him, and that thus he is not alone

---

73. Putnam, *Poem of the Earth*, 316ff.; Miles, 288ff. Contrast Spofford, 57ff., who wonders if the sequence of events related here is due more to luck than to justice.

like Orpheus. On the other hand, his mother, a goddess, counsels him to success through violence and guile. So the apotheosis that Aristaeus achieves appears ultimately to be the reward neither of virtue nor of sentiment, but simply an index of success and power in the world. Perhaps one could argue that his character and experience best ready him to deal with the ambiguity, cost, and exchange represented by the *bougonia*. Although Aristaeus expresses no sentiment, sense of guilt, or pity, he does become a god—a provocative comment on the nature of Iron Age divinity.

A vision of Iron Age reality is suggested in the triumph of Aristaeus. Through his vital ruthlessness of purpose he achieves his desired divinity (cf. 1.14, where he is invoked as a god), while Orpheus is the eventual victim of Aristaeus' passion and of his own. Bound to Eurydice by sentiment, he is incapable of compromise for survival. Rejecting any substitution, he preserves through song the memory of the ideal that he has lost. He remains unconsoled, his grief never solaced or relinquished. This myth of Aristaeus' success and of Orpheus' loss mirrors reality as the poet envisions it. In the Iron Age, beauty and sentiment, as embodied in Orpheus and other victims, are in tension with success and progress, represented here by divinity. Despite Orpheus' flaws of regressiveness, egocentrism, and sterility, the poet's clear intent is to engage the reader's sympathy with him. It is Orpheus' sorrow and not Aristaeus' triumph that moves the reader and resonates in memory.

With the closing vignette of the farmer who plunders the nightingale's nest, the *Georgic* poet further expands the reader's sensibility through pity and through apprehension of ambiguity. We saw in Book 1 that the reader was often identified (through first-person verb forms or direct address, such as at 50, 100, 155–59) with the farmer (*durus agrestis* 1.160), who struggled continually against deprivation and hardship, against enemies large and small that undermined his *labor*. At the concluding moment that same farmer (now the "harsh ploughman," *durus arator* 4.512) appears no longer as the sympathetic figure, but rather as predator and ravager of the nightingale's helpless young, the agent of destruction, loss, and sorrow. Thus we are made to feel, through the sorrows of Orpheus and the nightingale, the character and cost of Iron Age civilization, and hence to expand our moral and critical perspectives on our experience. This dual vision is the quintessence of the poem, for the poet shows man both as victim of the gods and nature (as in Book 1) and also as aggressor against nature and humanity. The poet makes the reader see with complexity and with pity that which otherwise might be seen, without reflection, as the unambiguous triumph of technology and mastery.

· · ·

The *Georgics* illuminates aspects of reality as the poet sees them and thus deepens the reader's sensitivity to those humane and artistic values that do not lead to quantifiable progress. The function of song in this poem, then—Orpheus', the nightingale's, and the *Georgic* poet's—is preservation of the memory of the ideal, variously of harmony and pity, and of its loss, since the ideal is continually seen in retrospect. As a whole, in the songs of its several poet voices, the *Georgics* preserves and values the memory of a retrospective ideal. This memory is preserved not only, if climactically, in the moving tale of Orpheus and Eurydice, but also in the repeated representations of and allusions to the Golden Age, which constitute reflections on an ideal beyond reach. It is the nature of these reflections on the Golden Age that I term "the poet's vision" and that forms the subject of the following chapter.

2

The Poet's Vision

The motif of the Golden Age is a recurrent one in the *Georgics*. In this chapter we will consider both those passages generally agreed to evoke the Golden Age and some others that (it will be argued) also relate to this motif, as we attempt to understand the significance of the Golden Age in this poem. Some scholars have felt that the Golden Age descriptions in the *Georgics* constitute Virgil's prophecy of or prescription for a renewed and perfected Roman society. Here I will argue that the Golden Age is not a prescription for political action but rather that it serves as a metaphor for a set of moral values that function in continuing and unresolved tension with Iron Age experience. Since it idealizes the past, the concept of a Golden Age necessarily criticizes the present, no matter how indirectly.[1] To use Raymond Williams's fine phrase in a slightly altered context, we may observe that the concept of the Golden Age allows the poet, reflecting critically upon aspects of contemporary experience, to turn "protest into retrospect,"[2] to focus the reader's attention upon the disparity between the present, as the poet sees it, and an ideal vision of alternative moral values. The Golden Age is a standard by which to evaluate and question the present, yet without indicting any particular class, policy, or individual. Indeed the poet takes a larger view of such problems as he sees and consequently does not propose solutions. Virgil allows the reader to

---

1. Some argue that the Golden Age was a heedless, lazy time and that man's lot is improved in the Iron Age, where he has opportunity for challenge and enlightened moral choices. See, for instance, Johnston, 50, 58, 69, 71; Richter, 137; Büchner, *RE* 8 A2 (1958): 1271; Perret, 81; Wilkinson, Georgics, 79; Klingner, *Virgil,* 189–91; Miles, 79. Contrast Perkell, "Vergil's Theodicy."

2. Raymond Williams, 83. Williams's entire study provides a perspective that is most illuminating of Virgil's work.

consider critically certain conventional values not by openly attacking them or by showing defeats of authority, but rather by suggesting the moral compromises that are necessary in order to preserve Iron Age values.

The Golden Age functions as a praise of absence, the absence of certain humane values that create moral community. Hence there is continual tension in the poem between any positively conceived ideal and its real opposite, such as spring vs. winter, peace vs. war, harmony vs. aggression, past vs. present.[3] Even the most positive Golden Age passages of the poem, the *laudes veris* ("praises of spring" 2.323ff.) and the *laudes ruris* ("praises of country life" 2.458ff.), conclude with the acknowledgment of winter or burning summer (2.343–45) and war (2.540), respectively, thus interrupting the compelling reverie of an alluring ideal. The poet does not imagine a paradisiacal past to have occurred historically, nor does he genuinely imagine such an event for the future. Rather he uses the motif of the Golden Age to express moral tensions central to the poem, thus illuminating certain oppositions between material progress and humane value.[4]

Virgil's Golden Age has a particular quality of community between man and nature and between man and man. City life, which epitomizes the present, is most different from the Golden Age precisely in its loss of community, that is, in the dissolution of bonds that (ought to) unite brothers (2.510) or neighbor cities (1.510). Instead, fratricide is expanded to civil war in pursuit of individual interests. It is the poet's special mission to create a moral community, to preserve and perpetuate the humane value of pity, to turn us into readers who would acknowledge Golden Age values as high and true. Thus the poet attempts to redress the moral omission of Jove (when he terminated the Golden Age, 1.121ff.) by restoring a moral content to the Iron Age. As has been noted by others, discrete Golden Age features do exist in the present communities of, for instance, the farmers (Book 2), the bees (Book 4), even the plague victims (Book 3).

---

3. Cf. Raymond Williams, 18.
4. Cf. Raymond Williams, 297, 293.

These communities do not, however, constitute a renewed Golden Age on earth, as most readers would agree. The reason, as will be argued, is that community remains morally inert without the enlightened, willed value of pity, which is the poet's special contribution.

THE GOLDEN AGE IN BOOK 1

The myth of the Golden Age,[5] since it is fundamentally opposed to progressivism, is a striking motif in a work ostensibly dedicated to agriculture. One might well assume that pride in and conviction of the value of agriculture would motivate a writer treating georgic themes. In Varro (1.2.16, 2.1.13), for example, one finds a positive, progressivistic expression of man's technology, knowledge, and ability to make nature productive for his own purposes.[6] With praise and enthusiasm for the development of agricultural technology, he represents man as coming from a primitive state and from an absence of skill and as progressing towards valuable knowledge. In the *Georgics,* however, allusions to past abundance (e.g., 1.127–32) compel the reader to envision the whole of civilization and its technology as a continuing attempt to compensate for the loss of the Golden Age. The very need of agriculture confirms the absence of this ideal (*ipsaque tellus/omnia liberius, nullo poscente, ferebat,* "Earth yielded

5. The myth of the Golden Age is familiar to us primarily from poetry: Hesiod *Works and Days* 109–20; Aratus *Phaen.* 96–114; Tib. 1.3.35–50, 1.10.1–12; Ov. *Met.* 1.89–112, *Am.* 3.8.35–36. Similarly Pind. *Pyth.* 10.38f., *Ol.* 2.68f. For an exhaustive compilation of relevant texts see A. O. Lovejoy and G. Boas, *Primitivism and Related Ideas in Antiquity* (Baltimore, 1935), 1–388. The myth of the Golden Age as it is represented in Hesiod is the oldest form of chronological primitivism in the Western tradition. On its moral quality see J. Fontenrose, "Work, Justice, and Hesiod's Five Ages," *CP* 69 (1974): 3ff. Cf. S. Benardete, "Hesiod's *Works and Days:* A First Reading," *Agon* 1 (1967): 156–57, on the absence of *eros* in the Golden Age. Pietro Pucci, *Hesiod and the Language of Poetry* (Baltimore, 1977), 82, sees the Golden Age as natural, the Iron Age as culture.

6. This progressivistic position is paralleled in many other writers; e.g., Aesch. *PV* 442–68, 478–506; Eur. *Supp.* 201–13; Diod. 1.8.1–7; *On Ancient Medicine* 3(1, 574–8 L.). For these and other references see W. K. C. Guthrie, *The Sophists* (Cambridge, 1971), 79–83.

all, of herself, more freely, when none begged for her gifts"
1.127–28).

The initial description in the *Georgics* of the Golden Age
(1.121ff.), with its ethic of sharing and harmony between men
and nature, establishes a standard set of features that recur in
subsequent variations on this theme. Of these I will discuss the
so-termed praises of Italy (2.136ff.), of spring (2.323–45ff.), and
of country life (2.458ff.) in Book 2; the passages on the Scythians
(3.349–83) and on the plague (3.478–566) in Book 3; and in Book
4 the passages on the bees (4.1–115, 149–218) and on the Corycian gardener (4.116–48). In Books 2 and 4 resemblances
between the Golden Age and the present are unmistakable, if
ultimately delusive. The passages on the Scythians and on the
plague in Book 3, however, take a different approach to the
Golden Age. These passages are perversions or travesties of
certain features typical of the Golden Age (as, for example,
property held in common, peace among usually predatory animals, and harmony between animals and men). By isolating
certain of these conventionally Golden Age features and thereby
revealing them to be insufficient in themselves to constitute or to
restore a Golden Age, the poet suggests that the elusive essential
of the Golden Age is a spiritual quality of mutuality or community. This vision of a moral community, without which discrete
Golden Age features remain morally inert, appears to be, as we
have seen, the exclusive preserve of the poet.

The Golden Age ideal, as it is first described at 1.125–35, sets,
by virtue of its initial position, the standard for the variations
that follow. The passage suggests the absence of aggression, of
private interest; it suggests sharing among men and a spontane-
ous giving from nature to man:

> ante Iovem nulli subigebant arva coloni:
> ne signare quidem aut partiri limite campum
> fas erat; in medium quaerebant, ipsaque tellus
> omnia liberius nullo poscente ferebat.
> ille malum virus serpentibus addidit atris,
> praedarique lupos iussit pontumque moveri,
> mellaque decussit foliis ignemque removit
> et passim rivis currentia vina repressit,
> ut varias usus meditando extunderet artis

paulatim, et sulcis frumenti quaereret herbam,
ut silicis venis abstrusum excuderet ignem.

(1.125–35)

Before Jove's time no settlers brought the land under subjection;
Not lawful even to divide the plain with landmarks and
    boundaries:
They sought the common good, and earth unprompted
Was freer with all her fruits.
Jove put the wicked poison in the black serpent's tooth,
Jove told the wolf to ravin, the sea to be restive always,
He shook from the leaves their honey, he had all fire removed,
And stopped the wine that ran in rivers everywhere,
So that practice by experiment might forge various crafts
Little by little, might seek the corn-blade in the furrow,
And strike the hidden fire that lies in the veins of flint.

In verses 125–28, two of which are negative statements and two
positive, the poet sketches the essence of his Golden Age. No
farmers "subdued" the fields, that is, man was not an aggressor
in his relationship to nature. Neither was he dominating or
possessive, for private ownership of nature by man was not
allowed (126–27). *Fas* ("right," "lawful" 127) is a strongly emotive, powerful term, indicating that this Golden Age had an
internal moral quality that functioned in such a way as to protect
man from moral compromise in his relationship with nature.
Among men there was sharing and pursuit of common interest
(*in medium quaerebant* 127) and from nature an abundance
of giving (*ipsaque tellus/omnia liberius . . . ferebat* 127–28)
even in the absence of demand.[7] What existed, then, was an ethic
of sharing and community among men as well as between men
and nature. Once, therefore, there existed a nonexploitive relationship between men and nature, when earth poured forth

7. *Ecl.* 4.18–25 reflects the same ideal. Earth brings forth crops spontane-
ously, grapes hang from uncultivated vines, lambs uncalled bring milk; there are
no poisons, no snakes, no hostilities between animals. Contrast the view of early
man in Lucr. 5.958–59:

        nec commune bonum poterant spectare neque ullis
        moribus inter se scibant nec legibus uti.

        For the common good they had no eye, nor knew
        Of the mutual uses of custom or of law.

plenty and men did not manipulate or do violence against nature in order to survive. Neither, consequently, was there competition or conflict between men, since all was abundant and given into the common store. While the Golden Age apparently accords no value or expression to individual strivings (this is, in any case, not mentioned in the text and seems to be precluded by *in medium quaerebant*), it also denies expression to individual competition and its worst consequences—murder and war (e.g., 1.505–14).

It has been possible, in reading this passage, to draw many inferences from few details. The qualities of this Golden Age (not even so termed by the poet)[8] must be inferred and defined from their absence, since their description is indirect. Readers cannot envisage this Golden Age from the poet's description, but must fill in the gaps created by negative statements from their own imagination, sentiment, and knowledge of literary tradition. For example, because Jove put poison into snakes, one must infer that once they had none. Because he struck honey from trees, one must infer that once it flowed freely from them. To describe the Golden Age in this way is to leave it to readers to imagine, to create or conceive in their own minds, the alternative values that the poet is indirectly suggesting. From its absence readers may conceive what they might desire and aspire to. The genius of the *Georgic* poet's description of the Golden Age is to have engaged the readers' own creative responsiveness on behalf of values or of a vision that they might not otherwise endorse.

A most powerful and ironic event in the history of the Iron Age is the role played by Jove.[9] As noted above, the character of the Golden Age was deeply moral, for it was not *fas* (a term that connotes in itself divine approbation) to subdue or even to possess the fields. There was no competition, since earth provided all in abundance and since men sought the common, not the individual, good. There is, therefore, no heedless or irrespon-

---

8. Johnston, 52, notes that Virgil "never modifies *gens, genus, aetas,* or *saeculum,* any of which might be used to denote an "age" or "race" of mortals, with adjectives denoting the metals of Hesiod's metallic myth."

9. For a more complete discussion of this passage see Perkell, "Vergil's Theodicy."

sible element in this vision of the Golden Age. Rather there is an ethic of sharing and responsibility towards others, explicit in *in medium quaerebant*. Because this period recalls the Golden Age, because it is characterized by *fas,* the reader is led to perceive it as positive. The irony (which is a function fundamentally of disparity)[10] of Jove's attitude towards the Golden Age is that in this period of moral harmony and absence of strife, he saw only *veternus* ("inactivity," "lethargy" 1.124). This perception of Jove's illuminates indirectly his own moral values:

> pater ipse colendi
> haud facilem esse viam voluit, primusque per artem
> movit agros, curis acuens mortalia corda
> nec torpere gravi passus sua regna veterno.
>
> (1.121–24)

> The father himself did not wish the way of
> agriculture to be easy, and he first stirred
> the fields through art, sharpening mortal hearts
> with care, not enduring his realms
> to be sluggish with lethargy.[11]

Jove creates conditions that compel man to material, but not to moral or spiritual, goals.[12] As represented here Jove is without

---

10. Quint. *Inst.* 8.6.54; Wayne C. Booth, *A Rhetoric of Irony* (Chicago, 1974), 183.

11. Author's translation.

12. A perception of ironic comment here would resolve long controversies on this verse. Most previous attempts to interpret it have assumed that Jove's intervention must have been for good—in the poet's and hence in the reader's eyes. Many critics assume without question that Jove acts beneficently towards man, stimulating him to creative action. Support for this reading is not actually in the text. As W. R. Johnson, 114–34, observes, Jove represents no moral principle at the conclusion of the *Aeneid* either. Rather he accedes chillingly to evil and becomes its agent. At 4.560–61 Thomas notes that Virgil is ambivalent towards Jupiter throughout the poem. Recently Karl Galinsky, "Vergil and the Formation of the Augustan Ethos," in *Atti del Convegno Mondiale Scientifico di Studi Virgiliani,* vol. 1 (Milan, 1984), 242–43, argued that Jupiter was "good" to wean men from their earlier stagnation, that *labor* "takes place under the aegis of a providential God," and that this passage is a "very personal statement" of Virgil's. I have attempted (Perkell, "Vergil's Theodicy") to show in detail that such thoughts are not actually implicit in Virgil's text but result rather from insufficient appreciation of his ironic and/or ambiguous expression. (Bodo Gatz,

concern for moral conscience or spiritual purpose in man. In order to compel man to activity Jove must make the world, initially hospitable towards man, inhospitable. He withdraws the natural abundance of honey, fire, and wine; he poisons and represses. In this way he drives man, whose survival is now in question, into an adversarial relationship with nature. As man must subdue the fields and conquer nature, so *labor* conquers him:

> labor omnia vicit
> improbus et duris urgens in rebus egestas.[13]
> (1.145–46)
> Labor conquered everything,
> perverse labor, and driving need in hard circumstances.

The military mode connoted by *vicit* (145) thus epitomizes the new regime, in which total community has been replaced by total combat. Man becomes simultaneously victim and victor, besieged by want, oppressed by labor. Man's technologies, represented as "the rending and perversion of natural things,"[14] force him into the role of predator (*captare*, "capture"), destroyer (*verberat*, "whip," *scindebant*, "rend"), deceiver (*fallere*, "deceive"), this last term suggesting the absence of an ethical component in the new age. Whereas in the Golden Age there was interest in the common good, in the Iron Age an individual who

---

Weltalter, Goldene Zeit und sinnverwandte Vorstellungen, Spudasmata 16 [Hildesheim, 1967], 162–65, takes a similar view of the passage and even sees Virgil as a proto-Christian.) Galinsky's assertion that the passage is a "very personal statement" of the poet is especially problematic. Cf. Annabel Patterson, *Pastoral and Ideology: Virgil to Valéry* (Berkeley, 1987), 4, on Virgil's dismemberment of his own voice and his shifting authorial presence in the *Eclogues*.

13. These familiar verses are often taken to mean that *labor* has overcome or made tractable all difficulties: see Klingner, *Virgil*, 204; Wilkinson, Georgics, 141. Putnam, *Poem of the Earth*, 34, argues persuasively against this interpretation. Altevogt, 28–29 and 43, states unequivocally that *labor* is an evil, but feels that ultimately all will be well because man's *labor* will restore the Golden Age. This is also the essential thesis of Johnston's book. Otis's view, *Virgil*, 153 and 213, is that the undoubted pessimism of this passage is outweighed by the optimism of Books 2 and 4.

14. Otis, *Virgil*, 157 n. 2.

fails to sustain himself is abandoned, envying others' private plenty, to starve alone:

> heu magnum alterius frustra spectabis acervum,
> concussaque famem in silvis solabere quercu.[15]
>
> (1.158–59)
>
> Vainly alas will you eye another man's heaped-up harvest
> and relieve your own hunger by shaking an oak in the woods.

Each man works only for himself, without responsibility, as previously, for the general welfare. As a result of Jove's intervention, then, man's moral relationship both to nature and to other men is compromised, for his survival requires continuing departure from the ideals of the Golden Age. Man's ambiguous moral position on the earth can never be resolved or ameliorated, but is a condition of the Iron Age.

As Jove's primary concern is for something other than morality or spiritual quality, so the *Georgic* poet does not show modern man making meaningful moral choices. Rather man is absorbed by care (*curis acuens mortalia corda* 1.123); overwhelmed by war (*saevit toto Mars impius orbe* 1.511), by passion (*in furias ignemque ruunt* 3.244), by disease (*contactos artus sacer ignis edebat* 3.566), or by failure (*ibi omnis effusus labor* 4.491–92). This view of man is corroborated by the adjectives that the poet attributes to him: *ignarus* ("ignorant" 1.14), *avarus* ("greedy" 1.47), *durus* ("hard" 1.63), *aeger* ("weak" 1.237), *acer* ("harsh" 2.405), *tristis* ("sad" 3.517), and *miser* ("wretched" 3.313). Men have transient joys when freed from work, but find themselves, overall, subject to destructive forces more powerful than they, such as universal decline (1.199–203) or pervasive war (1.511–14). Iron Age man relies on his *labor* for survival and for glory. Yet the failure of *labor* is a recurrent motif in the *Georgics* (1.324–26; 3.97–98, 525; 4.491–92).[16] This picture does contrast

---

15. Contrast Griffin, "*Haec super arvorum cultu,*" 32, who finds this line "gently humorous."

16. Cf. *Ecl.* 10.64:

> non illum nostri possunt mutare labores
>
> That god [i.e., Love] no labors of ours can change.

with Hesiod who asserts, on occasion (e.g., *Works and Days* 308–13), a correlation between work and prosperity.

In sum the poet represents early society as communal and generous, without sin or aggression. To this vision he juxtaposes, without explicitly qualifying them, technological achievements that are, by implication, of a violent and destructive character (1.139–45). Man's technology is not praised by Virgil, nor indeed is it qualified in any way. Since the poet uses no adjectives at all, he leaves the possibility open to the reader to see in the discovery of technology either a positive or a negative development. Thus the poet is deliberately uncommitted, allowing the ambiguous potential of *labor* and *ars* to suggest itself.[17]

Besides being morally ambiguous, the arts that man has been compelled to contrive are all aimed at material survival and therefore lead to visible and quantifiable, but not to moral or esthetic, progress. Under Jove's dispensation man pursues the material and practical, but lives without *fas* or art, a suggestive omission for a poet to allow. Virgil's description differs, in this respect, from those of his two major models, Lucretius and Hesiod. Lucretius, as we have seen, includes poetry, painting, and sculpture in his history of civilization (5.1448–53). Equally in Hesiod we find that Zeus likes poetry and is, indeed, the father of the Muses (e.g., *Theog.* 36–43, 53ff.). In the *Georgics*, however, Jove, like the farmers of *Georgic* 2 or the Romanized bees of *Georgic* 4, is indifferent to art. Poetry and song do not address the problem of material progress. It is most probably for this reason that Jove does not attend to them.

This passage on the development of civilization as we know it has several echoes in the concluding lines of Book 1, where the poet describes wars raging out of control. *Fas* recurs (127, 505), as do *robigo* ("mildew," "rust" 151, 495), *lupus* ("wolf" 130, 486), *arma* ("arms" 160, 511). These echoes suggest that the passages are in some way paired and, therefore, invite comparison. Thus the reader is invited to compare the life of Golden Age

---

17. Cf. Putnam, *Poem of the Earth*, 34: "There is no commendation of progress as virtuous or indication that in reality, or in Jupiter's thoughts, a new golden age is in prospect."

man with that of his contemporary Romans. Civilization has evolved from universal harmony to almost universal war, from the reign of moral law to the confusion of right and wrong (*fas versum atque nefas* 505). Jove appears more offended by *veternus* than by *nefas*.

In conclusion, the Golden Age in Book 1 is defined by community among men, who pursue the common good, and between men and nature, which gives forth bounteously. There is no domination or manipulation of nature. There is no agricultural *labor,* perhaps no *labor* of any kind (i.e., perhaps no poetry). Subsequent variations on the Golden Age motif echo and also question this initial version in various ways.

THE GOLDEN AGE IN BOOK 2

Turning now to the Golden Age passages of Book 2—the praises of Italy, spring, and country life[18]—we approach three of the best-known passages of the entire poem. These passages, often read independently of the poem as a whole, have been taken as expressions of the poet's uncomplicated confidence in various aspects of Roman life. All recall in numerous ways the Golden Age as it was described in Book 1. All also have features at variance with the Golden Age described there, and these discrepancies are equally important for the poet's purpose. While these passages express traditional Roman ideals and values, they do so in such a way as to provoke the reader's attention and to challenge his assumptions. In their provocative dissonance from Book 1, in their extravagant overstatement, or in their manifest untruth, these passages draw the reader's attention to those ways in which life's real ambiguities exceed the truth of facile formulations. Thus the *Georgic* poet is not uncritically limited to the bounds of conventional Roman patriotism, for his real purpose is to enlarge the reader's sensibility.

18. Cf. Richter, 233: "Saturnian land, Saturnian age, Saturnian life"; also Klingner, *Virgil,* 227; Büchner, *RE* 8 A2 (1958): 1280; Otis, *Virgil,* 163, 166.

THE PRAISES OF ITALY

The *laudes Italiae* (2.136–76), as it is often called, is frequently read as a set piece because, independent of the poem as a whole, it can be taken as a charming expression of Roman patriotism and as a vision of Italy as a contemporary embodiment of the Golden Age.[19] Indeed the poet explicitly uses the term *laudibus* ("praises" 138) in beginning the passage:

> Sed neque Medorum silvae, ditissima terra,
> nec pulcher Ganges atque auro turbidus Hermus
> laudibus Italiae certent
>
> (2.136–38)

> But neither the Median forests, that rich land, nor fair Ganges,
> Nor Hermus rolling in gold
> Compares in praise with Italy

and the vigorous apostrophe

> salve, magna parens frugum, Saturnia tellus,
> magna virum
>
> (2.173–74)

> Hail, great mother of harvests! O land of Saturn, hail!
> Mother of men!

in closing.

Let us first note the parallels between contemporary Italy as described in the following passage and the Golden Age of *Georgic* 1.125ff.:

> hic ver adsiduum atque alienis mensibus aestas:
> bis gravidae pecudes, bis pomis utilis arbos.
> at rabidae tigres absunt et saeva leonum

---

19. Wilkinson, Georgics, 52 n. 1, notes that even Varro's praise of Italy (which, unlike Virgil's, is restricted to the fertility of the land) "must not be taken *au pied de la lettre*." Contemporary passages show this to be a rhetorical set piece; cf. Strab. 6.4.1; Dion. Hal. *Ant. rom.* 1.36–37. Ross, *Virgil's Elements*, 110, rejecting a positive reading of all of these passages, considers them with the "sole purpose of watching for the Virgilian lie," that is, as untruths with negative implications for conventional formulations of ideals. Thomas, ad loc., also looks for untruths and implied criticism.

semina, nec miseros fallunt aconita legentis,
nec rapit immensos orbis per humum neque tanto
squameus in spiram tractu se colligit anguis.
$$(2.149-54)$$

Here is continual spring and a summer beyond her season;
Cattle bear twice yearly, apples a second crop.
No bloodthirsty tigers are found here, no fierce young lions roar.
No aconite grows to deceive and poison the wretch who picks it,
Nor does the scaly snake slither at such great length
On the ground or gather himself into so many coils here.

These verses suggest that contemporary Italy retains features of a primeval paradise, examples of which are her extraordinary fertility (149–50) and the absence of predatory animals (151–52), poisons (152), and snakes (153–54). These features have led critics to see here the poet's vision of a new Golden Age to come in Italy. A variation on this interpretation is that of Klingner, who sees Italy as representing the Golden Mean, a contrast to the excessive abundance of exotic growths of the decadent East.[20] In Italy, on the other hand, all is on a human scale, healthfully abundant, offering wholesome challenge, perfect for the farmer:

haec loca non tauri spirantes naribus ignem
invertere satis immanis dentibus hydri,
nec galeis densisque virum seges horruit hastis;
sed gravidae fruges et Bacchi Massicus umor
implevere; tenent oleae armentaque laeta.
hinc bellator equus campo sese arduus infert,
hinc albi, Clitumne, greges et maxima taurus
victima, saepe tuo perfusi flumine sacro,
Romanos ad templa deum duxere triumphos.
$$(2.140-47)$$

This land of ours has never been ploughed by bulls fire-breathing
Nor sown with dragon's teeth;
It has never known a harvest of serried helmeted spearmen;
Rather is it a country fulfilled with heavy corn and
Campanian wine, possessed by olives and prosperous herds.
Here the charger gallops onto the plain in his pride,

20. See Klingner, *Virgil*, 232–41. Contrast R. Syme, *The Roman Revolution* (Oxford, 1939; reprint, 1971), 25, who shows there must be some idealizing in Klingner's reading. "Italia" was a precarious concept and may have political overtones.

Here the white-fleeced flocks and the bull, a princely victim
Washed over and over in Clitumnus' holy water,
Lead Roman triumphs to the temples of the gods.

Klingner relates the passage also to the contemporary political situation, taking the East as an embodiment of "unmeasure" and hubris, of Antony's opposition to Rome and to her traditions of loyalty and manliness.

These observations have textual referents and are plausible. They do not, however, account for the entire content of this passage, which reflects as well a certain ambivalence towards Roman values. An undercurrent of verses of ambiguous import, too many to be easily ascribed to consistent carelessness (a concept difficult in itself), suggests a subtle tension determining the structure of this passage. In order not to lose the reader in tedious detail, let us restrict observations to some significant points of tension in this passage.

As a first example one may consider 140ff., in which the poet would seem to suggest that Italy is free from a mythologically monstrous past. Other lands, while fabled and wealthy, have disturbing, unnatural myths associated with their past, myths that, presumably, characterize in some real way aspects of their continuing present. Therefore these nations cannot compete with Italy for praise. This allusion to myths of the ancient past might, however, invite the reader to consider some of Rome's earliest myths, which, while offering nothing so fantastical as fire-breathing bulls, do offer their own kind of horror. Fraternal murder marks the founding of the Roman state, as all readers knew.[21] This myth was deeply disturbing to Virgil's contemporaries, since they saw in Romulus and Remus prototypes of the civil wars that had shattered their lives. Crime and violence, although not monstrous or fantastical, mark Rome's history

---

21. Cf. H. Wagenvoort, "The Crime of Fratricide," in *Studies in Roman Literature, Culture, and Religion* (Leiden, 1956), 169–83, who studies the disturbing quality of this myth for Romans. He cites Hor. *Epod.* 7.18 *scelus fraternae necis* ("crime of fraternal murder") as an illustration of contemporary concern with Romulus and Remus as prototypes of civil war. Cf. Steele Commager, *The Odes of Horace: A Critical Study* (New Haven, 1962; Bloomington, Ind., 1967), 181: "For what is civil war but expanded fratricide?"

from its very inception, a Roman version of original sin (cf. 1.502 and 2.537), so that the civil wars were perceived by some, and certainly treated in poetry, as proof of and payment for sin. This myth, then, to which the poet indirectly calls attention, was as fearful—in very real terms—to Roman eyes as any Eastern counterparts. Indeed it is a portrait of brothers rejoicing in the shedding of fraternal blood that closes this book (2.510), indicating the poet's present concern with fratricide and explicitly with the tale of Romulus and Remus (533) in this section of the poem.[22]

Another point of some ambiguity in this passage involves the question of cities and man's labor and technology. As we saw in the *labor improbus* passage of Book 1 (118ff.), man's technology, the defining feature of the Iron Age, has a rather destructive, aggressive character that renders it morally ambiguous in some of its expressions. *Labor* has vanquished or conquered all things (1.145; similarly 1.150), with the consequence that man's relationship to other men and to nature has the quality of combat more than harmony, as in the Golden Age. The praise, therefore, of Italian cities as creations of *labor* points to a certain unhappy dimension of their origin.[23] Cities are not natural or innocent but reflect the need for defensive posture that characterizes the Iron Age:

> adde tot egregias urbes operumque laborem,
> tot congesta manu praeruptis oppida saxis
> fluminaque antiquos subterlabentia muros.
>
> (2.155–57)

> Number our noble cities and the labor of our hands,
> The towns piled up on toppling cliffs, the antique walls
> And the rivers that glide below them.

The poet does not praise the city for its wealth of art or culture or as a refined expression of man's greatest creative acts; rather he praises it as a product of technology. Further to confirm the

---

22. Putnam, *Poem of the Earth*, 159, finely terms the suppression of the name of Romulus (*G.* 2.533) a "moral precipice."

23. Cf. *Ecl.* 1.19–25, 4.32–33. Putnam, *Poem of the Earth*, 101, notes that cities "are provocative objects for a singer of *georgica* to magnify."

poet's reticence or ambiguity here, we observe that this book concludes with an extended and thorough condemnation of city life for its pursuit of vain and destructive goals, the city absolutely epitomizing the dissolution of the Golden Age (2.503–12). Another example in this passage of the praises of Roman life coming into implicit conflict with the ethic of the Golden Age is Romans' treatment of their seas:

> an memorem portus Lucrinoque addita claustra
> atque indignatum magnis stridoribus aequor,
> Iulia qua ponto longe sonat unda refuso
> Tyrrhenusque fretis immittitur aestus Avernis?
>
> (2.161–64)

> Shall I mention our harbors, the wall that was built to bar the Lucrine
> And made the deep cry out in mighty indignation
> Where the Sound of Julius murmurs with the noise of the sea locked out
> And Tyrrhene tides flow through a canal into Averno?

Here enumeration of Italy's splendid resources modulates into the familiar motif of man's violation of the natural order. *Indignatum* (162) especially is a significant term here, given its other uses in Virgil.[24] Assuming its usage here to be consistent with these other occurrences, we infer that the poet is—if subtly—suggesting that Agrippa, as agent of Octavian, is (like Xerxes and Alexander) outraging the sea and exceeding mortal bounds in his violence against nature. The Romans' technology is, as in 1.139ff., represented as aggressive against natural things. Finally, the phrase *Iulia . . . unda* (2.163), with its implication that

24. Forms of *indignor* occur eleven times in Virgil: *Aen.* 1.55; 2.93; 5.229, 651; 7.770; 8.649, 728; 11.831; 12.786, 952; and *G*.2.162. Since ten out of eleven occur in the *Aeneid*, we infer that the word has an epic coloring. Four of the uses have to do specifically with natural forces restrained or inverted: *Aen.* 1.55; 7.770; 8.728; 12.786—in addition to *G*.2.162. The others express anger at loss of honor or life. *Aen.* 8.728 describes the Araxes River, which had destroyed the bridge Alexander had built over it; Augustus then built a new bridge in an effort to subdue the river (Serv. Auct. ad loc.). See R. D. Williams, ed., *The* Aeneid *of Virgil* (London, 1973) at 8.728; and M. C. J. Putnam, "Italian Virgil and the Idea of Rome," in *Janus: Essays in Ancient and Modern Studies*, ed. Louis L. Orlin (Ann Arbor, Mich., 1975), 185–92, for a similar discussion.

Caesar claims to own the waters, corroborates the notion that *fas* has been overturned (1.506), since, in the Golden Age, man did not claim for himself possession of the natural world.

A last example from this passage of discrepancy from the Golden Age is the portrait of Italian peoples:

> haec genus acre virum, Marsos pubemque Sabellam
> adsuetumque malo Ligurem Volscosque verutos
> extulit, haec Decios Marios magnosque Camillos
> Scipiadas duros bello
>
> (2.167–70)

> Fierce her breed of men—the Marsians and Sabellians,
> Ligurians used to hardship, Volscian javelin-throwers;
> Mother she is of the Decii, Marii, great Camilli,
> The Scipios relentless in war.

These tribes are defined by their harsh and military character. No other qualities are attributed to them. *Acre* ("fierce" 167), *adsuetum malo* ("accustomed to hardship" 168), *verutos* ("armed with a javelin" 168), *duros bello* ("relentless/hard in war" 169) are the phrases that occur here, making the Italians' aptitude for war and hardship their salient characteristic. Richter points out that this list of heroes parallels that in Horace *Epode* 16.1ff., which regrets Rome's apparently inexhaustible taste for war.[25] The list also anticipates the parade of heroes in *Aeneid* 6.756ff., which combines just the same tone of pride in Roman achievements with dismay at excessive actions committed on behalf of Rome and glory:

> infelix utcumque ferent ea facta minores:
> vincet amor patriae laudumque immensa cupido.
>
> (*Aen.* 6.822–23)

> Unhappy, however late ages will extol his deeds.
> Love of country will conquer and boundless passion for praise.

The patriotism of Anchises, speaker of these words, is ardent, yet he seems to imply that there is a danger in uncritical love of country.

---

25. Cf. Richter ad loc.: "Almost a literary symbol of Roman hero worship."

It is at this point that the poet asserts his intention of singing Hesiodic song throughout Roman towns, implicitly pointing to an absence in his homeland of art and all that it connotes in this poem (2.174–76). The poet's patriotism and commitment to Italy are also great, even if different in character from the soldier's.

In sum, while vital patriotic spirit resonates in this passage, most especially in 136–39, subsequent verses (e.g., 149–54), which reproduce *topoi,* or commonplaces, of the Golden Age, invite comparison of contemporary Italy with a previously stated ideal, and it is here that the ambiguities of the passage are found. More subtle and ambiguous than often assumed, the praises of Italy suggest a spirit moved, on the one hand, by deep sentiment for country and, on the other, inclined to a certain thoughtful perspective on its character and values.

THE PRAISES OF SPRING

Like the praises of Italy, the praises of spring recall the Golden Age.[26] Characteristic of the *Georgic* poet's retrospective point of view is the notion that spring recalls a former period of ideal vitality. Spring is conceived as the partial reenactment of the birth and primeval perfection of the world:

> non alios prima crescentis origine mundi
> inluxisse dies aliumve habuisse tenorem
> crediderim: ver illud erat, ver magnus agebat
> orbis et hibernis parcebant flatibus Euri,
> cum primae lucem pecudes hausere, virumque
> terrea progenies duris caput extulit arvis,[27]
> immissaeque ferae silvis et sidera caelo.
>
> (2.336–42)

So it was, I believe, when the world first began,
Such the illustrious dawning and tenor of their days.

---

26. Cf. Otis, *Virgil,* 166; Richter, 233, calls it the "Saturnian age." Klingner, *Virgil,* 258 parallels *G.*2.333–34 with *Ecl.* 4.22:

> nec magnos metuent armenta leones
>
> neither shall the herds fear huge lions.

27. Although most MSS read *ferrea,* both Mynors and Thomas print *terrea.*

> It was springtime then, great spring
> Enhanced the earth and spared it the bitter breath of an east wind—
> A time when the cattle first lapped up the light, and men
> Children of earth themselves arose from the raw champaign,
> And wild things issued forth in the wood, and stars in the sky.

Spring is lovely, but is compared to something lovelier and past. The present is positive in the degree to which it reflects a past perfection. The tenses are past, suggesting that earth's greatest vigor and clarity preceded altogether the creation of human beings. The vitality, joyousness, and fertility of spring are marked by the songs of birds (*avibus* . . . *canoris* 328) and by pathless thickets (*avia* . . . *virgulta* 328), which parallels the poet's joy at seeing fields untouched by man (2.438–39). This nostalgic placing of perfection in a period without mechanization or commerce is a characteristic note in this poem and absent from the Lucretian model of this passage, which will be discussed below.

Another characteristic note here, as also in English rural poetry, is the continuing tension between contrasting perspectives, as Raymond Williams puts it, "summer with winter, pleasure with loss, past or future with present."[28] In this passage spring represents only a transient peace for nature's creatures between the rigors of winter, on the one hand, and summer, on the other:

> nec res hunc tenerae possent perferre laborem,
> si non tanta quies iret frigusque caloremque
> inter, et exciperet caeli indulgentia terras.
>
> (2.343–45)

> Nor could so delicate creatures endure the toil they must,
> Unless between cold and heat there came such quietude
> And the gentleness of heaven embraced the earth and comforted
>   her.

One type of experience always implies its opposite in the continuing cycle of seasons and men's lives. This passage oscillates

---

28. Raymond Williams, 18.

between the alluring ideal of spring's peace and the impossibility of maintaining this peace in any permanent way.

Despite its clear relationship to the Golden Age motif, Wilkinson, for example, saw in this passage an essentially meaningless interlude "introduced with little particular relevance save that this is to be a happy book."[29] Klingner and Will Richter, on the other hand, see the passage as a kind of exalting proof of the immanence of God in nature, Richter adducing the epithet *omnipotens* (325) and the phrase *caeli indulgentia* ("heaven's gentleness" 345) to corroborate this reading.[30] One might feel, though, that *pater Aether* ("Father Air" 325) is an insufficiently emotive term to be the focus of such intense religious feeling as Klingner and Richter perceive here. One might feel that this term, since accompanied by such scientific and dispassionate language as *semina genitalia* ("seeds of new life," "generative seeds" 324), *tener umor* ("mild moisture" 331), and *ver utile* ("good, beneficial spring" 323), works to create a philosophical or scientific tone more than a religious one. The conception, expressed here in scientific language, of perfection as past is a scientific or philosophical analogue of the Golden Age myth and seems to invite comparison with its Lucretian models, especially Lucretius 1.10–20 and 250–61.[31] Virgil's regressive emphasis in his praise of spring and his emphasis on the absence of negative elements emerges clearly when juxtaposed to these Lucretian passages, one of which follows:

> postremo pereunt imbres, ubi eos pater Aether
> in gremium matris Terrai praecipitavit;
> at nitidae surgunt fruges ramique virescunt
> arboribus, crescunt ipsae fetuque gravantur;
> hinc alitur porro nostrum genus atque ferarum,
> hinc laetas urbes pueris florere videmus

29. Wilkinson, Georgics, 191. Cf. Perret, 65.
30. Klingner, *Virgil,* 257; Richter, 232.
31. On the debt of Virgil to Lucretius see Conington, 224; Richter, 231. See Merrill, 222–24, for echoes of Lucretius in G.2; also Klepl, 11–51, for Book 1 of Lucretius and G.2. Another similar passage in Lucretius is 5.780ff.

frondiferasque novis avibus canere undique silvas;
hinc fessae pecudes pingui per pabula laeta
corpora deponunt et candens lacteus umor
uberibus manat distentis; hinc nova proles
artubus infirmis teneras lasciva per herbas
ludit lacte mero mentes perculsa novellas.
                                    (Lucr. 1.250–61)

Finally, rains are lost when Father Heaven
Has dropped them into the lap of Mother Earth.
But shining grainfields sprout, and twigs grow green
On trees; the trees grow, too, and bear their fruits;
Hence our land and the animal kind are fed,
Hence we see happy cities bloom with children
And leafy woods all filled with young bird-song;
Hence flocks wearied with fat lay themselves down
Out in the fertile fields, and bright white liquor
Leaks from their swollen teats; hence newborn lambs
Gambol on wobbly legs through tender grass,
Their baby hearts tipsy with winy milk.

As Richter notes, Lucretius' concern is with the physical
power of nature, positive and vigorous, as manifest in renewed
growth every spring. The finely noted details of *artubus infirmis*
("wobbly legs" 260) and *mentes perculsa novellas* ("their baby
hearts tipsy" 261) reveal deep sympathy with animals and pleasure in their growth. There is no touch of retrospect or of
melancholy here. The notion of a Golden Age or past perfection
is antithetical to Epicurean doctrine. Through Epicureanism the
spiritual ideal of peace and the opportunity of a better life are
ever available. Though the physical condition of the world may
be morally flawed or degenerate, Epicurus' truth offers relief
from care and fear. Spiritual peace, the discovery of Epicurus,
results from an individual's insight into truths of existence (i.e.,
the gods are distant from human affairs; death, merely a rear-
rangement of eternal atoms, is not fearful). The ideal time for
human beings beckons in the future, a function of an individual's
conversion to Epicurus and as permanent as one's ability to

maintain one's conviction of Epicurean truth. The *Georgic* poet, however, offers no prescriptions for spiritual peace, in respectful deviation from the message of Lucretius (2.490ff.).[32]

THE PRAISES OF COUNTRY LIFE

The *laudes ruris,* or "praises of country life" (2.458ff.), the last Golden Age passage of Book 2, makes the points conventionally associated with that theme: he who lives simply avoids the vanities of political life, the dangers of war, the distress of envy and poverty; he experiences the uncorrupted pleasures of family, friends, and the bounty of nature. Since the farmer's life is free from political ambition, he—unlike his urban counterpart—is not driven to defile family ties or to abandon his country in criminal exile (511); rather it is he who sustains country and family (514). The farmer's relationships and purposes, in correspondence with the eternal motions of earth, endure, while political matters have only transient importance (498). Only nature is continually renewed, and the farmer, bound to nature's cycles, participates in its larger eternity. That these points are conventional detracts neither from their truth nor from their power to move readers.[33] Yet such a summary of the passage ignores its implication that the farmer's life, even as it epitomizes early Roman virtue, is, in its own way, flawed and limited. This passage, like many others in the poem, reflects a tension between the farmer's kind of knowledge and the poet's sensibility.

The first verse of the passage (*O fortunatos nimium, sua si bona norint,/agricolas!* "O happy, too happy, if they were to know their luck, are the farmers!") is suggestive for it recalls the ignorance that was adduced as the farmer's defining problem in

32. See Büchner, *RE* 8 A 2(1958): 1290; Richter, 265; Klepl, 9. For interesting discussions quite different from mine, see Ross, *Virgil's Elements,* 119–122; and Thomas ad loc.
33. On the morality and piety of the farmer see Cato *Agr.* Introduction 4; Varro *Rust.* 3.1.5; Cic. *Sen.* 51–60; Quint. *Inst.* 2.4.24. Hor. *Epod.* 2 constitutes a kind of satire of this tradition.

1.41 (*ignarosque viae mecum miseratus agrestis,* "pitying with
me the farmers who are ignorant of the way"). Farmers, as
representative of all men, lack illumined purpose in living. There
is much of mystery that we can never know, and this mystery
limits us. For farmers this inevitable epistemological limitation is
compounded by a certain narrowness of experience. Farmers live
a rural life and thus have a chance virtue, not virtue as the result
of deliberate moral choice. If farmers are fortunate or blessed in
their existence, yet without knowing it, they have no awareness
or knowledge of their situation in life. Their experience is inadequate to give them the perspective and conscious thoughtfulness
to come, for example, to a sophisticated rejection of the extravagance and urbanity of which they are involuntarily deprived.
That farmers are ignorant of their "blessings" suggests something of the restricted quality of their lives.[34]
   The next two verses

> quibus ipsa procul discordibus armis
> fundit humo facilem victum iustissima tellus
> (2.459–60)

> For them most just earth, of her own accord, far from discordant
> Arms, pours forth from the soil an easy living

are at variance with the truth of the farmer's life as it was
described in Book 1. There he is not "far from discordant arms,"
but is swept up into the whirlpool of war, exchanging pruning
hook for sword:

> non ullus aratro
> dignus honos, squalent abductis arva colonis,
> et curvae rigidum falces conflantur in ensem.
> (1.506–8)

> The plough has so little
> Honor, the laborers are taken, the fields untended,
> And the curving sickle is beaten into the sword that yields not.

---

34. Contrast Miles, 151–52, who says that rustics have learned to control
their appetites, terming rustic life a "contemplative ideal." See also the Introduction, note 32.

War is reality, and we have seen in Book 1 the easy exchange of
roles between farmers and soldiers. The effect of this discrepancy
between Books 1 and 2 is to create a tension between certain
conventional assumptions about rural virtues and perceived reality.[35]

Such verses as 2.460 (cited on p. 112), and

> at secura quies et nescia fallere vita
> (2.467)
> but calm security and a life that will not cheat

are starkly inconsistent with Book 1 and therefore similarly
create tension for the reader, who cannot rely on the narrator for
a unified perspective. Consequently the reader must come to an
independent perspective on these oppositions. As we saw in Book
1 the farmer's security is vulnerable to disease, storm, or political
intrusion, for example; his efforts to make earth productive must
be ceaseless (cf. *nec requies,* "no rest" 2.516) and can nevertheless be unavailing (e.g., 1.324–26). These inconsistencies thrust
upon the reader the real conflicts of experience and constitute a
challenge to his thoughtful awareness of which problems might
be solved by country life and which might not.

To confirm further the moral ambiguity of the whole, the poet
indicates that Justice, although planting her last steps among
rural people, has departed even the country (2.473–74). Nowhere
is there justice, not even among rural people. This ultimate
departure of justice from the earth remains unexplained—as is
consistent with the poet's method in this poem. A murky multiplicity of causes for the degenerate condition of man is suggested

35. Putnam, *Poem of the Earth,* 144, terms the *laudes ruris* ("praises of
country life") outright "false." (See note 19.) He states that 2.527–31 portray a
"make-believe georgic life." Contrast Antonio La Penna, "Esiodo nella cultura e
nella poesia di Virgilio," in *Hésiode et son influence,* Fondation Hardt Entretiens,
vol. 7 (Geneva, 1970), 239–40, who attributes the inconsistencies that he perceives
between the pictures of the farmer's life in *G.*1 and *G.*2 to Virgil's failure to
integrate successfully the Hesiodic tradition, his major source for Book 1, with
the pastoral idealization of country life that inspired him in Book 2.

in the poem's course: the will of Jove (1.121), Laomedon's perjury (1.502), the tendency of all things to deteriorate (1.199–200), the slaughter of animals for food (2.537). The essential thing to note in considering this passage is that, in closing, the poet reminds us that, despite rural virtues, Justice has departed even from the country and hence that no Iron Age life, not even the farmer's, is without moral ambiguity.

Analogous to the departure of Justice from the country is Rome's fratricidal history:

> hanc olim veteres vitam coluere Sabini,
> hanc Remus et frater, sic fortis Etruria crevit
> scilicet et rerum facta est pulcherrima Roma,
> septemque una sibi muro circumdedit arces.
> ante etiam sceptrum Dictaei regis et ante
> impia quam caesis gens est epulata iuvencis,
> aureus hanc vitam in terris Saturnus agebat—
>
> (2.532–38)

> Such was the life the Sabines lived in days of old,
> And Remus and his brother: thus it was, surely, that
> Etruria grew strong and Rome became of all things the finest,
> Ringing her seven citadels with a single wall.
> Before the rise of the Cretan
> Lord, before impious men slaughtered bullocks for the banquet,
> Such was the life that golden Saturn lived upon earth.

Romulus and Remus, although living a golden life in the Saturnian Age, nevertheless became the very symbols of fratricide.[36] Since Remus and the Sabines (2.532) were victims of violence even in the Saturnian Age, was Rome corrupt in some way from its inception? In the strengths and virtues of Rome's Saturnian or rural Golden Age, the very foundation of its power and glory, lay—evidently—the seeds of its dissolution:

> sic fortis Etruria crevit
> scilicet et rerum facta est pulcherrima Roma
>
> (2.533–34)

> Thus it was, surely, that
> Etruria grew strong and Rome became of all things the finest.

---

36. Miles, 162–63, notes the paradox of the Saturnian Age turning into the dreadful present, as did M. C. J. Putnam in "The Virgilian Achievement,"

For this difficulty no facile explanation is offered; the problem is only posed. Even in the Saturnian Age Romans built citadels that reflect the defensive posture characteristic of the Iron Age (2.535). As Richter points out here, *ensis* ("swords" 2.540) is the last word of the book proper. The poet does not allow the reader to forget, even in reverie, the reality of contemporary experience. While acknowledging the virtues that convention respects, the poet suggests the irresolvable ambiguities of Roman life in particular and of the human condition in general.

THE GOLDEN AGE IN BOOK 3

THE SCYTHIANS

Book 3, because of its horrifying passages on love and on the plague, is generally considered the most pessimistic book of the poem and, as such, may initially seem a strange quarry for treatments of the Golden Age.[37] In Book 3 the approach to the Golden Age seems to be parodic. For example, the passage on the plague (3.478ff.) has been widely recognized as a travesty of the Golden Age,[38] for it results in a harmony among animals that recalls the Golden Age (cf. *Ecl.* 4.22; *G.* 1.129–30), since predatory relationships among animals cease after the plague:

> non lupus insidias explorat ovilia circum
> nec gregibus nocturnus obambulat: acrior illum
> cura domat; timidi dammae cervique fugaces
> nunc interque canes et circum tecta vagantur.
> (3.537–40)

Wolves no longer lurk in ambush around the folds, nor lope
Towards the flock at night: more desperate the care

Arethusa 5 (1972): 36. On the multiplicity of causes for moral decline see R. O. A. M. Lyne, "Scilicet et tempus veniet . . . : Virgil, *Georgics* 1.463–514," in *Quality and Pleasure in Latin Poetry*, ed. Tony Woodman and David West (Cambridge, 1974), 47–66.

37. See, for example, Otis, *Virgil*, 151, 180; Perret, 68; Klingner, *Virgil*, 296; Wilkinson, Georgics, 74–75; Parry, 42.

38. By (among others) Wilkinson, Georgics, 208; Otis, *Virgil*, 179; Richter, 325. See also Putnam, *Poem of the Earth*, 210; Miles, 211.

> That makes them tame. Now timid fallow-deer and elusive
> Stags wander amongst the hounds and about men's houses.

This harmony, however, is not sustaining of community and spirit, but ironic, the bitter and brutalizing sharing of all creatures in death. The poet thus grimly parodies some conventionally conceived ideals with the effect of suggesting how they are, in themselves, incapable of creating or sustaining an enlightened moral community. Harmony, as above, can exist as an isolated and meaningless phenomenon, when achieved without deliberate moral choice or enlightened purpose.

Although this has not been commented upon previously, one could argue that the passage on the Scythians (3.349–83) also is a travesty or parody of certain Golden Age phenomena. The representation of remote and primitive peoples as living in a moral Golden Age was familiar practice to Roman readers. Horace (*Odes* 3.24) subsequently described the Scythians as living morally, in a contemporary Golden Age.[39] He represents them in particular as figures of virtue. For example, after observing that even great wealth is of no avail against death, he proceeds

> campestres melius Scythae,
>   quorum plaustra vagas rite trahunt domos,
> vivunt et rigidi Getae,
>   immetata quibus iugera liberas
>
> fruges et Cererem ferunt,
>   nec cultura placet longior annua,
> defunctumque laboribus
>   aequali recreat sorte vicarius.
>
> ille matre carentibus
>   privignis mulier temperat innocens,
> nec dotata regit virum
>   coniunx nec nitido fidit adultero.

---

39. See Lovejoy and Boas, especially 288–90 and 315–44, on the overall eulogistic treatment of the Scythians throughout antiquity for their "non-commercial and communistic life" and "general simplicity and lack of luxury" (327). Ross, *Virgil's Elements,* 176 and 177, takes the passage as genuinely idyllic— "scene of peace, ease, and delight," "strangely civilized wild men." With respect

> dos est magna parentium
> virtus et metuens alterius viri
> certo foedere castitas,
> et peccare nefas aut pretium est mori.
>   (*Odes* 3.24.9–24)

Far better live the Scythians of the steppes, whose wagons haul their homes from place to place, as is their wont; far better live the Getae stern, whose unallotted acres bring forth fruits and corn for all in common; nor with them is tillage binding longer than a year; another then on like conditions takes the place of him whose task is done.

There, matrons spare children of their mother reft, nor do them harm, nor does the dowered wife rule o'er her husband or put faith in dazzling paramour. Their noble dower is parents' virtue and chastity that shrinks in steadfast faith from the husband of another. To sin is wrong; or if they sin, the penalty is death.[40]

They live better (*melius* 3.24.9). Among the comparable Getae the poet notes the sharing of crops and the unpossessed fields. Particularly relevant to our theme is the moral quality of their lives: *virtus* ("virtue" 22), *castitas* ("chastity" 23), *certo foedere* ("sure bond" 23). They are conscious of wrong (*nefas* 24), which is punished by death. Their simplicity of life, lack of sophisticated culture, and distance from the city correlate with a morally pure life.

In the *Georgics,* by contrast, we find a different and more probing perspective on life among the Scythians. In the *Georgics* also they are without urban vice, competition, or war. Free from sophisticated criminality, they have no money and hold all in common. In these particular features they recall the Golden Age. Yet the poet suggests that despite these apparently Golden Age features the Scythians are more brutal and devoid of humanity than the animals whose skins they so aptly wear (*gens effrena virum,* "an unbridled race of men" 3.382). They sustain themselves virtually without *labor* or *ars* (contrast, for example,

---

to Horace, even if he is indulging in some irony here, this would not detract from the conventional nature of the thought.

40. C. E. Bennett, trans., *Horace: Odes and* Epodes, Loeb Classical Library (London and Cambridge, Mass., 1924).

1.122, 133, 145), for neither of these is required to trap animals
already immured in ice:

> intereunt pecudes, stant circumfusa pruinis
> corpora magna boum, confertoque agmine cervi
> torpent mole nova et summis vix cornibus exstant.
> hos non immissis canibus, non cassibus ullis
> puniceaeve agitant pavidos formidine pennae,
> sed frustra oppositum trudentis pectore montem
> comminus obtruncant ferro graviterque rudentis
> caedunt et magno laeti clamore reportant.
>
> (3.368–75)

> Cattle die, the bulky oxen stand about
> Shrouded in frost, and herds of deer huddling together
> Grow numb beneath new-formed drifts, their antlers barely
>   showing.
> Men hunt them not with hounds now, nor do they use the nets,
> No scarlet-feathered toils are needed to break their nerve;
> But the deer vainly shove at the banked up snow with their
>   shoulders,
> The men attack them at close quarters, they cut them down
> Belling loud, and cheerfully shout as they bring them home.

Here there is no harmony between men and nature, no pity, no
moral community. While these Scythians have an abundance of
food, secure leisure (*secura . . . otia* 376–77; cf. *secura . . .
quies* 2.467), games (*ludus* 379), and are joyful (*laeti* 379), they
lead a brutal life, without conscience or thoughtful consciousness. The image of animals, defenseless from cold (*torpent* 370),
that are raucously and callously killed (*magno laeti clamore
reportant* 375), repels. These people are not, in the *Georgics,* a
moral ideal but a *gens effrena,* a "wild race," as the poet says
(382). They have no Golden Age, since no humane or moral
purpose animates them. Their spiritual destitution is perhaps
reflected in their surroundings. They inhabit a place of *pallen-
tis . . . umbras* ("pale shadows" 357), rather like Hades, where
the sun never shines, where running water freezes, where the
sea's surface is solid, and wine must be split with axes (3.356–66).
These people, devoid of sensibility and pity, are in need of a
"lesson of poetry." Without this moral or spiritual quality animals, even if not predatory, or mankind, even if free from

modern crime, cannot live a humane, illumined existence. As we saw in chapter 1, spiritual illumination, sensibility, and pity are the province of the poet and essential to a humane age.

The passage on the Libyans, though far briefer, makes points comparable to those on the Scythians. As the Scythians live in the far north, so the Libyans live in the south, and thus Scythians and Libyans together could express a range of possibility. The Libyans have simple lives. Unencumbered by possessions, they take everything with them (*omnia secum/armentarius Afer agit* 343–44). They have no elegance, wealth, or competition and hence are free from the decadence of Rome. On the other hand, there is no suggestion of peace or happiness in their lives. They have no security of possessions or of spirit. The comparison of these shepherds to Roman soldiers suggests the menaced and difficult quality of their lives, as if spent in anticipation of enemy attack: *iniusto sub fasce* ("under an excessive load" 347), *et hosti/ante exspectatum positis stat in agmine castris* ("till the column is halted, the camp pitched, the foe surprised" 348). There is no illumined purpose in their lives, no community. The geographical expanse of vacant fields (*tantum campi iacet* 343) seems to parallel their own spiritual vacancy. The Golden Age in its essence, although not in all its particulars, eludes them.

THE PLAGUE

The plague that the poet describes in 3.478–566 is of exceptional horror.[41] An extract will suffice to suggest the gruesome details that the poet includes:

> Hic quondam morbo caeli miseranda coorta est
> tempestas totoque autumni incanduit aestu
> et genus omne neci pecudum dedit, omne ferarum,
> corrupitque lacus, infecit pabula tabo.

---

41. Virgil's primary models for this passage are Thuc. 2.49ff. and Lucr. 6.1138ff. See Jean Bayet, "Un procédé virgilien: la description synthétique dans les *Géorgiques*," in *Studi in onore di Gino Funaioli* (Rome, 1955), 9–18, for a useful examination of Virgil's method of synthesizing various sources and traditions in order to contrive one most dramatic event.

nec via mortis erat simplex; sed ubi ignea venis
omnibus acta sitis miseros adduxerat artus,
rursus abundabat fluidus liquor omniaque in se
ossa minutatim morbo conlapsa trahebat.
(3.478–85)

For here it was that once the sky fell sick and a doleful
Season came, all hectic with the close heat of autumn,
And it killed off the whole gamut of cattle and wild beasts,
Infected their drinking pools and put a blight on their fodder.
Death took them by two stages:
When parching thirst had seared the veins and shrivelled the poor
    limbs,
Watery humors broke out again in flux till the bones all
Rotted and melted piecemeal as the malady ran its course.

Nevertheless, as many critics have noted, the plague results in a renewed, if horrific, Golden Age. Echoes between this passage and the passage in Book 1 that describes the transition from the Golden Age to the Iron Age are unmistakable. The significant terms *ars, usus, cura,* and *labor* occur in both passages (there are many other echoes as well), and thus invite comparison. For example, in inaugurating the Iron Age, Jove ordered wolves, previously gentle, to become predators (*praedarique lupos iussit* 1.130). After the plague wolves become, once again, docile:

non lupus insidias explorat ovilia circum
nec gregibus nocturnus obambulat
(3.537–38)

Wolves lurk no longer in ambush around the folds, nor lope
Towards the flock at night.

But this docility is not gentle or blessed; rather the wolves have been tamed brutally:

acrior illum
cura domat
(3.538–39)

More desperate the care that makes them tame.

As another example, in the Iron Age, men had to contrive means to trap fish:

atque alius latum funda iam verberat amnem
alta petens, pelagoque alius trahit umida lina
(1.141–42)

One whips now the wide river with casting net and searches
Deep pools, another trawls his dripping line in the sea.

After the plague there is once again Golden Age plenty, and *labor* is not required. The earth recalls her Golden Age plenty only in parody, however, for the sea freely casts up quantities of fish, diseased and untouchable, a useless abundance of food:

iam maris immensi prolem et genus omne natantum
litore in extremo ceu naufraga corpora fluctus
proluit;
(3.541–43)

Now the deepwater tribes, yes, all the swimming creatures
Lie on the shore's edge, washed by the waves like shipwrecked
    bodies.

As a final example, we may consider the fearfulness of poisonous snakes, which originated in the Iron Age through Jove's intervention:

ille malum virus serpentibus addidit atris
(1.129)

Jove put the wicked poison in the black serpent's tooth.

This fear vanishes, since the snakes perish from disease, but it does not thereby renew the Golden Age:

interit et curvis frustra defensa latebris
vipera et attoniti squamis astantibus hydri.
(3.544–45)

The viper perishes too, in vain defense of her winding
lair; and the startled snake, his scales standing on end.

A certain harmony exists among animals:

timidi dammae cervique fugaces
nunc interque canes et circum tecta vagantur.
(3.539–40)

> Now timid fallow-deer and elusive
> stags wander amongst the hounds and about men's houses.

Harmony exists among animals and men as well, for oxen are no longer exploited for plowing:

> ergo aegre rastris terram rimantur, et ipsis
> unguibus infodiunt fruges, montisque per altos
> contenta cervice trahunt stridentia plaustra.
>
> (3.534–36)
>
> Painfully men scratched at the soil with mattocks, used their
> Own nails to cover in the seed corn, harnessed their necks
> To tug the creaking waggons over a towering hillside.

Yet these ancient enmities are not resolved with sympathy or felt community, but only by the terminal equality of death.

In sum, the aftermath of the plague shares with the Golden Age an absence of competition, of private property, and of predatory relationships among earth's creatures. Conventional *adynata,* such as harmony between sheep and wolves, ordinarily predicted only of a fantasized future, are realized.[42] Mankind is once again freed from vain concerns and artifice. The Iron Age ethic of usefulness stands revealed as ill conceived, for salvation lies precisely in abandoning technology:

> quaesitaeque nocent artes; cessere magistri
>
> (3.549)
>
> Cures (*artes*) they invented only killed; healers gave up

and in abandoning the Iron Age ethic of profitable materialism:

> nam neque erat coriis *usus*
>
> (3.559)
>
> the hides were of no *use.*

Yet, although Iron Age flaws are eliminated, a new Golden Age does not ensue. Iron Age values of *ars, usus,* and technological achievement are abandoned;[43] but they are abandoned through

42. Wilkinson, *Georgics,* 208.
43. Büchner, *RE* 8 A2 (1958): 1302, observes that man learned to deal with the plague not through the ethic of use but, paradoxically, of uselessness.

compelling disaster and without deliberate choice. Here, although without technology, man does not attain a new innocence but a new barbarism, as he is driven to dig the earth with his nails (3.534–35). *Quid labor aut benefacta iuvant?* ("Of what avail are work and good services?" 525).[44] The poet poses this question at the poem's grimmest moment, implying that the purpose of achievements and morality is unknown.

As a whole, then, this passage highlights the necessity of a certain spiritual quality or moral community, which alone might sustain Golden Age values. Such a quality does not exist as a consequence of the plague, for the harmony achieved there is grotesque and without spirit or volition. The poet has taken up conventional Golden Age features in successive isolation and permutation and finely revealed thereby what is absent—a spark of willed mutuality and illumined purpose.

THE GOLDEN AGE IN BOOK 4

THE BEES

In Book 4 the Golden Age passages, which are here considered to be those on the bees and the Corycian gardener, are not, as in Book 3, travesties of the Golden Age but again, as in Books 1 and 2, approximations of the Golden Age, in which disparities between real and ideal lead to subtle ironies and new perspectives on questions central to the poem.

As often noted, the bees of 4.1–115 and 149–280 recall in their selflessness and sharing the Golden Age ethic as described in Book 1. As a consequence they have been viewed at times as Virgil's model for the moral and political renewal of Rome, a new Golden Age. This interpretation, based upon an assumed equation of the bees with the Roman people and of Aristaeus with Octavian,[45] sees in the bees' "resurrection" an image of the

44. *Benefacta* had particular currency as a political term in the Roman party system. Cf. David Ross, *Catullus and the Traditions of Ancient Poetry* (Cambridge, 1969), 83–86.
45. E.g., Perret, 83–85; Steele Commager, ed., *Virgil: A Collection of Critical Essays* (New York, 1966), 3; Hellfried Dahlmann, "Die Bienenstaat in Vergils Georgica," in *Kleinen Schriften* (Hildesheim, 1970), 189.

rebirth of Rome under the leadership of Octavian. The perceived optimism of the poem as a whole resides especially in this conclusion to Book 4, where the miraculous birth of the bees is felt to resolve the tensions of the poem and to portend a positive future. This reading, although of long standing, has begun to meet with objections, for the bees appear seriously flawed as models of a renewed Golden Age.[46] Rather the portrait of them is a complex one in which strengths and weaknesses combine to form a morally ambiguous picture, identifying the bees as typical Iron Age creatures rather than as models for a moral Golden Age.

The *Georgic* poet devotes a disproportionate space to bees, given their relative lack of importance on a farm. Other small farm animals, such as dogs or fowl, omitted from this book, would reasonably deserve equal treatment. In addition, as Hellfried Dahlmann usefully noted,[47] the jussive form of the verb is infrequent in this passage, suggesting that here, as elsewhere, the *Georgic* poet does not have a conventional didactic purpose in mind. His focus is descriptive rather than prescriptive. It is the character of the bees' life, as he describes it, that is the focus of interest. His account derives in part from traditional wisdom about the bees and in part from an interest in certain of their behaviors that seem particularly Roman or, perhaps, in which Romans might well see themselves reflected, if obliquely and with some distance and perspective.

Aristotle (*Hist. an.* 5.21–23) classified bees with wasps, cranes, and men as political (living in a *polis*) and as having shared work (*koinon ergon*). Equally Varro (3.16.3, 3.16.6) noted their similarities to human beings and especially their talent for cooperative effort.

In the *Georgics* the analogy between bees and human beings is unmistakable from the book's opening verses, with their references to *magnanimosque duces . . . et populos et proelia:*

---

46. Putnam, *Poem of the Earth,* 245–63, and Griffin, "Fourth *Georgic,*" passim, write perceptively on the bees' flaws.
47. Dahlmann, 186.

admiranda tibi levium spectacula rerum
magnanimosque duces totiusque ordine gentis
mores et studia et populos et proelia dicam.
(4.3–5)

I'll tell of tiny
Things that make a show well worth your admiration—
Great-hearted leaders, a whole nation whose work is planned,
Their morals, strivings, tribes and battles—I'll tell you in due
    order.

Parallels between the bees' existence and that of human beings
are clear. Jove establishes for both the laboring way of life:

Nunc age, naturas apibus quas Iuppiter ipse
addidit expediam, pro qua mercede canoros
Curetum sonitus crepitantiaque aera secutae
Dictaeo caeli regem pavere sub antro.
(4.149–52)

Well then, let me speak of the natural gifts that Jove himself
Bestowed on the bees, their reward
For obeying the charms—the chorus and clashing brass of the
    priests—
And feeding the king of heaven when he hid in that Cretan cave.

(Cf. 1.121–24, cited on p. 96.) This intervention also entails
cura (4.178), *amor* (4.177), *ars* (4.56), *labor* (4.184), pursuit of
gloria (4.205), all without rest (*mora* 4.185): a collocation of
features that defines the Iron Age as represented in this poem.
Like men, bees have tiny enemies who undermine their *labor*
(4.13ff., 242ff., cf. 1.118–21, 178–86); they suffer from plague
(*casus . . . nostros,* "our ills" 4.251). All these features suggest
their similarity to mankind in general.

In other ways their ordered and religious society is represented
as specifically Roman, as the terms *larem* (43), *magnis . . .
legibus* (154), *patriam* and *penates* (155) suffice to suggest.[48]

In their sharing the bees certainly recall the Golden Age. Their
lives are very much communal experiences:

---

48. Contrast Thomas at 4.201 concerning *Quirites.*

> solae communis natos, consortia tecta
> urbis habent
>
> $$(4.153-54)$$
>
> They alone have their children in common, a city shared
> Beneath one roof
>
> et in medium quaesita reponunt[49]
>
> $$(4.157)$$
>
> and put their gains into a common store
>
> omnibus una quies operum, labor omnibus unus
>
> $$(4.184)$$
>
> For one and all one work-time and alike one rest from work.

Chastity, though not specifically a Golden Age feature, also distinguishes the bees from the Iron Age creatures of Book 3. The bees are apparently free of those destructive passions that characterize all other mortal creatures (*amor omnibus idem* 3.244). The poet emphasizes the bees' reputation for chastity by adducing the least scientific of contemporary hypotheses to explain their reproduction:

> verum ipsae e foliis natos, e suavibus herbis
> ore legunt, ipsae regem parvosque Quirites
> sufficiunt
>
> $$(4.200-2)$$
>
> But all by themselves from leaves and sweet herbs they will gather
> Their children in their mouths, themselves supply the succession
> And the tiny citizens.

(Cf. the suggestive contrast of *apibus fetis,* "mother bees" 4.139). The issue to consider is whether the bees' undeniable Roman and Golden Age features suggest that the Romans, to the degree to which they are symbolized by the bees, have or are to have a new Golden Age. Although some have assumed that the bees

---

49. Putnam, *Poem of the Earth,* 254, writes interestingly on the differences between *quaerebant* (1.127) and *reponunt* (4.157), inferring from *reponunt* that "the bees' existence is a decline from, rather than a reversion to, the Golden Age."

represent a Roman society perfected and renewed,[50] others have written perceptively about the bees' flaws, which are incompatible with a humane and creative society. The bees' undeniable virtues are in tension with failings that compromise them as moral models. For the Romans, therefore, the bees' flaws might be as instructive as their virtues; for while they embody to a degree a social and moral ideal, they represent equally a life without consciousness or pity.

The poet implies that the bees' sharing is achieved at the cost of individuality and reflection. For example, once their king dies, they are lost, incapable of individual or reflective action. Here total community is not necessarily a good, as it can lead to total self-destruction:

> praeterea regem non sic Aegyptus et ingens
> Lydia nec populi Parthorum aut Medus Hydaspes
> observant. rege incolumi mens omnibus una est;
> amisso rupere fidem, constructaque mella
> diripuere ipsae et cratis solvere favorum.
> ille operum custos, illum admirantur et omnes
> circumstant fremitu denso stipantque frequentes,
> et saepe attollunt umeris et corpora bello
> obiectant pulchramque petunt per vulnera mortem.
>
> (4.210–18)

Besides, they esteem royalty more than Egypt does or enormous
Lydia even, or the peoples of Parthia, or the Mede by Hydaspes.
Let the king be safe—they are bound by a single faith and
    purpose:
Lose him—then unity's gone, and they loot the honey cells
They built themselves, and break down the honeycomb's withy
    well.
Guardian of all their works he is. They hold him in awe.
Thick is their humming murmur as they crowd around and mob
    him.
Often they chair him shoulder high: and in war they shelter
His body with theirs, desiring the wounds of a noble death.

---

50. So Antonio La Penna, "*Senex Corycius,*" in *Atti del Convegno Virgiliano sul Bimillenario delle* Georgiche (Naples, 1977), 65: "That the society of the bees constitutes an ethical-political Augustan model is a truth which does not need to be confirmed."

Their uncritical obedience to their king is made to parallel that of the peoples of the (decadent, effeminate) East, whom the Romans did not admire and whose values were fundamentally opposed to Roman republican tradition. Thus, uniform community comes with a certain cost.

A lack of thoughtfulness in the bees accompanies their militarism. Bees' similarities to soldiers are implicit in such terms as *signa* ("standards" 108), *castris* ("camp" 108), *speculantur* ("are on watch" 166), *custodia* ("keeping guard" 165), *agmine facto* ("in martial array" 167) and in 4.193–94, which suggests military maneuvers and soldiers in a besieged town. The poet has imagined or created for bees this militaristic character since bees do not, in reality, behave as belligerently as is indicated here. The bee battle is a "literary flight of fancy"[51] that creates a correlation between militarism and absence of reflection. Bees prepare with excitement (4.69–70, 73) for wars without substance, sacrificing their lives with alacrity in battles that have no urgency (cf. *animasque in vulnere ponunt* 238). They die for glory, for the appearance of "beautiful" death (*pulchra mors* 218), thus adhering to the heroic code.[52] Yet to the poet their dramas appear more pathetic than heroic:

> hi motus animorum atque haec certamina tanta
> pulveris exigui iactu compressa quiescent.
>
> (4.86–87)

> And all these epic battles and turbulent hearts you can silence
> By flinging a handful of dust.

Further complicating the bees' claimed status as figures of moral renewal is that their lauded continence and lack of passion is more apparent than real, since they seem merely to have replaced sexual *amor* with another sort, that is, passion for gain:

> illum adeo placuisse apibus mirabere morem,
> quod neque concubitu indulgent, nec corpora segnes
> in Venerem solvunt aut fetus nixibus edunt.
>
> (4.197–99)

---

51. Wilkinson, Georgics, 263. Cf. Klingner, *Virgil*, 304, on the epic language used to describe the bee battle, as well as other differences from Varro's account.
52. Quinn, 1–22.

Most you shall marvel at this habit peculiar to bees—
That they have no sexual union: their bodies never dissolve
Lax into love, nor bear with pangs the birth of their young

Cecropias innatus apes *amor* urget habendi
(4.177)
An inborn love of possession impels the bees

(In *Aen.* 8.327 in the narration of Evander *amor habendi*, "love of gain,"[53] and *belli rabies*, "madness of war," bring about the dissolution of the Golden Age.) That the poet intends to represent the gathering of honey as a substitute for sexual activity is further indicated by the use of terms that denote passion and birth:

tantus *amor* florum et *generandi* gloria mellis
(4.205)
Such is their love for flowers and the glory of producing [generating] honey.

Thus, although bees do not weaken their bodies with sexual activity (198–199), they do expend them in battle (218) or in pursuit of honey (205) without consideration of their lives' value. Therefore the same drive that appears as sexual passion in other animals is expressed in the bees' lives as an urgent acquisitiveness or materialism and an unreflecting negligence of life (204, 218) in pursuit of glory.

While, then, the bees have the Golden Age virtues of community and sharing, in their case these come at the cost of their militaristic and appetitive passions. Although they are as flawed as human beings, yet they are without human virtues, such as song or poetry, which distinguish man from beast and serve to define human culture. Neglectful of individual lives, without individual satisfaction or sentiment, they achieve mere existence, existence without meaning. In comparison to the other important figures of this book, they are anonymous and lacking the unique creativity and devotion to beauty of the Corycian gar-

53. See Johnston, 101, who cites parallels: *amor terrae* of plants at G.2.301; *amor laudum* of horses at G.3.112, 185–86.

dener, the individual persistence of Aristaeus, and the potential for song and beauty of Orpheus. The bees as well as the human individuals of Book 4 have powerful and destructive passions that exist in tension with their virtues and achievements. None of these figures is a model for flawless existence; all embody conflicts that are illuminated but not resolved by the *Georgic* poet.

THE CORYCIAN GARDENER

In his harmony with nature, in his transcendence of natural constraints of time and place, and in his indifference to material goals, the Corycian gardener, most perfectly of any figure in the poem, approaches the spirit or morality of the Golden Age. From land abandoned by others as useless:

>   cui pauca relicti
> iugera ruris erant, nec fertilis illa iuvencis
> nec pecori opportuna seges nec commoda Baccho.
>   (4.127–29)

>   a few poor acres
> Of land once derelict, useless for arable,
> No good for grazing, unfit for the cultivation of vines

he contrives a miraculous and artistic fertility, his work thus reflecting the spiritual luminescence of his private Golden Age. The essence of his significance is that his achievement is miraculous and mysterious—not comprehensible, imitable, or possible to describe in conventional georgic *praecepta*. He makes sterile land productive. His hyacinths bloom while rocks shatter with winter's cold and streams are frozen (4.135–38); he is the first to pluck roses in spring (134); he is the first to gather honey (139–41). *Every* blossom on his trees survives to bear fruit (142–43). He alone can transplant fully mature trees:

> ille etiam seras in versum distulit ulmos
> eduramque pirum et spinos iam pruna ferentis
> iamque ministrantem platanum potantibus umbras.[54]
>   (4.144–46)

---

54. Conington states ad loc. that *seras, eduram, iam pruna ferentis, iamque ministrantem . . . umbras* are all emphatic. For fuller discussion see C. G. Per-

He had a gift, too, for transplanting in rows the far-grown elm,
The hardwood pear, the blackthorn bearing its weight of sloes,
And the plane that already offered a pleasant shade for drinking.

(In this feat he anticipates and parallels the poet-singer Orpheus.)
The gardener's moral relationship to nature recalls, as we see,
that of Golden Age man, for in each case nature, unassailed,
responds abundantly. The gardener's success is not attributed to
Iron Age technology. Although such terms as *captare* ("capture"), *fallere* ("deceive"), *insectari* ("assail"), *terrere* ("ter-
rify"), and *arma* ("weapons") characterize the Iron Age farmer
of *Georgic* 1, the gardener is not represented as being on the
attack. Neither do other terms denoting Iron Age technology or
anxiety (e.g., *labor, usus, ars, cura*) occur of his activities.[55] One
could reasonably argue that *labor, cura,* and *ars* are implicit,
for example, in the gardener's returning home late at night
(*sera . . . nocte* 132–33). The fact is, however, that the poet has
taken care to avoid the use of these particular terms, preferring in
this way to emphasize the miraculous, mysterious quality of the
gardener's achievements, which are not imitable through routine
georgic procedures. The farmer's feats are thus allowed to appear moral or spiritual more than technical. His success is not a
function simply of hard work.

Critics have seen in the gardener an embodiment of the fundamental value of agricultural life (Richter); a model, like the
farmers of *Georgic* 2, of wisdom (as they see it), who transcends
poverty through serenity and skill (Klingner); and an Epicurean
sage, exemplifying beauty and utility (Antonio La Penna).[56] My
thesis here, however, is that the gardener represents not so much
a rural or philosophical ideal as a poetic ideal. Neither does he
represent so much the simple life as the esthetic life, for he
pursues beauty and uselessness more than beauty and utility. The
gardener's values are at variance with the materialism and milita-

---

kell, "On the Corycian Gardener in Virgil's Fourth *Georgic*," *TAPA* 11(1981):
167–77.
    55. Cf. Klingner, *Virgil,* 309 n. 1, for a similar observation.
    56. Richter at 4.125–48; Klingner, *Virgil,* 309; La Penna, "*Senex Co-
rycius,*" 57.

rism characteristic of the Iron Age; and it is precisely his deviations from this tradition that identify him as a Golden Age figure.

In evaluating the gardener's achievement readers must realize that the garden in question is not the equivalent of a farmer's small vegetable patch. This garden does not provide produce particularly suited for consumption either by the gardener or by his bees;[57] rather it is described in such a way as to suggest a pleasure garden, an ornament, a timeless profusion of flowering trees and plants that is possible only in the imagination. In addition to its floral beauty the garden has also a formal artistic perfection, reflected in the words *in versum* (144) and *circum* (130), for example, which are tantamount to technical terms. These terms suggest, respectively, rows of well-aligned trees and borders of flowers (features "which constitute the grace of gardens . . . esteemed in Greco-Roman antiquity"[58]), thus indicating the artistic refinement of the garden. Therefore this garden is above all a symbol of beauty, beauty that serves no material function but that sustains and expands the spirit, like the beauty of art, song, or poetry. In growing flowers, the epitome of superfluous beauty, the gardener pursues (like the poet) an esthetic and spiritual ideal that ignores material function or profit. This is the essential significance of the old man's garden: to serve as an image of beauty that is nonmaterial, nonproductive, nonprofitable, and thus in opposition to the farmer's work, which is material and answers to physical needs.

The uselessness of the old man's garden is further underlined by his age. While many take the gardener's old age (*senem* 127)

---

57. The squash (*cucumis* 4.122) is not grown by the Corycian gardener, although La Penna, "*Senex Corycius*," 57, does not note this distinction. Contrast the plants recommended for bees at 4.30–32, 63, 109, 112. The character of this passage emerges clearly when it is compared with Varro's Veianius brothers, who turned their very small holding into a profitable apiary, as E. Burck notes in "Der korykische Greis in Vergils *Georgica* (IV 116–148)," in *Navicula Chiloniensis: Festschrift F. Jacoby* (Leiden, 1956), 160.

58. P. Wuilleumier, "Virgile et le vieillard de Tarente," *REL* 3 (1930): 326. A certain refinement is implicit also in the term *dapibus*. J. S. Clay, "The Old Man in the Garden: *Georgic* 4.116–148," *Arethusa* 14 (1981): 61, sees the flowers as reflecting "the love of the beautiful for its own sake."

to be an index of wisdom,[59] it is perhaps germane to recall the verses on the old stallion of *Georgic* 3.95–100, which set old age within a georgic, Iron Age context. There the old stallion, no longer able to procreate or to make war (his legitimizing functions within the georgic or material world), must be dismissed from the farmer's care and attention:

> Hunc quoque, ubi aut morbo gravis aut iam segnior annis
> deficit, abde domo, nec turpi ignosce senectae.
> frigidus in Venerem senior, frustraque laborem
> ingratum trahit, et, si quando ad proelia ventum est,
> ut quondam in stipulis magnus sine viribus ignis,
> incassum furit.
>
> (3.95–100)
>
> Yet even that horse, when he weakens from illness or weight of
>   years,
> You must pension off and spare no pity for age's failings.
> To be old is to be cold in rut, to prolong a loveless
> Labor impotently; and whenever it comes to the conflict,
> His passion is vain—a great fire in stubble, without strength.

In the farmer's world, dominated as it must be by material concerns, an old horse, since useless, has no value and cannot be redeemed by pity or sentiment. According, then, to the material standards implicit in the very nature of a georgic poem, the old Corycian would have no value, since he also is useless, not only for war or procreation, but for vigorous labor. Nevertheless, in the poet's vision he represents an experience of great value.

In contenting himself with unproductive land the gardener shows his negligence of profit, prestige, and convention. Although near the city (4.125–27), he pursues a life that excludes urban or, more generally, Iron Age values, as the absence from his life of commerce (*dapibus mensas onerabat inemptis,* "he loaded his board with unbought dainties" 133), appetitiveness, aggression, and ambition shows. As his old age makes clear the superfluous and inessential character of his activities, so his

---

59. Such as La Penna, *"Senex Corycius,"* 63. Cf. Clay, "Old Man in the Garden," 60, for a good discussion of the significance of the gardener's old age.

unique accomplishments do not translate into material profit or political power, to which concerns he is consistently indifferent. Content without *gloria, honor,* or *amor* and thus outside of Iron Age values and morality, he is distinct from the poem's other figures, including Aristaeus (4.325) and the *Georgic* poet (4.6), who are touched by Iron Age ambition and aspire variously to wealth, power, glory, or divinity. The gardener, by contrast, aspiring to nothing other than what he has, achieves enduring contentment (*regum aequabat opes animis* 132), unique in the poem.

The fourth *Georgic,* then, juxtaposes the impersonal, materialistic society of bees to the extravagant, individual passions of the variously failed and imperfect Orpheus and Aristaeus. Opposed to both is the fleeting ideal of the gardener, who has their strengths and not their flaws. Although an individual, he has neither Aristaeus' concern for mortal glory (*vitae mortalis honorem* 326) and hope of divinity (*quid me caelum sperare iubebas* 325) nor Orpheus' destructive passion (*quid tantus furor* 495). To place the Corycian gardener passage in this book, therefore, is to illuminate the tension between the imperfect reality of both farmer and poet and an ideal of human existence, creative in pursuit of beauty, at peace with nature, and free from urban corruption. It is not, then, the bees but the gardener who most closely embodies the Golden Age ideal. The city, although so near and in reality menacing, does not obtrude upon his existence. Unlike the conscripted farmers of *Georgic* 1 or the exiled poets of *Eclogues* 1 and 9, whose shattered lives exemplify the city's ascendancy, he lives—ideally and impossibly—free of the city's influence.

The gardener is different from the poet in his spiritual contentment (*regum aequabat opes animis* 4.132) and in his indifference to those drives for power, profit, honor, or glory that define variously the city, the poet, and the Iron Age. Although the gardener lives alongside the city (4.125), he is untroubled by its needs. Equally without rural connections, he pursues his isolated and marvelous creations. In growing flowers, the epitome of superfluous beauty, the gardener pursues, like the poet, an esthetic or spiritual ideal that ignores material function or profit. One might sense that the gardener's appeal is precisely his freedom from the limiting realities, internal and external, that trouble the *Georgic* poet. He is free from ambition and longing; he does not idealize an irretrievable past, nor does he seek to escape the present. Neither does he conceive artistic goals comparable to the poet's desires to understand the mysteries of the universe or to be in Greece. Creative in pursuit of beauty, in harmony with nature, free from urban corruption and rural constraint, the gardener embodies an ideal of contentment and withdrawal that appeals powerfully to the poet. Of all the figures in the poem he lives closest to the morality of the Golden Age, feeling the challenge neither of mystery nor of mission.

Even the gardener, however, is not a perfect embodiment of the Golden Age, for there are ways in which he too diverges from the Golden Age ethic of Book 1. His pursuit of beauty identifies him most significantly as a poet. We may infer from the learned and Alexandrian adjective *Oebalia* for Tarentum that he is a poet of a particular sort.[60] As *Oebalia* evokes Hellenistic poetry and abstruse mythological reference, so the gardener is subtly associated with the highly self-conscious and refined Alexandrian tradition. Again, he inhabits a city Greek in origin, renowned for its beauty (cf. Hor. *Odes* 2.6.9–24) and at the greatest remove from Rome. We may infer from these attributes that the cultural value that he is meant to embody is one of high refinement and is defined by the free and timeless pursuit of beauty for its own sake. In his artistic aspects the gardener is learned, graceful, and without mission. As he is untouched by the city's influence, so he is also untroubled by its needs. His "art" is not political, not for the group, but for himself alone.[61] In his individuality and

60. Cf. Klingner, *Virgil*, 309, for *Oebalia* as evocative of ancient Greek poetry and mythology. Thomas ad loc. specifies the particularly Alexandrian style of this difficult periphrasis for Tarentum. (Oebalus was a king of Sparta, and it was Spartans who founded Tarentum.)

61. Cf. La Penna, "*Senex Corycius*," 65, who thinks the gardener blamably indifferent to society, and Clay, "Old Man in the Garden," 60, who notes his "apolitical solitude."

indifference to others he reflects a lack of group consciousness and concern. Even he, therefore, is not entirely a Golden Age figure, for he does not have the ethic of sharing or cooperation essential to its spirit.

His indifference to others raises a question critical for understanding the nature of the relationship of the artist to the Golden Age. In this poem it is only individuals, namely, Proteus, Orpheus, the *Georgic* poet, and the Corycian gardener, who are shown as creative and artistic. The place of art in the Golden Age is equivocal, then, for although it is not explicitly excluded as a component of the Golden Age, neither is it explicitly included. The mystery of its origin remains unexamined. This is an important point, contrasting significantly with Lucretius, for example, who does include song as a natural development in his history of civilization (5.334, 1379–1411). Perhaps we are to infer that art is only an Iron Age phenomenon, just as in Lucretius philosophy belongs only to a highly developed political age. Both the *Georgic* poet and Orpheus, as we have seen, are Iron Age figures in that each is touched by ambition and discontent. Yet these are not qualities prerequisite to pure art since the Corycian gardener is represented both as content (132) and artistic; they may be prerequisite to politically conscious art. Through the combined experience of these figures the poet would seem to imply that the artistic personality does not form part of a group and that, therefore, the Golden Age ideal, in which all is shared and there are no distinctions, is not compatible with individual artistic endeavor. The gardener, as the only happy figure in the poem, embodies a vision of escape from political and moral questions; but this ideal is realized neither in society nor for society. Secluded in time past, in distance from Rome, and in exile (he is a foreigner, not Roman like the apian *Quirites*), he is an isolated figure. Significantly the *Georgic* poet qualifies this vision of the artist in apolitical isolation as impossible of realization for himself. He cannot pursue this vision, as he says, precisely because of constraints—of time and of responsibility (116, 147–48). He implies that a substantive distinction exists between himself and the gardener when he indicates that he is not able to pursue his vision of the gardener as he would wish. The freedom to pursue an entirely esthetic ideal is the gardener's privilege and not the *Georgic* poet's.

While the gardener, then, both in his harmonious relationship to nature and in the spiritual dimension of his life, of any figure in the poem most closely approaches the Golden Age model, he nevertheless fails of it. He too is disparate from the ideal, since he is alone, while in the Golden Age all was shared. In his individuality and absorption with art, he resembles Orpheus and the *Georgic* poet, both, to a degree, Iron Age figures. While artistic creativity is not necessarily incompatible with the Golden Age, the poet may be suggesting his sense—in thus restricting art to individual figures—that it cannot come out of an undifferentiated community. The irony and pathos of this vision for the *Georgic* poet is that he is alien not only in the present, as we have seen, but also even in the Golden Age past that he himself creates and idealizes. The ideal of the Golden Age would not exist without his poetry and without the tradition from which his poetry derives; yet he himself could not exist in the Golden Age of which he sings. The poet is the carrier of the values of pity, humanity, and art; but the simultaneous conception of these values exists, apparently, only in the Iron Age, thus creating an ironic play of absence and presence that questions all values and ideals.

• • •

In summarizing the poet's treatment of the Golden Age overall, we may observe that in Book 1 he sets forth a miniature meditation on the nature of human society and how it evolved from an ethic of morality, sharing, and harmony with nature to an ethic of egocentric materialism, requiring a certain aggression against nature and other men. In Book 2 the praises of Italy, spring, and country life are all, ultimately, discrepant from the Golden Age as adumbrated in Book 1, because of the lack within them of a moral community. The Scythians and the plague of Book 3, outright travesties of the Golden Age, point as well to the absence of spirit and sensibility requisite to a perfected society. The harmony achieved in Book 3 is a bitterly ironic harmony of unwilled animality and death. While the bees of Book 4 do share, they are materialistic, militaristic, and without reflection. The gardener, on the other hand, creates beautiful things and is at peace with himself, isolated as he is. For him there is no sharing and no community. Therefore no model exists in the poem for the perfect relation to nature and to other men. An ideal is conceived in the poem but not shown as capable of realization. The conflicts of life to which the poet points appear incapable of resolution. This view, while tragic, is not sentimentalized in the poem or pathetic. The poet sees evenly, with clear-eyed vision.

· · ·

In the following chapter we will consider further the character of the poet's vision. As we see, it is the poet who emerges as the most troubled and also as the most challenging figure of the poem. Alienated both in the present and in the idealized past, he wishes to bring his poetry—and all it connotes of reflective sorrow, of capacity for pity, of community, and of mystery—to Italy and, of course, to all readers. Yet it is difficult to understand how he can feel this mission with such urgency, given his apprehension that neither the world of power nor fundamental existential problems will be changed by it. In pursuit of some response to this question we will consider in chapter 3 the value and continuing power of the poet's vision and the quality of his truth.

3

The Poet's Truth

The purpose of this chapter is to examine the nature and value of the poet's truth. My essential thesis is that there is a tension within the poem, most clearly reflected in the poem's final book, between two types of knowledge and value. The one is materially useful and real, the farmer's knowledge, based—to use the poem's terms—on observed *signa* ("signs") and distilled into *praecepta* ("maxims" or "precepts"). The other knowledge, the poet's, is not aimed at material usefulness, but, embodied in myth and mystery, it adumbrates a vision of the quality of human experience. This knowledge, the insights of which are intuitive and imagistic, aims at qualities of spirit and emotion and thus is antithetical to the farmer's, which is rational and material. In the *Georgics* the farmer's truth, as embodied in *praecepta,* and his values of material survival and utility are in tension with the figure of the poet and his values, as represented by Orpheus and the *Georgic* poet and as embodied both in myth and in the particular morality, harmony, and community of which the *Georgic* poet sings. Although this poem is called *Georgica* and would, therefore, be presumed to emphasize and value *ars* ("skill" or "craft"), we see—clearly at the poem's conclusion—the poet's ultimate concern not with knowledge appropriate to a practical, agricultural handbook, which the *Georgics* initially proclaims itself to be, but rather with mystery, myth, and divine revelation. This explains why the poet has chosen to conclude an ostensibly practical poem with the fabulous tale of *bougonia,* a precept completely without georgic truth.[1] To conclude a geor-

1. For a more elaborated discussion of *bougonia* see chapter 1. It may help the reader to know that a number of other of the poet's "facts" and precepts in this poem are without georgic truth. Wilkinson, Georgics, 235ff., for example, observes that not all of the information in the passage on signs is accurate. The

gic, didactic poem in this way seems necessarily to pose an alternative to the very presumptions and values of the genre, and thus to point to a tension between the poet, who appears as a figure in the poem, and the values implicit in the genre that he has chosen. It poses the question of poetic truth and the role and function of the poet in the practical, material, Roman world. It poses also the question of the nature of society and of the real value of technology (*artes*) and man's work (*labor*).

As we have seen, the poem opens with a series of questions (1.1–4) and closes with mystery (i.e., with the *bougonia*, of unexperienced reality, imperfectly understood). The ultimate revelation of the poet's truth and values is precisely the *bougonia*, which concludes the poem with a powerful and significant paradox: the *bougonia* is unreal but true. The carcass of a calf, no matter how treated, will not yield bees; but *bougonia* as an image, as a representation of the poet's vision of Iron Age existence—with its message of the brutality of success, of the cost of survival, of the pathos of loss—is true, and thus reveals the limitations of the merely real. This paradox of being unreal but true reveals the essence of the opposition between the farmer's knowledge and the poet's knowledge, for the poem concludes with the new myth of Aristaeus and Orpheus, created by the poet, and the image of *bougonia*, which as *praeceptum* is false or useless but as symbol is true. Thus the farmer and the poet

---

"seacoot is a non-bird" and, similarly, the *marina fulica* may not exist. He calls this a "literary blend." Wilkinson also speaks of impossible grafts described by Virgil (243–44). Ross, *Virgil's Elements*, 105f., also says Virgil makes claims for grafts that could never have been accomplished. He later refers to the "Virgilian lie" in the praises of Italy, spring, and country life of Book 2 (110ff.). The signs at Caesar's death (for discussion see pp. 158–62) are, with one exception or possibly two, not historical. (Cf. also L. A. S. Jermyn, "Weather-Signs in Virgil," *G&R* 20 [1951]: 32 and 59.) Untruth is, therefore, a pervasive motif in the poem. M. S. Spurr, "Agriculture and the *Georgics*," *G&R* 33 (1986): 164–87, has recently argued, on the contrary, that Virgil's agricultural data are correct for the time. While I am in no way qualified to assess the validity of his arguments as opposed to those of Pliny, Seneca, Jermyn, Wilkinson, or Ross, for example, I would argue that Virgil's representation of *bougonia* alone suggests its unreal and symbolic value. Once even this is acknowledged, we are free to begin to apprehend a pervasive pattern of unreal but (in some other way) true or useful assertions in the poem.

engage in two different modes of discourse, aiming at two different claims to truth. The poet's truth, as embodied in myth, unverifiable and impractical, is consequently at variance with the assumptions of a georgic poem, which must esteem as valuable such *praecepta* as are aimed at tangible, profitable ends. The magnificence of this paradox is that, in this georgic poem, it undermines the values of the "real," thus using the form of the genre to challenge its own values.

The myth of *bougonia* embodies a truth higher than the merely useful, because man's life is shown in the poem to be defined and limited by unanswerable questions, by a spiritual or metaphysical ignorance that *praecepta* do not address. Farmers are described at 1.41 as *ignarosque viae* ("ignorant of the way," i.e., ignorant of an enlightened way of life) and at 2.458 as ignorant of their blessings (*o fortunatos nimium sua si bona norint/agricolas!*). Further, the placing of the farmer at the primal moment of cutting an unknown field (1.50) epitomizes the condition of ignorance with which the *Georgic* poet is absorbed throughout the poem. Here the poet is returning the reader to the paradigmatic moment of man's initial confrontation with nature, the moment when, without the aid of obfuscating tradition or others' labor, we (*at prius ignotum ferro quam scindimus aequor*, "but before *we* plough an unknown plain" 1.50) confront our primal and defining ignorance. The poet's use of the first-person plural here expresses the universality of this moment and of this undertaking.

Unanswerable, troubling questions such as the following are among the most resonant verses of the poem:

> quid labor aut benefacta iuvant? quid vomere terras
> invertisse gravis?
>
> (3.525–26)

> Of what avail are toil or services? Of what avail to have
>   turned the difficult
> Earth with the plough?

> quid faceret? quo se rapta bis coniuge ferret?
> quo fletu Manis, qua numina voce moveret?
>
> (4.504–5)

> What could he do, where go, his wife twice taken from him?
> What lament would move death now? What voice might alter
>   Heaven's will?

When, for example, the very purpose of labor and accomplishment is, as especially in the first citation here, unknown, the relative unimportance of *praecepta* is necessarily implied. *Praecepta* do not acknowledge or touch upon the unresolvable and defining mysteries of existence to which above all the poet is sensitive and to which he responds through the image of *bougonia*. While the farmers are "ignorant of the way" and "do not know their blessings," the poet aspires precisely to knowledge—not of *praecepta* but of *causae* ("causes"), that is, of ultimate truths, which he represents as the gift of the Muses (2.475–82). Significantly, the poet does not look to the scientific method, that is, to the Epicurean atomism, materialism, and rationalism of Lucretius to reveal these ultimate truths, but rather to the poetic tradition and mode of experience, as we infer from his explicit assumption that the Muses are privy to the mysteries of nature's functioning. This association of the Muses and of poetry with knowledge of mystery is a significant conception here since it implies that the Muses transcend *praecepta*, which are expressions of the Iron Age—material, rational, useful, and limited. The poet, although he professes to know and to be able to hand on *praecepta*, implies that these are in themselves low and vulgar. Perhaps others will disdain them also:

> Possum multa tibi veterum praecepta referre,
> ni refugis tenuisque piget cognoscere curas.
>
>   (1.176–77)

> I can repeat for you many ancient precepts
> Unless you recoil and are loath to learn slight cares.

The poet's truth, therefore, is other than georgic, material truth, for his ultimate concern is with metaphysical, moral questions—urgent and essential—that *praecepta* do not address. The poet, however, acknowledges these most urgent questions and responds to them through myth and image, his poetry aiming at divine revelation (as from the Muses or Proteus) and at apprehension of mystery. By opening with questions (1.1–5) and closing with mystery (4.548–58), by posing unanswerable questions, the poet suggests the primacy of mystery and thereby touches upon the limitations of the merely real and hence also suggests his own true value. As poet he apprehends and represents mystery, through myth and metaphor, in all its ambiguity, complexity, and contradiction.

In the final half of the poem's final book, the poet portrays himself as the agent of the Muses, of a tradition and of a power greater than and outside of himself. Knowledge comes to him from the Muses, that is, from inspiration or revelation, rather than from trial and error. This contrasts importantly with the farmer's random and experimental mode:

> ut varias usus meditando extunderet artis
> paulatim
>
> (1.133–34)

So that practice, by taking thought, might forge man's various
  crafts
Little by little.

Similarly we encounter in this book Proteus, the divine seer, who knows all—everything that is, was, or will be:

> novit namque omnia vates,
> quae sint, quae fuerint, quae mox ventura trahantur;
> quippe ita Neptuno visum est
>
> (4.392–95)

> for as a seer he knows all
That is, that has been, and all that is about to be—knows all by
  the god Neptune's
Grace.

In knowledge (but not in power, significantly) he is the most privileged figure in the poem; and his knowledge, as it is Neptune's gift, also comes from divine revelation, not experiment and discovery. Proteus is not interested in and hence does not hand on *praecepta,* rather he reveals *causae,* as Cyrene indicates:

> ut omnem
> expediat morbi causam eventusque secundet.
> (4.396–97)

> so that he'll tell you
The whole cause of your bees' sickness and put things right.

Proteus' focus on *causae* is confirmed by his own words:

> haec omnis morbi causa
> (4.532)

Here is the whole cause of your bees' sickness.

It is left to Cyrene, Aristaeus' mother, to prescribe the remedy, to give *praecepta* (e.g., 534–547, 548; cf. 448), thus to deal in the material and corporeal:

> 'quattuor eximios praestanti corpore tauros,
> qui tibi nunc viridis depascunt summa Lycaei,
> delige, et intacta totidem cervice iuvencas.
> quattuor his aras alta ad delubra dearum
> constitue, et sacrum iugulis demitte cruorem,
> corporaque ipsa boum frondoso desere luco.
> post, ubi nona suos Aurora ostenderit ortus,
> inferias Orphei Lethaea papavera mittes,
> et nigram mactabis ovem, lucumque revises:
> placatam Eurydicen vitula venerabere caesa.'
> haud mora: continuo matris *praecepta* facessit.
> (4.538–48)

"Choose four bulls of excellent body that now on the heights of
Green Lycaeus are grazing,
And as many heifers whose necks have never felt the yoke.
Build for these four altars beside the lofty shrines
Of the goddesses, and let the sacred blood from their throats,
Then leave the oxen's bodies alone in a leafy thicket.
When the ninth day has dawned
You shall send oblivion's poppies as a funeral gift to Orpheus,
Slay a calf in honor of Eurydice placated,
Slaughter a black ewe and go to the thicket again."
Without delay he acts at once on his mother's prescriptions.

The need for this distinction between inspiration or revelation and instruction or maxim may explain why Proteus does not, in fact, give *praecepta* as Cyrene had said he would.[2]

---

2. Johnston, 113 n. 12, among others, notes that the presence of two narrations (Cyrene's and Proteus') has bothered critics. (Cyrene's speech is not really a narration.) Parry, 51–52, sees a useful distinction between the practicality of Cyrene and the "poetry" of Proteus. Aristaeus, he feels, must learn "a lesson of poetry." This is surely true, although whether he in fact does learn a lesson is debatable. Cf. Putnam, *Poem of the Earth,* 13 and 314 n. 61.

The conclusion of the poem, then, brings sharply into focus the contrast between the farmer's practical, Roman, Iron Age knowledge, embodied unambiguously in *praecepta,* and the poet's visionary knowledge, embodied in myths both traditional and of his own creation. These constitute his revelation in mythic image of the nature of human existence. The poem, therefore, is not protreptic in that it does not prescribe specific measures to restore the state to political or moral health. Rather it expresses an apprehension of certain oppositions that are not capable of resolution: victor vs. vanquished, material vs. spiritual, agricultural vs. poetic, Iron Age vs. Golden Age.

The poet is, as we have already seen in other ways, in tension with the Iron Age agricultural ethic, that is, with the implicit assumptions of the genre of a didactic poem. This tension manifests itself not only in his having pity or compassion as his mission (as expressed in 1.41), not only in his preserving as a moral ideal his Golden Age vision of the past, namely, of a harmonious, noncombatant community among men and between men and nature; but above all in his perpetuating a mode of thought and value that poses an alternative to contemporary convention.

This tension between, on the one hand, mystery and the poet's truth and, on the other, *praecepta* and the farmer's truth can be approached and confirmed in a variety of ways.[3] While the *bougonia* image, emphatically placed as it is at the end of a major

3. This study proposes that such manifestations of the divine as are suggested in the poem are subsumed under the larger category of mystery. The possibility of religious truth and of divine responsiveness to human prayer or piety appears not as central to this poem as is the opposition between science and mystery, which comprehends the category of religious mystery. Of course, the extent to which the poet's religious expressions, such as invocations (1.5–42) and prayers (1.498–501) or exhortations to prayer (1.100, 338) are formal and traditional as opposed to genuinely pious is a complex and arguable question—as are virtually all major issues in Virgil. (Contrast, for example, Thomas ad loc., who argues for the former position, with R. M. Ogilvie, *The Romans and Their Gods in the Age of Augustus* (New York, 1969), 113, who assumes the latter.) As an illustration of the overall ambiguity of the status of religion in the poem, we may note that although the poem begins with prayer and closes with sacrifice, the poet also indicates that prayer is futile (3.455–56) and denies the probability of divine causality (in bird song, 1.415–23).

dramatic episode and at the poem's conclusion, is the best example of the primacy of mystery and of the inadequacy of *praecepta,*
there are also other motifs that illuminate this vision in the poem.
After discussing the symbolic value of *bougonia* I would like to
treat the motif of ignorance and knowledge in the poem overall.
As noted above, the poem opens with questions and closes with
mystery. We can see upon reflection, however, that the entire
poem moves towards enhancement of mystical, mysterious, or
poetic modes, which are insufficiently acknowledged by Iron Age
materialism. The poem is punctuated by troubling, unanswered
questions that reflect the urgency of mystery in our lives. The
presence of mystery and of the unique (as in the unprecedented
portents of civil war following upon the assassination of Caesar)
demonstrates the limitations of the farmer's human knowledge.
As the poet contrives to show, past experience, that is, knowledge or science, is inadequate for controlling or even understanding the present and future.

Another motif we will consider, also reflective of the limits of
knowledge, is prayer. In the context of an agricultural poem, the
ritual of prayer necessarily implies dependency and ignorance.
The act of prayer is especially dramatic as it opens and closes
Book 1, thus setting the natural, political, and divine worlds (the
subjects, variously, of both prayers) as the major fixed points of
mystery, of the unknown, in the poem.

I will also look at mythical vs. "scientific" explanations of
various phenomena in the poem and at how the poet implicitly
challenges the power of the latter. The effect of this, it will be
argued, is to suggest the limitations of scientific knowledge and
to enhance the power of myth. Thus the poet adumbrates the
value of the poetry that preserves and even creates the mythological vision.

Finally I shall look at the poet's share in mystery—that is, his
unique power to create new myths, to structure the poem and its
episodes, and thus to reveal meaning in experience through the
medium of myth, of metaphor, and of the nonmaterial. In so
doing the poet suggests most powerfully the limitations of *praecepta,* for it is through mystery and myth that he reveals his
ultimate truths.

ON THE *BOUGONIA*

In chapter 1 I treated the image of *bougonia* in terms, first, of its unreality and, second, of its dynamics as a process. This is important because the dynamics of the process of *bougonia* contribute to its ultimate symbolic value in the poem. To review my earlier arguments, we must not assume that the ancients, without ever having witnessed or practiced *bougonia,* believed uncritically in its reality. Rather it occasioned scepticism among them, as may be seen in Varro (3.16.4, 37–38) and Columella (9.14.6). Further, several features of the poet's telling of the tale suggest that he intends the reader to be distanced from and doubtful about it. These include an unusually impersonal style ("a place is chosen," "they enclose it" 4.295ff.); the setting of the tale in a distant country from which there is only hearsay; and the representation of the tale as *fama* (286, 318), thus unverified, something of which neither he nor his compatriots had experience. The poet would, then, be only repeating a story told by others, which he himself declines to authenticate. Of the *bougonia* he does not assert masterfully "I sing" (*cano*)[4] but rather, at this point alone in the poem, asks the Muses to tell him what to sing (4.315).

The unreality of *bougonia* relates to the second important point about it, namely, its symbolic value. While a common view is that *bougonia* signifies resurrection and a positive future for Rome, the dynamics of *bougonia,* as the ancients appear to have understood them, do not seem to support this interpretation. *Bougonia* was not, as scholars have inferred, thought to bring about rebirth or resurrection from death to life but rather an exchange of death and life, since the soul of the slain calf is required in order to animate the new bees. Further, in Aristaeus' case, new bees are indeed born, but they are not *re*born, as there is no regeneration of the bees that he had previously lost. These remain irretrievable. As a symbol, therefore, the process of *bougonia* embodies the ambiguous qualities of Iron Age culture in this poem—characteristically aggressive, destructive, and neg-

---

4. Compare instances such as 1.12; 2.176; also 1.5; 2.2; 3.1; 4.559, 566.

ligent of cost. The effect of crediting Aristaeus, a culture hero, with this suspect and distasteful process of contriving life out of death is to comment, if obliquely, on the particular quality or character of the culture that he is made to epitomize. In emotional tension with Aristaeus stand the figures of the *Georgic* poet, the Corycian gardener, Orpheus, Proteus, Eurydice, and the nightingale (4.511–15), all of whom have—variously—sentiment, appreciation of beauty, or capacity for sorrow and pity.

In this chapter the central importance of *bougonia* is its relationship to the tension between the farmer's and the poet's knowledge and truth. Through the paradox of being unreal but true, *bougonia* as symbol suggests the limitations of the materially real, as embodied in *praecepta,* and consequently the higher value of the poet's truth as it is revealed in myth and mystery. Here the effect is to clarify the distinction between the farmer's and the poet's truth, and, in some sense, to validate the latter. The material truth of profit and productivity is ultimately less urgent than poetic truth. The significance of *bougonia,* then, is critical for the entire poem, not only as a representation of the quality of Iron Age culture but also as a demonstration of the limitations of the useful and material and of the transcendent nature of the poet's truth and value. This is the essential vision of the poem.

PRAYER

The *Georgics* are punctuated by questions—implicit and explicit—that are unknowable and unresolvable. This persistent motif of the unknowable is one of the ways in which the poet suggests the presence of mystery in life. The prayers that open and close Book 1 are another expression of mystery in the poem, for prayer necessarily implies ignorance and dependence with respect to some greater force. The ritual of prayer reveals a vulnerability that is not eliminated by technology, by *praecepta,* no matter how sophisticated. Particularly in a didactic and georgic poem, the act and counsel of prayer reveal man's dependence on powers that exceed his control and understanding. Even so practical a man as Cato, always confident in his instructions for dealing with difficulties, nevertheless counsels sacrifice and prayer to the gods.[5] Thus he acknowledges the reality that technology is not, in fact, in complete control.

Through the prayers that bracket Book 1 the poet touches on the mysteries of the political, natural, and divine worlds. The opening prayer invokes particularly Greek and rural gods, while the closing prayer addresses uniquely Roman and essentially political gods. The opening prayer speaks for the farmer in his confrontation with the mysteries of nature and of the gods. This prayer is a highly literary—but not, therefore, necessarily meaningless—expression of a stance of dependency and ignorance because the poet invokes those rustic gods who are in charge of things not controlled by man (e.g., 22–23). While this prayer opens spiritedly, with the poet expressing high confidence in his ability to sing with knowledge of those subjects that he has set for himself (1.1–5), the major motif of man's ignorance, both of nature and of the ultimate causes of those forces that determine his life, emerges in the address to Caesar:

> tuque adeo, quem mox quae sint habitura deorum
> concilia incertum est, urbisne invisere, Caesar,
> terrarumque velis curam et te maximus orbis
> auctorem frugum tempestatumque potentem
> accipiat cingens materna tempora myrto;
> an deus immensi venias maris ac tua nautae
> numina sola colant, tibi serviat ultima Thule,
> teque sibi generum Tethys emat omnibus undis;
> anne novum tardis sidus te mensibus addas,
> qua locus Erigonen inter Chelasque sequentis
> panditur (ipse tibi iam bracchia contrahit ardens
> Scorpius et caeli iusta plus parte reliquit):
> quidquid eris (nam te nec sperant Tartara regem,
> nec tibi regnandi veniat tam dira cupido,
> quamvis Elysios miretur Graecia campos
> nec repetita sequi curet Proserpina matrem).
> (1.24–39)

You too, whatever place in the courts of the immortals
Is soon to hold you—whether an overseer of cities

And warden of earth you'll be, Caesar, so that the great world
Honor you as promoter of harvest and puissant lord
Of the seasons, garlanding your brow with your mother's myrtle:
Or whether you come as god of the boundless sea, and sailors
Worship your power alone, and the ends of the earth pay tribute,
And Tethys gives all her waves to get you for son-in-law:
Or whether you make a new sign in the zodiac, where amid the
Slow months a gap is revealed between Virgo and Scorpio
(Already the burning Scorpion retracts his claws to
Leave you more than your heaven):—
Become what you may—and Hell hopes not for you as king
And never may so ghastly a ruling ambition grip you,
Though Greece admire the Elysian plains, and Proserpine
Care not to follow her mother who calls her back to earth.

We note that when the poet invokes rural gods, their names and functions are clearly delineated, as is characteristic of Greek and Roman invocations. In this sense all appears known. Octavian, addressed as a god, is invoked in a period, lavish and elaborate, whose formal opulence sets in relief its one substantive element: the poet does not know the nature of Octavian's destiny or future power. Although Octavian is perhaps a god, the poet is ignorant of what form his power will take in the future—*incertum est* (25), *quidquid eris* (36). Will it be on earth? On the sea? In the sky? Even Hades (*dira cupido* 37) is possible. While the functions of the rural gods are apparently known and defined, Caesar's are not. Unknown yet surely momentous, his will be the future of Rome. Thus the reader, along with the poet, is drawn from the opening of the poem into acknowledging his own ignorance of this major determinant of his future.

Additionally, the call to Caesar for pity (1.41) surprises, as it is a discordant note following the spirited, positive invocation of nurturing gods, along with the positive world view it implies, that opens the poem. If startling, however, it is also suggestive of the truth of the Romans' desperate situation, which is further elaborated in the closing prayer.

Significantly, both prayers are identical in expressing uncertainty as to Octavian's future power:

di patrii Indigetes et Romule Vestaque mater,
quae Tuscum Tiberim et Romana Palatia servas,

hunc saltem everso iuvenem succurrere saeclo
ne prohibete! satis iam pridem sanguine nostro
Laomedonteae luimus periuria Troiae;
iam pridem nobis caeli te regia, Caesar,
invidet atque hominum queritur curare triumphos;
quippe ubi fas versum atque nefas

(1.498–505)

O gods of our fathers, native gods, Romulus, Vesta
Who guard our Tuscan Tiber and the Roman Palatine,
Hinder not our young prince from rescuing this shipwrecked
    era!
Long enough now have we
Paid in our blood for the promise Laomedon broke at Troy.
Long now has the court of heaven grudged you to us, Caesar,
Complaining that you care only for mortal triumphs.
For Right and Wrong are confused here.

The second prayer, however, is depressed throughout and negative in tone, thus different from the first prayer. In the second prayer the poet asks the gods only to refrain from prohibiting Octavian from saving his homeland. Therefore there is implied a fear of divine menace rather than a confident hope of divine nurturance, as in 1.21, for example. The poet senses that the Roman people are marked by—and still expiating through suffering—some primal crime. And perhaps, it is delicately suggested (504), Caesar himself, too influenced by political ambitions, is not appropriately concerned about moral questions. Impious or unholy Mars rages throughout the world (1.511), and Jove's intervention in human history may well have allowed the confusion of *fas* and *nefas* (1.505). Hence we infer that the gods do not sustain the moral order. There is no necessary coincidence or relationship between the divine and the moral or scrutable. The whole world, overwhelmed by criminal and civil wars (*vicinae ruptis inter se legibus urbes/arma ferunt* 1.510–11), is experiencing the gravest moral upheaval, to which Caesar may be responding inadequately. The prayer concludes with an image of the world as a chariot out of control, dragged by a horse that is powerful, passionate, and irrational (1.512–14). This prayer to Roman gods, then, in its ambiguity and anxiety, mirrors the desperation and confusion of the present moment. It expresses uncertain hope for future peace, not a conviction of fulfillment of that hope. If prayer in itself expresses ignorance and dependence, this prayer, in particular, expresses massive, monumental uncertainties, thus confirming the original description of farmers (and, indeed, all persons) in 1.41 as *ignarosque viae*. The natural, political, and divine orders are in gravest upheaval. Caesar's potential impact on any of these is unknown. His future, and equally that of Rome, is imponderable.

An illuminating progression emerges from comparison of the two prayers. In the first, the relationship of the farmer to nature illuminates with unique clarity the human condition as a whole. The farmer is subject continually to immense, imponderable natural upheaval that limits his productivity and impinges upon the quality of his life. The closing prayer speaks for political, Roman man as he confronts war and moral disorder, that is, his own nature out of control. From one to the other prayer, then, the movement is from the external and universal (man in confrontation with nature) to the internal and particular (Roman man in confrontation with the consequences of his political life). Thus the intractable realities of the natural, human, and divine worlds are the fixed points of mystery for the poem, the poles that generate the poem's major themes.

SCIENTIFIC EXPLICATION

In this section it is suggested that the poet uses the language of science in such a way as to question, if subtly and discreetly, its truth value for the reader, with the result that he can ultimately privilege the value of his own mode of myth and mystery. The poet, it is argued, exploits scientific terminology and the formal qualities of scientific explication in a consistently compromised fashion, thus suggesting the limitations of the scientific method and of truth acquired through science. That is to say, in those passages where the poet alludes in form or in language to scientific or technical reasoning, he significantly and suggestively fails to achieve a result that is substantively sound.

In an attempt to demonstrate this thesis, I will discuss the poet's use of particular scientific modalities: sign theory, Epicurean explanation by plural causes, and primary opposites. I shall argue that the implication of the poet's use of the language of signs is that sign theory is often inadequate to reality as we experience it, for the unique phenomenon confounds previously established hypotheses or correlations. With respect to the (largely) Epicurean practice of explanation by plural causes, I shall argue that Virgil, diverging from the characteristic practice of Epicurus or Lucretius, adduces plural causes that are contradictory or mutually exclusive, thus undermining the potential truth value of any and allowing the method of explanation by plural causes to seem inferior to the unitary vision of myth. Finally, I will suggest that in his use of primary opposites he is deliberately vague, thereby declining to advance in any substantive way our understanding of the phenomenon in question. To his presentation of myth, however, he gives a fine resonance and emotional impact, which allow it to outweigh in significance and power the scientific insights sketched in the poem.

SIGN THEORIES

To suggest the primacy of mystery and the inadequacy of *praecepta,* the poet has given to each book its share of mysteries or happenings whose cause is not known or that exceed previous knowledge and experience.[6] Nature is therefore seen to remain unencompassed by *praecepta* or previously observed *signa.* Unprecedented outbursts—of storm, for example, or passion or plague—defy previous experience and controvert familiar, trusted signs (*signa*). Therefore nature's power is seen to remain mysterious, vaster than man's ability to catalogue.

From the several possible examples of unprecedented and disordering phenomena in the poem, I would like to consider two: the signs at Caesar's death in 1.427–97 and the Noric plague in 3.478–566, also marked by signs.

There are twenty-two occurrences of *signa* or the verbal form *signare* in the *Georgics.* While *signa* once denotes sculptures

---

6. Examples are 1.86ff., 415ff.; 2.103–8, 475–82; 3.272–77; 4.197, 554.

(3.34) and twice denotes military standards (3.236, 4.108), its primary uses in the poem are clustered around the two meanings of constellations as weather signs (1.229, 239, 257, 351, 354, 439 [twice], 463) and of symptoms of disease (3.440, 503; 4.253). That Virgil's use of signs clusters around astronomy/astrology and medicine suggests that he is alluding to or making use here of sign theory as it reflected and expressed the field of natural scientific inquiry from the pre-Socratic philosophers through the Roman period.[7] While the method of inference from signs characterized many fields, from zoology to metaphysics, popular interest in signs focused above all on astrology and medicine, with knowledge of mathematics and other areas of natural science being restricted to an intellectual elite.[8]

There was a variety and complexity of sign theory in the ancient world with which Virgil might have been familiar. For our purposes it is not necessary to distinguish between Stoic and Epicurean sign theories or to distinguish, for example, the commemorative from the indicative sign.[9] It suffices to know that sign theories constituted an important and characteristic dimension of philosophy and natural scientific inquiry in the ancient world. For natural scientists in general, who were seeking an "alternative, naturalistic, rationalist framework"[10] for understanding experience, sign theory provided one form of systematic inquiry and discourse. Sextus Empiricus expressed the thought that the method of inference by signs is of the very essence of human intelligence:

> They [the doctrinaire philosophers] say that it is not uttered speech but internal speech by which man differs from non-rational (ἀλόγων) animals; for crows and parrots and jays utter articulate sounds. Nor is it by the merely simple impression that he differs . . . but by impressions produced by inference

7. 4.219 is also a scientific use. I will discuss its significance as a portent at 1.471. Varro and Cato also use the term "sign." For references see Thomas at 4.440.

8. Lloyd, 331–32.

9. See Elizabeth Asmis, *Epicurus' Scientific Method* (Ithaca, N.Y., 1984), 175–266; or A. A. Long and D. N. Sedley, *The Hellenistic Philosophers*, 2 vols. (Cambridge, 1987), s.v. "signs."

10. Lloyd, 47.

(μεταβατικῇ) and combination (συνθετικῇ). This amounts to his possessing the conception of "following" and directly grasping, on account of "following," the idea of sign (σημείου). For sign is itself of the kind "If this, then that." Therefore the existence of signs follows from man's nature (φύσει) and constitution (κατασκευῇ).[11]

(*Math.* 8.275–76)

Hellenistic epistemology attributed particular significance to signs, which it defined as evident or manifest facts that serve to disclose other nonevident facts. The essential characteristics of the method of inference from signs were the distinction between what is evident and what is nonevident, and the use of the evident (τὸ ἐναργές, in Epicurus' terminology) as a "witness" of the nonevident (τὸ ἄδηλον). Sextus Empiricus defines the (commemorative) sign as consisting in something evident that reminds us of something not evident at present but having been observed with it previously, as smoke with fire.[12] An example of a sign in medicine is roughness of the tongue, indicating fever,[13] or a wound in the heart, indicating death. In astrology an example of a sign, here based only on a sense of empirical data and not on an understood causal relationship, is that people born at the Dog Star do not die at sea.[14] Knowledge of weather signs, what Lévi-Strauss would call "concrete science,"[15] is acquired through this same empirical method, to which the *Georgic* poet alludes in Book 1:

> Atque haec ut certis possemus discere signis
> aestusque pluviasque et agentis frigora ventos,
> ipse pater statuit, quid menstrua luna moneret,
> quo signo caderent Austri, *quid saepe videntes*
> *agricolae propius stabulis armenta tenerent.*

(1.351–55)

11. Long and Sedley, trans., 2:319.
12. Asmis, 181.
13. Asmis, 216.
14. Long and Sedley, 264 (passage 38E: Cic. *Fat.* 12). Cf. also David Sedley, "On Signs," in *Science and Speculation: Studies in Hellenistic Theory and Practice*, ed. J. Barnes, J. Brunschwig, M. Burnyeat, and M. Schofield (Cambridge, 1982), 254 n. 38; Sedley points out that Cic. *Div.* 1.25 and 126 acknowledge that astrological rules are fallible.
15. Lévi-Strauss cited by Lloyd, 51.

So that we might be able to predict from manifest signs
These things—heatwaves and rain and winds that bring cold
  weather,
The Father himself laid down what the moon's phases should
  mean,
The cue for the southwind's dropping, the sign that often noted
Should warn a farmer to keep his cattle near their stalls.

Aratus, author of the *Diosemeiae,* or *Weather Signs,* an important source for *Georgic* 1, includes in his poem the caution that one should look for sign confirming sign, as there is greater certainty in two or three. From two signs indicating the same outcome one may have hope, from three real confidence:

καλὸν δ᾿ ἐπὶ σήματι σῆμα
σκέπτεσθαι· μᾶλλον δὲ δυοῖν εἰς ταὐτὸν ἰόντων
ἐλπωρὴ τελέθοι, τριτάτῳ δέ κε θαρσήσειας.
        (*Diosemeiae* 410–12=*Phaen.* 1142–44)

More generally he adds that the universal way of mortal men is to live from inferences from signs:

οὕτω γὰρ μογεροὶ καὶ ἀλήμονες ἄλλοθεν ἄλλοι
ζώομεν ἄνθρωποι. τὰ δὲ πὰρ ποσὶ πάντες ἑτοῖμοι
σήματ᾿ ἐπιγνῶναι καὶ ἐσαυτίκα ποιήσασθαι.
        (*Diosemeiae* 369–71=*Phaen.* 1101–3)

For thus do we poor, changeful mortals win in diverse ways our livelihood, and all are ready to mark the signs at their feet and adopt them for the moment.[16]

The method of prognosis and prediction is similar in what we would call both scientific and nonscientific endeavors, such as medicine and astrology/divination. For this reason those Hippocratic writers, for example, who sought to distinguish themselves from diviners argued that there was a genuinely scientific character to their prognoses, founded precisely on the reliability of the signs on which they based their predictions or forecasts. G. E. R. Lloyd cites a medical writer who denies that he is a diviner but

16. G. R. Mair, trans., *Callimachus: Hymns and Epigrams; Lycophron; Aratus,* Loeb Classical Library (London and Cambridge, Mass., 1921; reprint, 1969).

asserts rather that he makes inferences from reliable signs about the outcome of a given disease:

ἐγὼ δὲ τοιαῦτα μὲν οὐ μαντεύσομαι, σημεῖα δὲ γράφω οἷσι χρὴ τεκμαίρεσθαι τούς τε ὑγιέας ἐσομένους τῶν ἀνθρώπων καὶ τοὺς ἀποθανουμένους, τούς τε ἐν ὀλίγῳ χρόνῳ ἢ ἐν πολλῷ ὑγιέας ἐσομένους ἢ ἀπολουμένους.

(*Prorrhetic* 2.1(L) 9.8.2–4)[17]

I will not prophesy such things, but I will set out signs from which it is necessary to infer those who will recover and those who will die, and whether they will do so in a short or a long time.[18]

The conception of the reliability of signs and of the predictability of routine, seasonal, or annual events forms the very basis of the assumption of a knowable world and of georgic endeavors. A georgic poem requires the assumption of cyclical experience, of the validity of past experience as a guide to the present and future. It therefore seems of great significance that two of the most dramatic events in the *Georgics,* the portents after Caesar's death (1.463–97) and the Noric plague (3.478ff.), both marked by signs, are represented as unique and unnatural occurrences, for which there is no rational, material, natural, or atomic explanation.[19] These events are marked by signs, but the signs are

---

17. Cited by Lloyd, 42 n. 137.
18. Author's translation.
19. E. L. Harrison, "The Noric Plague in Vergil's Third *Georgic,*" *PLLS* 2 (1979): 1–65, assumes, despite lack of textual evidence, that both events are manifestations of divine anger. Certainly portents and plagues were typically interpreted as manifestations of disturbance in the relationship between men and gods. Further, the poet's use of moral and religious terms (e.g., 1.468, 491; 3.513) would seem to imply that there is or could or should be a correlation between morality or piety and events. However, the poem as a whole does not bear out such a hypothesis. Rather it appears that the innocent are punished (as the beasts in Book 3) and the criminal are allowed to atone and prosper (as Aristaeus in Book 4). Therefore one must say that the gods, if they are there, are not consistent or moral from a human perspective. Thomas observes that agrarian failure is never preceded by impiety or religious flaws; that prayer, in and of itself, never brings success (at 3.486–93); and that the moral status of Jove is ambiguous throughout the poem (at 4.560–61). Therefore, even if Harrison were correct in stating that there must be a religious explanation of the portents of Book 1 and of the plague in Book 3, this too would be insufficient to prove, as Harrison also contends (e.g., 27, 34–39), that Virgil believes in a moral universe and in the value of piety and virtue.

unique, thus suggesting that all experience is not routine and that, therefore, it has not yet been explained or even catalogued. The premise of a knowable world is clearly questioned by the occurrence of an unprecedented, unexperienced event. The realm of mystery has not yet, it appears in this poem, receded beyond the horizon of scientific discovery. We see that the poet undercuts the impact and persuasiveness of the conception of the knowable world expressed through reliable signs by focusing on events that are unique and whose signs are unfamiliar.

The portents attendant upon Caesar's death and presaging civil war are preceded by a lengthy passage on weather signs (351ff.), based largely, although not exclusively, on Aratus' *Diosemeiae,* as noted earlier. This passage is introduced by verses (cited on p. 155) that indicate that relationships between signs and heat, rain, or winds are securely predictable; the signs are "sure" (*certis*), since they are based on frequent observation of correlation between sign and consequence (*quid saepe videntes / agricolae* 355). Similar passages concerning the sun (e.g., 1.424–26 and 438–40) indicate that the relationships between sun, moon, and weather are also ordered and sure. Indeed, the sun gives the surest signs (*certissima signa* 439), both at its rising and at its setting. Therefore the sequence of natural events attendant upon various signs of all sorts is represented as a reliable basis for human undertakings.

With these passages as background, then, we may find the passage on the sun signs (or solar eclipse) and other portents

---

Harrison is, however, very right to point out (e.g., 11, 36) that there is a congruence between certain signs of plague and events, such as failed sacrifices, which are in themselves prodigious. (See Bruce MacBain, *Prodigy and Expiation: A Study in Religion and Politics in Republican Rome* [Brussels, 1982], 83–104, for a list of prodigies and expiations from 504 B.C. to 17 B.C. Plague is the most common.) The doubleness of signs, a pervasive motif in the poem, intensifies the reader's sense of cognitive and moral ambiguity. (I intend to pursue this topic elsewhere.)

Finally, the scientific context of weather signs in Book 1 and of plague signs in Book 3, in addition to the largely scientific pose and context of the *Georgics* as a whole, inclines readers to attribute scientific value to the signs in question.

following the assassination of Caesar to be striking and surprising:

> tempore quamquam illo tellus quoque et aequora ponti,
> obscenaeque canes importunaeque volucres
> signa dabant. quotiens Cyclopum effervere in agros
> vidimus undantem ruptis fornacibus Aetnam,
> flammarumque globos liquefactaque volvere saxa!
> armorum sonitum toto Germania caelo
> audiit, insolitis tremuerunt motibus Alpes.
> vox quoque per lucos vulgo exaudita silentis
> ingens, et simulacra modis pallentia miris
> visa sub obscurum noctis, pecudesque locutae
> (infandum!); sistunt amnes terraeque dehiscunt,
> et maestum inlacrimat templis ebur aeraque sudant.
> proluit insano contorquens vertice silvas
> fluviorum rex Eridanus camposque per omnis
> cum stabulis armenta tulit. nec tempore eodem
> tristibus aut extis fibrae apparere minaces
> aut puteis manare cruor cessavit, et altae
> per noctem resonare lupis ululantibus urbes.
> non alias caelo ceciderunt plura sereno
> fulgura nec diri totiens arsere cometae.
>
> (1.469–88)

Though at that time the earth as well, the waves of the sea,
Mongrels and birds morose gave signs.
How often we saw Mount Aetna deluge
The fields of the Cyclops with lava from her cracked furnaces,
Rolling up great balls of flame and molten rocks!
In Germany they heard a clash of fighting echo
Through the whole sky; the Alps shook with unnatural shudders.
Likewise in stilly woods a voice was heard by many—
A monster voice, and phantoms miraculously pale
Were met at the dusk of night, and cattle spoke—an omen
Unspeakable! Rivers stopped, earth gaped, and ivories
In temples wept sad tears and brazen images sweated.
Po, the king of rivers, in maniac spate whirled round
Forests, washed them away, swept all over the plains
Herds and their byres together. A time it was when the guts of
Woe-working victims never failed to reveal the worst
Nor wells to seep with blood
Nor high-built cities to sound all night with the wolves' howling.
Never elsewhere have lightnings flickered so constantly
In a clear sky, or baleful comets burned so often.

A number of features of this passage are important to note. First, these portents or signs are not predictable but unique (e.g., *non alias,* "never" 487) and *un*natural (*insolitis . . . motibus,* "unnatural shudders" 475). As they fall outside of known, reliable *signa,* they undermine the premises of the georgic genre, namely, the very notion of an ordered world, suggesting how ignorant man is of the great forces that shape his life.

Lucretius, for his part, is very aware of the impact of irregular or unique occurrences on the religious sensibilities of his readers. He knows their inclination to interpret such events as instances of divine anger or intervention of other sorts. He, therefore, particularly devotes Book 6 to giving an atomic explanation or an explanation from natural causes for phenomena such as thunder and lightning (6.96–422), routinely associated with Jove's anger, and also for the occasional or unique occurrences to which popular superstition attributed religious significance, such as earthquakes (6.535–607), volcanoes (639–711), and pestilences (1090–1137).[20]

In our passage, however, the *Georgic* poet adduces no natural explanation, but rather, above all, a mysterious or mystical one. He implies that the cause of the solar eclipse, the eruption of Aetna, and the other portents was the "sympathetic" revulsion of nature and of the whole cosmos at murder and war (*miseratus* 1.466). Nature reflected man's own moral disturbances (cf. *impia . . . saecula* 1.468), translating them into a physically disordered reality.[21] While nature's laws are presumed to be eternal (*continuo has leges aeternaque foedera certis/imposuit natura locis,* "Nature imposed these laws, a covenant everlasting, on different parts of the earth right from the earliest days" 1.60–61), in this instance they are seen as disorderable, controverted by man's depravity. *Obscenaeque canes importunaeque volucres/signa dabant* (470–71): dogs and birds gave *signs,* the

20. See Bailey ad loc. In the case of the *Georgics* passage, however, not all of the prodigies are paralleled even in the pontifical prodigy lists. See MacBain above.

21. See Lloyd, 44 and n. 150, on sympathetic relationships between heavenly bodies and earth.

term here clearly having the sense of portents. To the extent, then, that observation of signs reflected man's belief in an ordered and rational world, the correlation of Caesar's assassination and consequent civil war with irregular or unique phenomena would be subversive or troubling. And here, of course, the poet signs the event not only with solar eclipse, as was testified to by historians, but also with literary and/or unnatural signs, such as cattle speaking, ivory images weeping, blood in wells, and pale phantoms at dusk.

Virgil's list of prodigies following Caesar's assassination is the first and one of the longest in ancient literature. Since attempts to find literary antecedents for the prodigies in this passage have not been wholly successful, we may infer that in his selection or creation of marvels for this passage the poet is seeking the very unusual if not the unique.[22] Furthermore, the collocation of literary or contrived portents with real phenomena, such as the solar eclipse or the (possible) eruption of Aetna in 44 B.C., results in a striking confusion of real and supernatural or inscrutable phenomena surrounding a historical event. There is, therefore, a consequent confusion here of what is knowable and/or persuasive and how it comes to be so. Familiar scientific or weather signs modulate into portents and hence into mystery. As the poet conflates real and mysterious events, real and literary phenomena or prodigies, he suggests a mode of truth different from the historical or scientific—different, but not without truth value of an alternative sort. Beasts speaking is perhaps undocumented in history, but true as metaphor in poetry. Signs, such as metaphors, in poetry may be without literal truth, but not without literary or poetic truth, valid in the poet's discourse if not the historian's or scientist's. The poet offers, perhaps creates, a series of signs that show nature as disordered and hence as disorderable. The experience of the unprecedented and unnatural must tend to subvert confidence in the possibility of true scientific knowledge and must suggest also that man's ability to interpret

22. See also Lyne, 53ff.; and both Richter and Thomas ad loc. on the primacy and possible originality of Virgil's account of the portents.

signs is limited by his experience and perhaps even by his intelligence. It would not suffice, as a counterargument, to suggest that routine signs signal routine events, unique signs unique events, thus leaving the method of inference by signs intact as a scientific methodology; for the point is that nature is disorderable, our experience and comprehension limited. The portents at Caesar's death have no natural or rationalist cause, but are rather a mysterious, unexplained collusion of celestial and terrestrial events. Ultimately mysteries elude scientific explanation and cataloguing.

The second event in the poem that is unprecedented and characterized by signs (as symptoms of disease) is the plague of Book 3.478ff. Though scholars have studied the poet's description of the plague's symptoms and compared them with the findings of modern veterinary science, it appears that, whatever historical basis there might possibly have been, this plague is a literary fiction, a creation of the poet's reading of Lucretius (6.1138–1286) above all and of his own imagination.[23] Like the portents of civil war, which involve a grand expanse of territory, from Rome to the Alps and even into the heavens, this plague is represented as widely involving sea animals, snakes, and birds. The devastation occurred without discernible cause, without precedent, and without cure. It overwhelmed and poisoned lakes, pastures, cattle, dogs, pigs, birds, "melting bones with disease" (3.484–85). The plague is a *furor* or madness in nature (*furiis* 511), its manifestations recalling those of storm (cf. storm as *pestes,* or "diseases" 3.471) and love. Like the omens at Caesar's death, this plague is unnatural and unprecedented (*insolitae* 3.543), which recalls the unnatural movements (*insolitis* 1.475) of the earlier passage. Pervasive, wild, and deadly, this plague exceeds previous experience. Through his intensity and extravagance of detail the poet suggests how new experience may confound precedent.

---

23. Wilkinson, *Georgics,* 207. See Thomas at 3.474–77, commenting on Virgil's clear debt to Lucretius there. E. Flintoff, "The Noric Cattle Plague," *QUCC* 42 (1983): 85–111, argues that the plague has historical validity, as it would constitute an "indictment" (86) of Virgil were the plague to be false.

A significant irony in this passage is that all man's technology, that is, the knowledge that he believes to be most useful, is worse than useless, even harmful:

> quaesitaeque nocent artes; cessere magistri
> (3.549)
> Cures (*artes*) they invented only killed: healers gave up.

Relief comes only through relinquishing the whole ethic of usefulness and profit[24] upon which Iron Age culture is based. Thus, again, the poet suggests the limitations of Iron Age values. In the face of death Iron Age acquisitiveness and domination are irrelevant. Unable to eat the flesh or wear the skins of infected animals, man had to abandon his drive to put things to use. *Ars* (549), *usus* (559), and the whole conquering ethic—as with *vincere* (3.560), where one cannot "conquer" the disease with fire, recalling how *labor* "conquered" all things (*labor omnia vicit improbus* 1.145– 46)—are inadequate to this disaster. Hence the poet reasonably asks:

> Quid labor aut benefacta iuvant?
> (3.525)
> Of what avail work or services?

The plague illuminates man's ignorance in another way as well. Not only is the form of the disease unprecedented, but it also by implication appears to punish some crime of which man is unaware. Such terms as *culpa* ("evil," "fault" 468) and *vitium* ("fault," "crime" 454), which the poet attributes to the diseases of sheep, or the phrase *di meliora piis* ("May gods grant better to the pious" 513) suggest this notion. Yet religious practices also fail as diviners cannot interpret the signs of disease (*nec responsa potest consultus reddere vates* 3.491).

Because the cattle are represented as innocents, uniquely soft and vulnerable (299), an intense pathos and horror attaches to

---

24. Cf. Büchner, *RE* 8 A 2 (1958): 1302: man had to abandon his ethic of acquisitiveness.

their deaths.[25] Innocence characterizes also the dying bull, whose freedom from worldly vanity recalls the farmers of Book 2. Parallels between the bull and the farmers are numerous. There is the emphasis on work (e.g., 2.61–62, 397, 412, 514–15; cf. 3.515, 519); the beauty of pastoral scenes, which constitute the essential appeal of the simple life (2.467–71, 3.520–22, 528–30); and the avoidance of wine and lavish feasts (2.472; cf. 3.526–27). The moral and epistemological problem is apparent and grave. This plague, like that of Lucretius in Book 6,[26] has specifically moral overtones. Yet it is not fear and desire, most especially deplored in Epicurean thought, that bring about suffering here. Rather the cause is unknown; ignorance, therefore, becomes the greatest terror. Innocence and simple virtue neither guarantee reward nor protect against suffering. Rather, some other, unknown set of correlates is operative. From the human perspective there is no conviction of a moral universe, for if the universe were just, these creatures of simple virtue would be rewarded.[27] The

25. Cf. Otis, *Virgil*, 177, "passive victims." Sheep are traditional examples of innocent and helpless creatures, e.g. *Iliad* 4.422–56. Cf. Soph. *Trach.* 530 for Deianeira as a lost calf. See W. Liebeschuetz, "Beast and Man in the Third Book of Virgil's *Georgics*," *G&R* 12 (1965): 75. Similarly Richter at 527ff. Contrast Griffin, "*Haec super arvorum cultu*," 33, who trivializes this scene: "Not, one might think, the poet's happiest thought, to tell us that oxen do not go in for gourmet cookery and yet die; the facile moralizing of some Imperial writers is all too clearly foreshadowed."

26. See Steele Commager, "Lucretius' Interpretation of the Plague," *HSCP* 62 (1957): 108.

27. Cf. *Aen.* 1.603–5:

> di tibi, si qua pios respectant numina, si quid
> usquam iustitia est, et mens sibi conscia recti,
> praemia digna ferant.

> May the gods, if any divine powers have regard
> for the good, if justice has any weight anywhere—
> may the gods and the consciousness of right bring
> thee worthy rewards.

We might parallel this situation with that of Job, who thinks he is innocent, who thinks, further, that it is even a question of guilt or innocence. His musings and plaints are inappropriate, as his thoughts cannot be commensurate with those of God, as God's voice points out (Job 38.2–40.2). There is no way for human understanding to encompass universal experience or the divine will. Hence gods can be "moral" or "immoral," rational or random, as they choose.

suffering of the guiltless remains unexplained and epitomizes man's ignorance of forces that determine his life. As the unparalleled virulence of the plague demonstrates the limitations of experience, so the terms *culpa, vitium,* and *piis* hint at unresolvable epistemological and moral questions. Since all human efforts ultimately dissolve in death, the plague here may be seen to represent any and all death; and the necessity of death inevitably poses the fundamental question of the purpose and value of life—the most intense and urgent mystery that all people face.

Along these same lines one should note also that the poet observes that one cannot know all things (2.103–8). Significantly, he cites as mysteries, which he wishes that the Muses would reveal to him, a number of phenomena that Epicurus and Lucretius had already claimed to explain. The *Georgic* poet asks that the Muses

> caelique vias et sidera monstrent,
> defectus solis varios lunaeque labores;
> unde tremor terris, qua vi maria alta tumescant
> obicibus ruptis rursusque in se ipsa residant,

A similar example and one that would have been familiar to Virgil is Sophocles' *Oedipus Rex,* which deals with the limitations of human intelligence, no matter how powerful and grand, to understand the conditions of existence. In his fine treatment of the second stasimon of the play in "The Second Stasimon of *Oedipus Tyrannus*," *JHS* 91 ([1971]: 119–35) (reprinted with modifications in *Sophocles: An Interpretation* [Cambridge, 1980], 179–204), R. P. Winnington-Ingram shows how the chorus seeks to interpret experience in terms of familiar moral parameters: *hubris,* as traditionally defined, leads to punishment. Yet the experience of Oedipus does not quite fit the chorus' paradigm, and so its members, like Job's advisors, are confused. Their traditional religious view of causality is inadequate to explain their experience. Nevertheless, there is an urgent drive in human beings to fit their experience into a moral framework that they can understand and accept. The possibility of a rational, if punitive, universe is less terrifying than the conception of an altogether irrational one. To return to Harrison's argument, he assumes that (1) Virgil is genuinely religious; (2) the plague must, therefore, have been caused by a "reasonably consistent" and not "amoral" god (34); (3) the farmers must have been impious and brought the plague on themselves somehow. He hypothesizes ritual error. Clearly, however, the guiltless suffer in Virgil. Consider the deaths of Rhipeus and Galaesus, *iustissimus unus,* who perish unjustly in the *Aeneid* (2.426–28 and 7.535–39). (Dante felt constrained to correct this error by placing Rhipeus in paradise [*Par.* 20.67–69, 118–29].)

quid tantum Oceano properent se tinguere soles
hiberni, vel quae tardis mora noctibus obstet.
(2.477–82)

reveal heaven's pathways, the stars
The several eclipses of the sun, the travails of the moon
The cause of earthquakes and the force that compels the deep sea
To swell, to break all bounds, to fall back on itself again;
The reason why winter suns race on to dip in ocean,
And what delays the long nights.

Yet Lucretius gives a series of explanations precisely of eclipses of the sun and moon (*solis item quoque defectus lunaeque latebras* 4.751–70). Similarly he explains earthquakes (6.535–607) and the varying lengths of day and night (5.680–704). To the *Georgic* poet these phenomena endure as mysteries, since he remains, apparently, unenlightened by Epicurean scientific explanation.

Lucretius attempts to explain these phenomena and others with a series of natural hypotheses, in this way following the Epicurean procedure of adducing plural causes to explain obscure phenomena. This practice is, evidently, not persuasive to the *Georgic* poet, as we have seen above and will consider further now.

PLURAL CAUSES

Another way in which the poet suggests the primacy of mystery and the consequent value of the mythical or poetic mode is by vitiating or undermining the persuasiveness of such scientific explications of various phenomena as he does offer. "Scientific" explanations in the poem are outweighed in number and in impact by the mythical tales. Let us examine the two occurrences of scientific explanations in the poem (to which Richter also pointed ad loc.) as examples of the poet's method of attempted scientific explication or overview. These are 1.84ff., where the poet attempts to explain mechanistically the enhanced fertility of fired fields, and 1.415ff., where, affecting to doubt divine intervention or fate, he speculates in scientific terms on the causes of birds' apparent foreknowledge of weather changes, an indication of their mysterious sentience or sensibility.

Here in the first of the passages, the poet's presumed purpose is to explain why it is useful to set flame to barren fields. As we read the passage, however, we sense how the incompatibility of suggested causes (86–93) in fact detracts from the real power of any:

> Saepe etiam sterilis incendere profuit agros
> atque levem stipulam crepitantibus urere flammis:
> sive inde occultas viris et pabula terrae
> pinguia concipiunt, sive illis omne per ignem
> excoquitur vitium atque exsudat inutilis umor,
> seu pluris calor ille vias et caeca relaxat
> spiramenta, novas veniat qua sucus in herbas,
> seu durat magis et venas astringit hiantis,
> ne tenues pluviae rapidive potentia solis
> acrior aut Boreae penetrabile frigus adurat.
>
> (1.84–93)

> Or again it profits to burn the barren fields,
> Firing their light stubble with crackling flame: uncertain
> It is whether the earth conceives a mysterious strength
> And sustenance thereby, or whether the fire burns out
> Her faults and sweats away the profitless moisture,
> Or whether that heat opens more of the ducts and hidden
> Pores by which her juices are conveyed to the fresh vegetation,
> Or rather hardens and binds her gaping veins against
> Fine rain and the consuming sun's fierce potency
> And the piercing cold of the north wind.

The language that the poet uses here, with its alternative hypotheses, has the ring of science to it. Yet he suggests the limitations of scientific thought in his selection of two sets of mutually exclusive explanations. Why do fired fields become more fertile? Either something goes into the earth from the fire (86–87) or something goes out (87–88). Either the earth becomes more porous (88–90) or less (91–92).

This passage, because it has seemed lacking in overall clarity, has perplexed and troubled commentators. T. C. Page, yielding to puzzlement, summarizes by saying that "it is hard to believe that the reasons here suggested are anything but fanciful."[28] J. Conington is representative in thinking that the various expla-

28. Page at 87.

nations are intended for various kinds of soil.[29] Miles writes: "It is not immediately clear how many distinct alternatives Virgil is offering here—whether the later alternatives (89–93) are to be taken as new possibilities or as elaborations of earlier statements."[30] However, it is very important to note, as Richter does, that this is the only place in the poem "where such a compendious overview of a philosophical topic is offered."[31] Another way of stating this, perhaps, is that this is the poem's most elaborated exposition of the scientific method. The quality of argumentation, then, that the poet allots to this overview is reflective of his response (and of the desired response from the reader) to the scientific method.

Commentators (e.g., Richter and Wilkinson, following him)[32] have noted that this passage has formal parallels with the Epicurean practice of adducing multiple causes to explain obscure (typically, celestial) phenomena. Yet their method was not characterized by the proffering of mutually exclusive possibilities.

The most important sources for this practice are Epicurus' *Letter to Pythocles* 85–88 and Lucretius Books 5 and 6. In order to understand the nonapparent, particularly in the heavens, Epicurus endorsed the procedure of adducing several hypotheses, as long as they were consistent with the phenomena, that is, not contested or "counterwitnessed" by our sense perception or direct experience. For Epicurus it is appropriate to consider all these explanations useful—as they serve our "freedom from disturbance and our firm confidence"—and true. While some things, such as the existence of matter and void or the existence of atoms, have only one explanation, "in the case of celestial events this is not the case: both the causes of their coming to be and the accounts of their essence are multiple. . . . Now in respect of all things which have a multiplicity of explanations consistent with things evident, complete freedom from trepida-

29. Conington at 91; similarly, Richter at 85ff.
30. Miles, 75.
31. Richter, 132. Thomas ad loc. notes that stubble burning is nowhere advised before this passage. He interprets it as a redressing of elemental imbalances.
32. Richter at 1.85ff.; Wilkinson, Georgics, 229.

tion results when someone in the proper way lets stand whatever is plausibly suggested about them" (*Ep. Pyth.* 86–87). For the purposes of this study the next assertion of Epicurus is critically important:

> ὅταν δέ τις τὸ μὲν ἀπολίπῃ, τὸ δὲ ἐκβάλῃ ὁμοίως σύμφωνον ὂν τῷ φαινομένῳ, δῆλον ὅτι καὶ ἐκ παντὸς ἐκπίπτει φυσιο-λογήματος ἐπὶ δὲ τὸν μῦθον καταρρεῖ.
>
> (*Ep. Pyth.* 87)

> But when someone allows one explanation while rejecting another equally consistent with what is evident, he is clearly abandoning natural philosophy altogether and descending into myth.

That is to say that to have one explanation only instead of several is the mode of myth rather than science. Let us consider, in contrast, an example of the practice of Epicurus, who does not adduce mutually exclusive causes.

> Clouds may form and gather either because the air is condensed under the pressure of winds, or because atoms which hold together and are suitable to produce this result become mutually entangled, or because currents collect from the earth and the waters; and there are several other ways in which it is not impossible for the aggregations of such bodies into clouds to be brought about.[33]
>
> (*Ep. Pyth.* 99–100)

While Elizabeth Asmis observes that no ancient source accuses Epicurus of rejecting the principle of noncontradiction, scholars have noted that, although not attested, the possibility of Epicurus' having offered mutually exclusive hypotheses as being equally true could be a logical danger of his method. Therefore they have proposed alternatives to the possibility of contradiction. They incline to interpret "no counterwitnessing" loosely, as a criterion of possible, but not necessary, truth. (Epicurus held a scientific theory true whenever there was "no counterwitnessing" or contradiction by the phenomena, false when there

33. Long and Sedley, trans., 1:92, for *Ep. Pyth.* 86–87, 87. R. D. Hicks, trans., *Diogenes Laertius: Lives of the Ancient Philosophers*, vol. 2, Loeb Classical Library (London and Cambridge, Mass., 1925; reprint, 1979), for *Ep. Pyth.* 99–100.

was "counterwitnessing.") Also, they give important acknowledgment to the concern of Epicurus to show not only compatibil-
ity of theory with the phenomena, but also "an incompatibility of
the contradictory of the theory with the phenomena," thus
assuring to a great degree that mutually contradictory theories
not be found true.[34]

Lucretius, in his use of plural causes, differs somewhat in
focus from Epicurus. He appears to think only one cause to be
true of any given incident, although many may be true either in
general or in other worlds:

> Sunt aliquot quoque res quarum unam dicere causam
> non satis est, verum pluris, unde una tamen sit;
> corpus ut exanimum siquod procul ipse iacere
> conspicias hominis, fit ut omnis dicere causas
> conveniat leti, dicatur ut illius una.
> nam neque eum ferro nec frigore vincere possis
> interiisse neque a morbo neque forte veneno,
> verum aliquid genere esse ex hoc quod contigit ei
> scimus. item in multis hoc rebus dicere habemus.
>
> (Lucr. 6.703–11)

There are also a number of things for which it is not enough to
name one cause, but many, one of which is nevertheless the true
cause: even as if you should yourself see some man's body lying
lifeless at a distance, you may perhaps think proper to name all the
causes of death in order that the one true cause of the man's death
be named. For you could not prove that steel or cold had been the
death of him, nor disease, or it may be poison, but we know that
what has happened to him is something of this kind. We can say
the same thing in many cases.[35]

Here he concludes his several explanations of the causes of the
movements of the heavenly bodies:

> nam quid in hoc mundo sit eorum ponere certum
> difficile est; sed quid possit fiatque per omne
> in variis mundis varia ratione creatis,

---

34. See Asmis, 194, on the principle of noncontradiction. See Sedley, 266–72,
for further discussion of plural causes and noncontestation.

35. W. H. D. Rouse, trans., *Lucretius: De Rerum Natura*, Loeb Classical
Library (London and Cambridge, Mass., 1924; reprint, 1966).

id doceo plurisque sequor disponere causas,
motibus astrorum quae possint esse per omne;
e quibus una tamen sit et hic quoque causa necessest
quae vegeat motum signis; sed quae sit earum
praecipere haudquaquamst pedetemptim progredientis.

(Lucr. 5.526–33)

For which of these causes holds in our universe it is difficult to say
for certain; but what may be done and is done through the whole
universe in the various universes made in various ways, that is
what I teach, proceeding to set forth several causes which may
account for movements of the stars throughout the whole universe; one of which, however, must need be that which gives force
to the movement of the signs in our universe also; but which may
be the true one, is not his to lay down who proceeds step by step.[36]

As Asmis puts it, Lucretius implies that the goal of science is to
narrow the range of possible explanations.[37] These passages
show that Lucretius himself is aware of the limitations of his
science. When one is too far away, one does not know enough to
make distinctions between hypotheses. If one could be closer or
could know more, one could make better inferences. Lucretius'
passage on the moon's light illustrates the problem with the
method. He says, to summarize, that the moon may shine (1)
with reflected light from the sun or (2) with its own light, which
may at times be obscured by some other opaque body passing in
front of it. Alternatively it may be revolving and dark on one
side, light on the other. Finally (3), a new moon may be made
each day in succession, like the seasons (5.705–50). We see from
this example that knowing the list of possible causes—even the
correct one—is not the same as knowing the truth since there is
here an inability to discriminate between the true and the untrue
and to select the correct hypothesis.

We note that while the *Georgic* poet follows the form of this
method (*sive . . . sive . . . seu . . . seu . . .*), he does not
follow the substance of it. The plural causes that he adduces are
problematic since they are mutually exclusive, and as we can see
from reading through the *Letter to Pythocles* or Lucretius Books

36. Rouse, trans.
37. Asmis, 322.

5 and 6, this is not the characteristic practice of either Epicurus or Lucretius. Yet the *Georgic* poet proposes two stark opposites: something goes into the earth or something goes out; the earth becomes more porous or less. We are advanced not at all in our understanding; rather we recognize to what degree the fertility of fired fields remains, in fact, mysterious to us. I am proposing that the poet here is neither discussing different soil types nor being fanciful or incompetent. Rather he is outlining a problem for which there are only pairs of mutually exclusive solutions and hence no real solution at all. A list of possibilities of plural causes is apparently the greatest state of confusion to which an Epicurean can admit. In this regard, as in others, Epicureanism is an optimistic philosophy. The *Georgic* poet, however, through his imperfect imitation of this method of scientific explication, finishes, in fact, by illuminating the pervasiveness of mystery in our experience.

There may also be some further irony intended here. Ordinarily the method of plural causes is directed at celestial phenomena. In this passage the method cannot clarify even the earth at our feet. In truth, even science cannot eliminate ambiguity and mystery from our world. The mysterious fertility (*occultas vires* 86 and *caeca spiramenta* 90) of the fired fields remains mysterious.

Primary Opposites

Let us move on to the other passage of scientific tone, in which the poet discusses birds' mysterious sensitivity to oncoming changes in weather:

> tum liquidas corvi presso ter gutture voces
> aut quater ingeminant, et saepe cubilibus altis
> nescio qua praeter solitum dulcedine laeti
> inter se in foliis strepitant; iuvat imbribus actis
> progeniem parvam dulcisque revisere nidos.
> haud equidem credo, quia sit divinitus illis
> ingenium aut rerum fato prudentia maior;
> verum ubi tempestas et caeli mobilis umor
> mutavere vias et Iuppiter umidus Austris
> denset erant quae rara modo, et quae densa relaxat,
> vertuntur species animorum, et pectora motus

nunc alios, alios dum nubila ventus agebat,
concipiunt: hinc ille avium concentus in agris
et laetae pecudes et ovantes gutture corvi.

$$(1.410-23)$$

Then rooks, the guttural talkers, three times or four repeat
A clear cool note, and often up there in the treetop cradles
Charmed by some unfamiliar sweet impulse we cannot guess at
Gossip among the leaves; they love, when rain is over,
To visit again their baby brood, their darling nests.
It's not, to my belief, that god has given them
A special instinct, or fate a wider foreknowledge of things;
But when the weather and the inconstant moisture
Of the atmosphere shifts its course, and Jove
Wet with south winds makes dense what up to now
Was rare and rarifies what up to now
Was dense, the images of their minds are changed,
Their sense feels motions other than it felt
While the wind was herding the clouds.
Hence, the countryside over, begins that bird-chorale,
Beasts rejoice, and rooks caw in their exultation.

Here again Richter is sensitive in noting the similarity of scientific tone between this passage and 1.86–93.[38] In this passage the poet, affecting to doubt divine intervention in the birds' behavior, suggests instead the material or physical cause of atmospheric changes (415–423). The poet affects to explain scientifically or mechanistically the birds' sensibilities, choosing, with the terms "rare" and "dense," one of the typical correlates of primary opposites as proposed by Aristotle, for example. Aristotle says that "it seems evident that [these four primary opposites of hot and cold and dry and wet] are practically the causes of death and of life, as also of sleep and waking, of maturity and old age, and of disease and health" (*Part. an.* 648b4ff.).[39] He believes that other qualitative differences, among which are "rare" and "dense" and "heavy" and "light," correlate with and can be subsumed by these. In alluding to primary opposites, then, the poet appears to participate in one of the

38. Richter at 415ff.
39. Cited by Lloyd, 195. Primary opposites are a major focus of interest in Ross, *Virgil's Elements,* although he does not discuss this passage.

central scientific discourses of the ancient world. As with the instance of plural causes, however, he compromises the scientific power of his explanation, this time by thoroughgoing vagueness. The essence of his explanation is that when things change, things change. When what was rare becomes dense and what was dense becomes rare, the birds feel different ("the images of their minds are changed"), and consequently they make different sounds, begin to sing. Thus changes in weather produce changes in their moods. I propose that the lack of clarity or substance here prevents the explanation from being illuminating or persuasive. Other terms of the discussion intensify its vagueness. For example, the wetness of the sky is *mobilis* ("inconstant" 417), therefore perhaps, implicitly, not susceptible to rational analysis. The birds' minds "are changed" (*vertuntur* 420), the passive verb form revealing no agent and hence obscuring understanding. *Alios, alios* ("sometimes one motion, sometimes another" 421) also tends to suggest that the procedure in question here is random and again, therefore, possibly not susceptible to rational analysis.

Further compromising the scientific substance of this passage, the poet introduces Jupiter as the personified and divine cause of storms. Richter understands this Jupiter as merely "meteorological" and as a touch of "poetic coloring." However, this remark takes insufficient note of the inappropriateness, in a passage that affects exclusive commitment to mechanistic explication, of an equation of Jupiter with storm.[40] In the very moment of proffering a mechanistic or purely physical theory of factors affecting birds' responses, the poet implicitly challenges it by injecting the notion of god and of divine presence into the experience of mortal creatures. Additionally, the words *motus* and *species* (420) are deliberately ambiguous, each connoting not only physical movement and appearance but also emotional changes and visionary or phantom appearances.[41] Therefore, even the terms that the poet uses for his ostensibly physical explanation of the

40. Contrast Miles, 103, who sees Jupiter as "the archaic sky god, little more than a symbolic equivalent of wind and rain." Both Richter and Miles sense the incongruity of the presence of Jupiter in this ostensibly scientific passage.

41. Cf. Page ad loc.

birds' sentience connote as well something of a spiritual sort. Again we can only conclude that the poet has consistently compromised the persuasiveness of proffered scientific or mechanistic theories.[42]

By contrast we may consider the following passage from Lucretius, part of his proof of the existence of unseen particles. This is an admirable example of scientific thought, which allows the reader to grasp an idea and evaluate its plausibility:

> denique fluctifrago suspensae in litore vestes
> uvescunt, eaedem dispansae in sole serescunt:
> at neque quo pacto persederit umor aquai
> visumst nec rursum quo pacto fugerit aestu.
> in parvas igitur partis dispergitur umor
> quas oculi nulla possunt ratione videre.
> quin etiam multis solis redeuntibus annis
> anulus in digito subter tenuatur habendo,
> stilicidi casus lapidem cavat, uncus aratri
> ferreus occulte decrescit vomer in arvis,
> strataque iam volgi pedibus detrita viarum
> saxea conspicimus; tum portas propter aena
> signa manus dextras ostendunt adtenuari
> saepe salutantum tactu praeterque meantum.
> haec igitur minui, cum sint detrita, videmus.
> sed quae corpora decedant in tempore quoque,
> invida praeclusit speciem natura videndi.
> . . . .
> corporibus caecis igitur natura gerit res.
>   (Lucr. 1.305–321, 328)

To continue, clothing hung where breakers clash
Grows damp, then dries when spread out in the sun.
And yet, how water-moisture settled there,
Cannot be seen, nor how heat drove it off.
Into small parts, then, water is disposed,
Parts that the eye in no way can perceive.
Still more: as years and years of sun roll round,

---

42. Contrast Epicurus' denial of animal sentience: "The fact that weather is sometimes foretold from the behavior of certain animals is a mere coincidence in time. For the animals offer no necessary reason why a storm should be produced; and no divine being sits observing when these animals go out and afterwards fulfilling the signs which they have given. For such folly as this would not possess the most ordinary being if ever so little enlightened, much less one who enjoys perfect felicity" (*Ep. Pyth.* 115–16, trans. Hicks).

> The inner side of a ring is thinned by wearing;
> Water-drip hollows rock, the iron plow
> Grows imperceptibly smaller in the field,
> And paving stones we see worn down by feet
> Of people passing; then, near city-gates,
> Bronze statues show their right hands worn away
> By touch of the many who greet them and pass by.
> Once they're worn down, we see these things are smaller,
> But how many particles leave at given times,
> A niggard nature has blocked our power to see.
> . . . .
> Therefore nature works by means of bodies unseen.

This passage is one from among many that one could cite from Greek or Latin writers that demonstrates the possibility of tight and persuasive scientific reasoning. The *Georgic* poet has, however, not availed himself of the most powerful and cogent insights that ancient science had to offer. He has declined, ultimately, to bring his poetic discourse and the mental world that it entails into congruence with scientific value and methodology.

MYTHOLOGICAL PARADIGMS

I have suggested, then, that the scientific explanations in this poem are not and are not meant to be as compelling as the mythical tales, which function in a more frequent and more powerful way in the poem as paradigms or alternative illuminations of human experience. Through their power to absorb the imagination, to resonate in memory, and to suggest meanings beyond themselves the mythical tales have great emotional impact and value as a mode of perceiving and interpreting experience.

Myths figure with increasing importance in the poem. One proceeds, for instance, from Book 1 with its brief allusion to Deucalion (1.61–63), to the somewhat more elaborated stories of Bacchus and the centaurs (2.455) and Hero and Leander (3.258–63), to give only two examples, and finally to the Aristaeus epyllion, which fills half of Book 4. While the notable scientific passages of the poem are restricted to Book 1, as we come to

Book 4, the close of the poem, we enter a world of nymphs, of descents variously to life or death, of an enthralling poet-*vates*—Orpheus—whose music animates the woods and charms the dead. Allusions to Homer openly recall the world of poetry. The stories of Jupiter's birth and of Aristaeus, Orpheus, and Eurydice absorb the reader's attention with myth's powerful appeal. Poetic and mysterious processes dominate the book. For example, only here does the poet ask for knowledge from the Muses:

> Quis deus hanc, Musae, quis nobis extudit artem?
>
> (4.315)
>
> What god was it, O Muses, who forged for us this craft?

In thus presenting myth the poet suggests his agreement with Epicurus' view of the similar purposes of myth and science, although he differs as to what value to assign to each of them. Epicurus asserted, for example, that if one makes correct inferences from signs, there is no use for myth:

> μόνον ὁ μῦθος ἀπέστω· ἀπέσται δέ, ἐάν τις καλῶς τοῖς
> φαινομένοις ἀκολουθῶν περὶ τῶν ἀφανῶν σημειῶται.
>
> (*Ep. Pyth.* 104)

Only let myth be excluded [from explanation of thunderbolts]; and it will be excluded if one properly makes inferences from signs consistent with the phenomena concerning the unseen.[43]

We observe, then, the extent to which Epicurus conceived of both science and myth as modes—but antithetical modes—of interpreting experience. And we have already noted his view that the choice of a single explanation—as opposed to multiple explanations—characterizes the (low) mode of myth. To envision only one cause is neither rational nor thorough, in his opinion. The *Georgic* poet also, it appears, views science and poetry as competing modes of interpreting experience, yet he accords the higher value to the modality of myth, which he chooses for the expression of his truth.

---

43. Hicks, trans., with my alterations.

A good starting point for understanding the functioning of myth in the poem is the description of the zones of heaven:

> quinque tenent caelum zonae: quarum una corusco
> semper sole rubens et torrida semper ab igni;
> quam circum extremae dextra laevaque trahuntur
> caeruleae, glacie concretae atque imbribus atris;
> has inter mediamque duae mortalibus aegris
> munere concessae divum, et via secta per ambas,
> obliquus qua se signorum verteret ordo.
> mundus, ut ad Scythiam Riphaeasque arduus arces
> consurgit, premitur Libyae devexus in Austros.
> hic vertex nobis semper sublimis; at illum
> sub pedibus Styx atra videt Manesque profundi.
> maximus hic flexu sinuoso elabitur Anguis
> circum perque duas in morem fluminis Arctos,
> Arctos Oceani metuentes aequore tingi.
> illic, ut perhibent, aut intempesta silet nox
> semper et obtenta densentur nocte tenebrae;
> aut redit a nobis Aurora diemque reducit.
>
> (1.233–49)

> Five zones make up the heavens: one of them in the flaming
> Sun glows red forever, forever seared by his fire:
> Round it to right and left the furthermost zones extend,
> Blue with cold, ice-bound, frozen with black blizzards.
> Between these and the middle one, weak mortals are given
> Two zones by grace of the gods, and a path was cut through both
> Where the slanting signs might march and countermarch. The world,
> Rising steeply to Scythia and the Riphaean plateaux,
> Slopes down in the south to Libya.
> This North pole's always above us: the South appears beneath
> Our feet, the darkling Styx and the deep-dead shadow people.
> Here the great snake glides out with weaving, elastic body
> Writhing riverwise around and between the two bears—
> The bears that are afraid to get wet in the water of Ocean.
> At the South pole, men say, either it's dead of night,
> Dead still, the shadows shrouded in night, blacked out forever;
> Or dawn returns from us thither, bringing the day-light back.

Here, what we see in the sky is balanced by what we do not see in Hades or below. The visible modulates subtly and without acknowledgment into the mythological or rather into what can be described only in myth since it is not perceptible with the eye.

What one must note in observing the poet's technique is that this modulation from the real into the mythical is unacknowledged by the poet and thus catches the reader unaware. He is led, without consciousness or volition, into envisioning his world as informed by myth.[44]

Similarly at 1.404ff. the myth of Nisus and Scylla is subtly integrated into a description of weather signs:

> at nebulae magis ima petunt campoque recumbunt,
> solis et occasum servans de culmine summo
> nequiquam seros exercet noctua cantus.
> apparet liquido sublimis in aëre Nisus
> et pro purpureo poenas dat Scylla capillo:
> quacumque illa levem fugiens secat aethera pennis,
> ecce inimicus atrox magno stridore per auras
> insequitur Nisus; qua se fert Nisus ad auras,
> illa levem fugiens raptim secat aethera pennis.
>
> (1.401–9)

> Rather do mists hang low and crouch along the plain,
> And the little owl, perched on a gable, watching the sun go down,
> Keeps at her crazy night-call.
> Aloft in the lucid air Nisus
> Appears, and Scylla pays for that purple hair she stole:
> Wherever in flight she parts the thin air with her wings,
> Look! her enemy, cruel, down the wind loudly whistling,
> Nisus follows her close; where Nisus zooms upwind,
> Frantic in flight she parts the thin air with her wings.

Here again there is no acknowledgment of transition to another, mythical mode of thought. As a useful contrast we may consider the description of the bees' work (4.169–78), a rare example in this poem. In this passage the phrases *ac veluti* ("just as when")

---

44. Contrast Wilkinson, *Georgics*, 204: "Here Virgil has intruded into a scientific description of the globe the idea of the Styx and the Greek mythology of Hades, with a literary reminiscence from Lucretius (3.25ff.), and others from Homer (*Il.* 18.489; *Od.* 5.225). He must have known what he was doing. It was simply that he enjoyed such juxtapositions and had no scientific conscience." Willi Frentz, *Mythologisches in Vergils Georgica*, Beitr. zur klass. Philol. 21 (Meisenheim, 1967), has made an extensive study of myth in the *Georgics*. His primary interest is to demonstrate the Hellenistic/Alexandrian source of Virgil's myths. Additionally he argues that myth functions as more than learned play since it adds vividness, beauty, and charm to Virgil's poem.

and *non aliter* ("not otherwise" or "even so") signify to the reader that a comparison is being made between two things that, although similar, are not in fact identical. The simile is an apparent poetic artifice of which the reader is made aware. In the passages on the zones of heaven and on weather signs, typical of the poet's method in this poem, the subtle modulation from real to mythical results in the unacknowledged pervading of the entire poem by mythical modes of vision, that is, the invasion and even the appropriation of the real by myth.[45]

The value or truth of myth as paradigmatic of experience is illustrated in the poem by the way in which the poet makes myth become real. By allowing myths to be realized and reiterated in the poem, he makes mythical paradigms become the poem's reality. For example, one first reads of lightning in 1.278–82, when Jupiter uses his thunderbolt to punish the hubris of the Giants:

> tum partu Terra nefando
> Coeumque Iapetumque creat saevumque Typhoea
> et coniuratos caelum rescindere fratres.
> ter sunt conati imponere Pelio Ossam
> scilicet atque Ossae frondosum involvere Olympum;
> ter pater exstructos disiecit fulmine montis.
>
> (1.278–82)

> Then Earth spawned the unspeakable
> Coeus and Iapetus and the ogre Typhoeus
> And the brothers who leagued themselves to hack the heavens down.
> Three times they tried, three times, to pile Ossa on Pelion—
> Yes, and to roll up leafy Olympus on Ossa's summit;
> And thrice the father dashed apart the heaped-up hills with a thunderbolt.

Because the storm incident recounted in 1.278–82 is the first description of a storm in the poem, the reader is implicitly invited or may be predisposed to perceive in storms a reiteration of a mythological paradigm. This storm prefigures the occurrence of another storm, real within the poem's action, which is described

---

45. For other similar examples, see 1.61f., 276ff.; 3.89–94, 113–17, 152–53, 267–68, 391–93, 549–50; 4.149–52.

shortly thereafter (1.316–27) in an awesome scene, the reality of which the poet personally confirms with the words *ego . . . vidi* ("I have seen" 1.318). After these initial descriptive verses, the storm is most powerfully imagined or revealed as Jove hurling lightning and casting terror upon all creatures:

> ipse pater media nimborum in nocte corusca
> fulmina molitur dextra, quo maxima motu
> terra tremit, fugere ferae et mortalia corda
> per gentis humilis stravit pavor; ille flagranti
> aut Atho aut Rhodopen aut alta Ceraunia telo
> deicit; ingeminant Austri et densissimus imber;
> nunc nemora ingenti vento, nunc litora plangunt.
>
> (1.328–34)

> The Father, enthroned in midnight cloud, hurls from a flashing
> Right hand his lightning: the whole
> Earth trembles at the shock; the beasts are fled, and human
> Hearts are felled in panic throughout the nations; on Athos,
> Rhodope or the Ceraunian massif his bolt flares down:
> The south wind doubles its force and thicker falls the rain.
> Now wail the woods with that gale tremendous, now the shores
>   wail.

The presence of Jove as agent of this lightning storm would seem to corroborate the paradigmatic value of the myth of Jove and the Giants at 1.278–83. Consequently the reader is implicitly or by suggestion invited to envision storms, most especially violent ones, as the flashing anger of Jove.[46] For the issue of scientific vs. mythological knowledge, which is our subject here, this image of Jove hurling lightning is especially significant because Lucretius had selected for particular ridicule the notion of Jove hurling his thunderbolt as a cause of storms (e.g., Lucr. 2.1093–1104; 6.379–422). The *Georgic* poet would, then, be reasserting the symbolic value of this notion, reasserting the validity of mythology (or, as Lucretius would say, of superstition) over the scientific mode.

Myth serves as a paradigm of real experience, as seen above, and also as a paradigm of the poet's new myth of Aristaeus, Orpheus, and Eurydice. The myth of Hero and Leander is a

---

46. A similar example is that of the myth of Io, in which the *pestis* ("plague" 3.153) that attacks her is realized at 3.478ff.

typically Hellenistic tale of destructive passion, which the poet tells in, as we may infer, a conventional way:[47]

> quid iuvenis, magnum cui versat in ossibus ignem
> durus amor? nempe abruptis turbata procellis
> nocte natat caeca serus freta, quem super ingens
> porta tonat caeli, et scopulis inlisa reclamant
> aequora; nec miseri possunt revocare parentes,
> nec moritura super crudeli funere virgo.
>
> (3.258–63)

> What of the young man, burning with cruel love to the bones?
> Late in the blindfold night he swims the narrows
> That are vexed by headlong gales, while above his head the huge
> Gates of heaven thunder and the seas collide with a crash
> Against the capes: powerless to recall him his sorrowful parents
> And the girl who is soon to die of grief over his body.

In its tragic ending (there are no happy love stories in Virgil), it prefigures the outcome of the newly cast stories of Aristaeus and Orpheus, both of which are structured by the poet to be equally compelling and fresh paradigms of experience. Thus the poet selects and creates his myths to reiterate the same truth. The myths have a unitary vision. The tale of Glaucus, also one of unhappy sexuality, is a variation on this motif of sexuality and tragic passion; and we may note that Virgil alone makes the tale an *aition* of the love-fury of mares.[48] Because Glaucus refused to allow his mares to breed, he was torn apart by them when they were maddened by Venus:

> scilicet ante omnis furor est insignis equarum;
> et mentem Venus ipsa dedit, quo tempore Glauci
> Potniades malis membra absumpsere quadrigae.
>
> (3.266–69)

> But of all, beyond doubt, the fury of mares is the most
>   remarkable:
> Venus herself incited
> The chariot-team that day they champed the limbs of Glaucus.

47. Miles, 198 n. 19, is useful. The names of Hero and Leander do not occur until Ovid *Her.* 18 and 19 and *Am.* 2.16.31. It is not clear whether Virgil is suppressing names, otherwise well known, in order to generalize the value of the story or if no specific names were in fact associated with the story. Thomas, at 258ff., assumes an Alexandrian original; see also Frentz, 129.

48. Frentz, 60.

We may see, further, that the Glaucus myth prefigures the story of Orpheus in another way as well. Orpheus attempts a lonely denial of sexuality and refuses to mate. He suffers dismemberment, just as does Glaucus. In the case of Orpheus dismemberment results from refusal to mate, since the spurned (*spretae*) Ciconian women, in fury, tear him apart. Punishment comes roughly from Venus to mortals who struggle against the powerful drive that she represents. The poet's myths reiterate and embody similar visions, and therefore, as Epicurus says, to envision one truth is the practice of myth. Yet in the *Georgics* the fact that mythical visions are continually reiterated appears to be a subtle affirmation of their truth.

To summarize the poet's use of myth in this poem, we may suggest first that through his fine integration of the mythological into the real he seductively informs the reader's whole vision of the world with mythical images. Second, he contrives to adumbrate the truth and value of myth by allowing certain myths to become real within the poem's reality. Third, he structures the poem in such a way that familiar, traditionally told myths parallel his own newly created myth so that the truth, value, and impact of both old and new myths seem corroborated.

The poet seeks to address the mysteries of existence most powerfully through the medium of myth and not, as we have seen, through scientific inquiry. Myths for him seem to have greater power than science because, first, they have emotional impact and resonance in the imagination, absorbing the reader's feelings and memory. Second, they do not have alternatives as the scientific explanations do, but rather they present a reiterated singleness of vision. Hence we see that the poet's use of myth in this poem serves to rival the value of the technological mode that the poem purports to esteem. Myth's powerful presence in this ostensibly practical tract is part of the poet's compelling argument for his own value and truth.

THE POET'S TRUTH

Thus far we have seen the poet-figures in the poem, Orpheus and the *Georgic* poet, as essentially parallel, most especially in their nonmaterial goals and in their idealized vision of the past. For Orpheus this idealized past is embodied in Eurydice; for the *Georgic* poet it is embodied in the Golden Age. Orpheus and the *Georgic* poet are parallel also in daring. Orpheus is courageous in descending alone to the fearfulness of hell and in never abandoning his ideal of Eurydice. Instead he sings forever of his sorrow, pure and uncompromised, at her loss. His music, like that of the nightingale to which he is compared (4.511–15), does not solace suffering but rather preserves it. The beauty of his song, at variance with the tragedy of which it sings, makes a beautiful thing of tragedy itself. Beauty is a value that the poet lends to the present. Similarly the *Georgic* poet terms himself daring (1.40, 2.175, 4.565). He too, throughout the *Georgics,* memorializes a retrospective ideal in his vision of the Golden Age. Both of these figures are different from Aristaeus, who never looks back but only forward—to success, to power, to apotheosis. If Eurydice does in some way embody an ideal, whether of nature or of the past, Aristaeus surely does not observe that fact. Much less, then, can he mourn it.[49] From Orpheus' point of view, as well as from the *Georgic* poet's, Aristaeus would necessarily appear obtuse, ignorant of the true value of things, indifferent to beauty, without insight or pity. He expresses neither understanding nor regret; he does not see the consequences of the tale of Proteus for himself. These must be interpreted for him by his mother.[50] (We remember that the original request that the poet makes of Caesar is that he have pity. Aristaeus never pities, but only succeeds.) In sum, Orpheus and the *Georgic* poet have some parallel visions and also differ in similar ways from Aristaeus.

If, however, we wish to understand the poet's truth, we must appreciate an important distinction between Orpheus and the *Georgic* poet, for they do not see entirely the same vision. The *Georgic* poet's truth, as reflected in his creation of the Aristaeus epyllion, with its myth of Aristaeus, Orpheus, and Eurydice and

---

49. See Miles, 270f., for good remarks on the indifference of Aristaeus to Eurydice's fate.

50. Contrast Putnam, *Poem of the Earth,* 11f., who feels that Aristaeus achieves a "unity of physical strength and mental understanding."

also with its image of the *bougonia,* reflects a vision more penetrating and subtle than that attributed to Orpheus.

Orpheus' song, as we have seen, is powerfully moving, sad, and nostalgic, as expressed in 4.464–66, 471–74, 481–84, and 510. His vision seems to linger on sorrow since he sees in Hades scenes of particular pathos (4.475–77). He sings what he sees, and consequently his song is continually of loss. Although there is a haunting, sorrowful beauty to his song, it is perhaps limited by its lack of complexity. Orpheus seems more interested in the past and in the tragic than in the true.

The *Georgic* poet's vision is subtler and more inclusive than that of Orpheus, for the Aristaeus epyllion, which he creates, expresses ambiguity and exchange, not only loss. The *Georgic* poet's vision is of the exchange of calf for bees, of death for life, of loss for gain. To the question of how to perceive the relative value of these terms he has no explicit answer, although the deaths of the calf and of Orpheus and Eurydice are presented with pathos, while the bees merely exist, undifferentiated and unreflective. They do not elicit the poet's (or, consequently, the reader's) involved sympathy. Orpheus and Eurydice perish definitively, while new bees take the place of those lost.

The poet intends to reveal true things (2.45–46) and not trite things for the thoughtless (3.3–4). He wants, therefore, something true and new, and he does not aim at *vacuas mentes* ("idle minds"). He explicitly disdains commonly told myths (3.4–8). The myth of Aristaeus and Orpheus as told here is his truth: a new myth, especially for Romans, a myth that embodies the oppositions between power and beauty, profit and art, material and spiritual in their society. It shows the brutality of victory and the pathos of loss, for the tragedy of Orpheus and Eurydice is only imperfectly redeemed by the birth of the impersonal swarm of bees. Aristaeus, while ultimately successful, appears unreflective, insensitive, and without regret. Although responsible for the deaths of his original bees, of Eurydice, and of Orpheus, he voices no understanding of guilt nor regret for his actions once their consequences have been revealed to him. Significantly, the poet engages the reader's sympathy with the victims—with Orpheus, flawed as he too is, with Eurydice, and with the struggling calf—and thus expands the reader's sensibility. The reader learns identification with victims and losers, and thus learns compassion and pity. The poet does not suggest an alternate route to survival or victory, for there is none. That is to say, he does not propose the elimination of Aristaeus and what he stands for. The effect of his poem is rather to suggest compassion in confronting the truth of experience, to make readers sensitive to loss, and to create a "community of pity."

To appreciate the value of the poet's truth, we must observe that the outcome of the poem affects the figures in the poem differently from the way in which it affects the readers. Neither Aristaeus nor Orpheus learns a lesson, but readers can; for the fates of Aristaeus and Orpheus are related and meaningful to us, if not to them. The poet has shaped the poem to show the immediate triumph of material man—Aristaeus or the analogous figure of Caesar—while simultaneously eliciting from the reader an appreciation of and pity for Orpheus (and similarly for Proteus, Eurydice, and the nightingale) as a figure of poetry, music, and beauty. The *Georgics,* through its representation of the Golden Age and most especially through the story of Orpheus, expands the reader's awareness of life's ambiguity, his sensitivity to loss, and his capacity for sorrow. Hence the sensitive reader becomes morally superior to Aristaeus and Cyrene, who never experience or express regret. Moral superiority, however, does not bring change; it is not an exhortation to action. It merely makes possible the apprehension of tragic conflict.

Aristaeus is successful and forfeits the reader's sympathy. While he has the immediate triumph, since he and not Orpheus is allowed atonement, and while his questions have answers (4.321–25) as opposed to those of Orpheus (4.504–5) and Eurydice (4.495), which do not, he nevertheless does not triumph through merit:

> haud quamquam ad meritum poenas, ni fata resistant[51]
> (4.455)

---

51. Reading with Conington, Page, and Wilkinson *ad* of the Palatine MS for *ob* (although the latter is more frequently attested), since, as they argue, it gives better sense. Wilkinson's remarks are found ad loc. in his translation, *Virgil: The Georgics* (Harmondsworth and New York, 1982).

This vengeance against you—if fate did not
interpose—far short of your deserts.

Aristaeus has Proteus to reveal *causae* (4.532) and Cyrene to
teach *praecepta* (4.534-47). Thus fate is not just.[52] On the other
hand, the loss of Orpheus, with what he represents of sentiment
and beauty, is not solaced. The poem ends, as the reader is made
to feel, in unresolved and unresolvable tragedy: in the loss of
Orpheus and Eurydice and in the defeat of their love. Orpheus
perishes somehow wrongly, since Hades does not know of pity or
forgiveness:

> nesciaque humanis precibus mansuescere corda
> (4.470)
> The hearts that know not how to be touched by human prayer

> ignoscenda quidem scirent si ignoscere Manes
> (4.489)
> Pardonable indeed, if Death knew how to pardon.

Yet the beauty of Orpheus' song, with its memory of Eurydice,
endures eternal, through the song of the *Georgics*. The tragic
vision of the *Georgics* is undermined only by the beauty of the
poetry that sings the tragedy.

Since the tragedy of Aristaeus, Orpheus, and Eurydice is not
resolved by the poet, the poem is not protreptic. Art is useless,
and therefore, as noted above, it does not occur in the theodicy of
Book 1, since it has no practical value. The poem simply shows
the truth. Neither consoling nor false, it is tragic and true. The
poet tells the truth and therefore is truly *audax* ("bold" 4.565).
To Page this adjective signifies only that Virgil was the first to
sing pastoral poetry in Latin; but perhaps it relates rather to his
function as poet overall. In the opening of Book 3 he had already
described his projected poetic achievements in heroic terms:

52. See Wilkinson, Georgics, 120, who also notes that the experience of
Orpheus is not presented as just. Spofford, 56ff., ruminates on the great role of
luck and status, as opposed to justice, in the destiny of Aristaeus and observes:
"Complication about justice is beginning to be developed in the *Georgics*" (58).

> temptanda via est, qua me quoque possim
> tollere humo victorque virum volitare per ora.
> primus ego in patriam mecum, modo vita supersit,
> Aonio rediens deducam vertice Musas;
> primus Idumaeas referam tibi, Mantua, palmas.
>
> (3.8–12)

> Now, I must venture a theme will exalt me
> From earth and give me wings and a triumph on every tongue.
> If life enough is left me,
> I'll be the first to bring the Muses of song to my birthplace
> From the Aonian peak; the first to wear the Idumaean palm for
>   Mantua.

At 4.565 the term *audax* is even emphatic, since it is juxtaposed to Caesar's military feats, which are not described as requiring courage (4.560–62). While Caesar triumphs over the *volentis* ("willing" 4.561) and his enemies are *imbellem* ("war-worthless" 2.172), the poet's challenges are awesome. (We recall Orpheus' descent to the sorrow and fearfulness of hell, where he sees the king explicitly described as fearful [*regem . . . tremendum* 4.469].)

.   .   .

The truth of the poet's myth of Aristaeus and Orpheus is confirmed in the epilogue, for the relationship there described between the historical figures Caesar and Virgil[53] is analogous to that between Aristaeus and Orpheus. While we see in the epilogue the poet's graceful acknowledgment of Caesar's success in the political world, we see also his magnificently subtle assertion of his own difference from the farmer and the conqueror, those more conventional embodiments of Roman virtue:

> illo Vergilium me tempore dulcis alebat
> Parthenope studiis florentem ignobilis oti,
> carmina qui lusi pastorum audaxque iuventa,
> Tityre, te patulae cecini sub tegmine fagi.
>
> (4.563–66)

---

53. This is emphatic, for the name Vergilius appears only here (4.563) in the entire corpus of Virgil's works.

This was the time when I, Virgil, nurtured in sweet
Parthenope, did flower in pursuits of inglorious ease,
And dallied with songs of shepherds and, by youth emboldened,
Tityrus, sang of you in the shade of a spreading beech.

The clear echo in the concluding verse of the *Georgics* of the first
verse of the first *Eclogue*

Tityre, tu patulae recubans sub tegmine fagi
(*Ecl.* 1.1)

Tityrus, you, lying under the covert of your spreading beech

further corroborates the political ramifications of the relationship between the poet and Caesar.[54] Caesar is immediately
victorious, yet the *Georgic* poet has a power other, perhaps even
greater, than his. Through his poetry he suggests to his readers
how to perceive, interpret, and value experience. In structuring
the readers' visions of experience he creates their values. Caesar
aspires to divinity, but the *Georgic* poet concludes his poem by
affirming his own characteristic and enduring boldness and song
(4.565–66). Nevertheless, we cannot take as wholly ironic the
poet's derogation of his own achievements in relation to Caesar's
(*studiis florentem ignobilis oti, carmina qui lusi*), for the poet is
not deluded with respect to his own power in the political world.
As we have seen, despite his beautiful song, Orpheus is impotent
in the world. Similarly, for the *Georgic* poet the mission of pity,
while in one sense daring, is also easy and even self-gratifying, as
poet and readers risk feeling complacent in their superior sensibility, while the world's conflicts remain unresolved and its losses
inadequately redeemed.

54. This allusion to the *Eclogues* returns us to a world "in which the spiritual
polarity of the political and poetic worlds and the nullificatory impact of the
former on the latter are affirmed and exhibited (esp. *Ecl.* 1, *Ecl.* 9, *Ecl.* 10),"
Boyle, 80.

CONCLUSION

In sum, while the poem purports to be didactic and to teach *praecepta,* it embodies, in fact, a whole range of values that function in tension with the conventional, material, and Iron Age values upon which a georgic poem might be expected to be based. The poem privileges mystery, not solution; complexity and ambiguity, not certainty. The overall effect of this poem is to highlight the mysteries of existence, to challenge and even to transcend the values of the technological mode that it ostensibly accepts and endorses. In the *Georgics,* then, the ultimate meaning is at variance with the assumed or implicit values of the form. The *Georgic* poet is more like Proteus than like Cyrene, for he too is more interested in *causae* than in *praecepta.* Hence the *bougonia,* although false as *praeceptum,* does embody the poet's sensed truth of the quality of Iron Age existence. The Aristaeus-Orpheus story, parallel in significance to the *bougonia,* constitutes the poet's revelation in mythic image of the nature of human experience.

The poem should be seen neither as an agricultural tract nor as prescriptive of a return to country values.[55] Rather it expresses an apprehension of certain oppositions that are not capable of resolution (e.g., victor vs. vanquished, agricultural vs. poetic, Iron Age vs. Golden Age, material vs. spiritual). The poem is not antimaterial or anti-imperial as much as it is an apprehension of the cost of material progress and imperial expansion. The poem provokes the responsive reader to a sense of compassion and of sorrow for loss that is the essence of humanity. The poem forges a community of readers sensitive to loss and capable of pity. It enlarges and deepens the reader's appreciation of those spiritual and artistic values that do not lead to quantifiable progress. In the poem's tragic and beautiful conclusion we see reflected the opposition between the truth of myth and poetry and the value of the agricultural, material poem that the *Georgics* on its surface professes to be.

55. Similarly the poetry of the poet-singer Proteus also is not protreptic, since he sings only of *causae* and not of *praecepta.* Orpheus' song likewise is not concerned with *praecepta;* he sings only the truth of his experience.

Bibliography

Alpers, Paul. *The Singer of the* Eclogues: *A Study of Virgilian Pastoral.* Berkeley, 1979.

Altevogt, H. *Labor Improbus: Eine Vergilstudie.* Münster, 1952.

Anderson, W. S. "The Orpheus of Virgil and Ovid: *flebile nescio quid.*" In *Orpheus: The Metamorphoses of a Myth,* edited by John Warden, 25–50. Toronto, 1982.

Asmis, Elizabeth. *Epicurus' Scientific Method.* Ithaca, N.Y., 1984.

Bailey, C. R., ed. *Titi Lucreti Cari* De Rerum Natura *Libri Sex.* 3 vols. Oxford, 1947. Reissued, 1986.

Bayet, Jean. "Un procédé virgilien: la description synthétique dans les *Géorgiques.*" In *Studi in onore di Gino Funaioli,* edited by E. Paratore, 9–18. Rome, 1955.

———. Les premières *Géorgiques* de Virgile." *RPh* 56 (1930):128–50, 227–47.

Benardete, S. "Hesiod's *Works and Days:* A First Reading." *Agon* 1 (1967):150–74.

Betensky, Aya. "The Farmer's Battles." *Ramus* 8 (1979):108–19.

Bloom, Harold. *A Map of Misreading.* New York, 1975.

Booth, Wayne C. *A Rhetoric of Irony.* Chicago, 1974.

Bowra, C. M. "Orpheus and Eurydice." *CQ* 2 (1952):113–26.

Boyle, A. J. "*In Medio Caesar:* Paradox and Politics in Virgil's *Georgics.*" *Ramus* 8 (1979):65–86.

Bradley, A. "Augustan Culture and a Radical Alternative: Virgil's *Georgics.*" *Arion* 8 (1969):347–58.

Buchheit, Vinzenz. *Der Anspruch des Dichters in Vergils* Georgika: *Dichtertum und Heilsweg.* Darmstadt, 1972.

Büchner, K. "P. Vergilius Maro." *RE* 8 A 1 (1955):1021–1264; *RE* 8 A 2 (1958):1265–1486.

Burck, E. "Der korykische Greis in Vergils *Georgica* (IV.116–148)." In *Navicula Chiloniensis: Festschrift F. Jacoby,* 156–72. Leiden, 1956.

———. "Die Komposition von Vergils *Georgica.*" *Hermes* 64 (1929):279–321.

Burkert, Walter. *Homo Necans: The Anthropology of Ancient Greek Sacrificial Ritual and Myth.* Translated by Peter Bing. Berkeley, 1983.

Camps, W. A. *An Introduction to Virgil's* Aeneid. Oxford, 1969.

Cavell, Stanley. " 'Who does the wolf love?': *Coriolanus* and the Inter-
pretations of Politics." In *Shakespeare and the Question of Theory*,
edited by P. Parker and G. Hartman, 245–72. New York, 1985.
Clay, J. S. "The Old Man in the Garden: *Georgic* 4.116–148." *Arethusa*
14 (1981):57–65.
———. "The Argument of the End of Virgil's Second *Georgic*." *Phi-
lologus* 2 (1976):232–45.
Commager, Steele, ed. *Virgil: A Collection of Critical Essays*. New
York, 1966.
———. *The Odes of Horace: A Critical Study*. New Haven, 1962.
Reprint. Bloomington, Ind., 1967.
———. "Lucretius' Interpretation of the Plague." *HSCP* 62 (1957):105–
18.
Conington, John, and Henry Nettleship, eds. *The Works of Virgil*.
London, 1898. Reprint. Hildesheim, 1963.
Conte, Gian Biagio. *The Rhetoric of Imitation: Genre and Poetic Mem-
ory in Virgil and Other Latin Poets*. Edited by Charles Segal. Ithaca,
N.Y., 1986.
Dahlmann, Hellfried. "Die Bienenstaat in Vergils *Georgica*." *AAWN*
10 (1954):548–62 (=*Kleinen Schriften* [Hildesheim, 1970]).
Davis, P. J. "Virgil's *Georgics* and the Pastoral Ideal." *Ramus* 8
(1979):22–33.
Derrida, Jacques. *Of Grammatology*. Translated by G. C. Spivak. Balti-
more and London, 1976.
Detienne, M. *The Creation of Mythology*. Translated by Margaret
Cook. Chicago and London, 1986.
———. "Orphée au miel." *QUCC* 12 (1971):3–23.
———. *Crise agraire et attitude religieuse chez Hésiode*. Brussels, 1963.
Duckworth, George E. "Virgil's *Georgics* and the Laudes Galli." *AJP* 80
(1959):225–37.
Eagleton, Terry. *Literary Theory*. Minneapolis, 1983.
Empson, William. *Some Versions of Pastoral*. London, 1935. Reprint.
New York, 1974.
Fish, Stanley E. "Interpreting the Variorum." *Critical Inquiry* 2
(1976):465–85 (reprinted in Jane P. Tompkins, ed., *Reader-Response
Criticism from Formalism to Post-Structuralism* [Baltimore and Lon-
don, 1980]).
———. "Literature in the Reader: Affective Stylistics." *New Literary
History* 2 (1970):123–62 (reprinted in Tompkins).
Frayn, Joan M. "Subsistence Farming during the Roman Period: A
Preliminary Discussion of the Evidence." *G & R* 21 (1974):11–18.
Frentz, Willi. *Mythologisches in Vergils* Georgica. Beitr. zur klass.
Philol. 21. Meisenheim, 1967.
Galinsky, Karl. "Vergil and the Formation of the Augustan Ethos." In

Atti del Convegno Mondiale Scientifico di Studi Virgiliani, vol. 1, 240–54. Milan, 1984.

Gatz, Bodo. *Weltalter, Goldene Zeit und sinnverwandte Vorstellungen.* Spudasmata 16. Hildesheim, 1967.

Griffin, Jasper. "*Haec super arvorum cultu.*" *CR* 31 (1981):23–37.

———. "The Fourth *Georgic*, Virgil, and Rome." *G & R* 26 (1979):61–80.

Grimal, Pierre. *Les jardins romains à la fin de la république et aux deux premiers siècles de l'empire.* Paris, 1948.

Guthrie, W. C. K. *Orpheus and Greek Religion.* London, 1952.

Harrison, E. L. "The Noric Plague in Vergil's Third *Georgic*." *PLLS* 2 (1979):1–65.

Heurgon, Jacques. "Orphée et Eurydice avant Virgile." *MEFR* 49 (1932):6–60.

Hiller v. Gaertringen, Friedrich. "Aristaios." *RE* 2 (1896):852–59.

Iser, Wolfgang. *The Act of Reading: A Theory of Aesthetic Response.* Baltimore, 1978.

Jacobsen, H. "Aristaeus, Orpheus, and the *Laudes Galli.*" *AJP* 105 (1984):271–300.

Jermyn, L. A. S. "Weather-Signs in Virgil." *G & R* 20 (1951):26–37, 49–59.

Johnson, W. R. *Darkness Visible: A Study of Vergil's Aeneid.* Berkeley, 1976.

Johnston, Patricia A. *Vergil's Agricultural Golden Age: A Study of the Georgics.* Mnemosyne Supp. 8. Leiden, 1980.

Klepl, Herta. *Lukrez und Virgil in ihren Lehrgedichten: Vergleichende Interpretationen.* Darmstadt, 1967.

Klingner, F. *Virgil: Bucolica, Georgica, Aeneis.* Zurich, 1967.

Kromer, Gretchen. "The Didactic Tradition in Vergil's *Georgics*." *Ramus* 8 (1979):7–21.

La Penna, Antonio. "*Senex Corycius.*" In *Atti del Convegno Virgiliano sul Bimillenario delle Georgiche*, 37–66. Naples, 1977.

———. "Esiodo nella cultura e nella poesia di Virgilio." In *Hésiode et son influence.* Fondation Hardt Entretiens, vol. 7, 213–70. Geneva, 1970.

Lau, D. *Der lateinische Begriff "Labor."* Munich, 1975.

Leach, Eleanor W. "*Georgics* 2 and the Poem." *Arethusa* 14 (1981):35–48.

Liebeschuetz, W. "Beast and Man in the Third Book of Vergil's *Georgics*." *G & R* 12 (1965):64–77.

Linforth, Ivan. *The Arts of Orpheus.* Berkeley, 1941.

Lloyd, G. E. R. *The Revolutions of Wisdom: Studies in the Claims and Practice of Ancient Greek Science.* Berkeley, 1987.

Long, A. A., and D. N. Sedley. *The Hellenistic Philosophers.* 2 vols. Cambridge, 1987.

Lovejoy, A. O., and G. Boas. *Primitivism and Related Ideas in Antiquity.* Baltimore, 1935.

Lyne, R. O. A. M. "Scilicet et tempus veniet . . . : Virgil, *Georgics* 1.463–514." In *Quality and Pleasure in Latin Poetry,* edited by Tony Woodman and David West, 47–66. Cambridge, 1974.

MacBain, Bruce. *Prodigy and Expiation: A Study in Religion and Politics in Republican Rome.* Brussels, 1982.

Marx, Leo. *The Machine in the Garden: Technology and the Pastoral Ideal in America.* Oxford, 1964. Reprint. 1981.

Merrill, W. A. "Parallels and Coincidences in Lucretius and Virgil." *University of California Publications in Classical Philology* 3 (1918):137–264.

Miles, Gary B. *Virgil's Georgics: A New Interpretation.* Berkeley, 1980.

Newman, J. K. *Augustus and the New Poetry.* Collection Latomus 88. Brussels, 1967.

Nichols, James H., Jr. *Epicurean Political Philosophy: The* De Rerum Natura *of Lucretius.* Ithaca, N.Y., 1976.

Norden, E. "Orpheus und Eurydice." *Sb. Ak. Berlin phil.-hist. Kl.* (1934):626–83 (=*Kleine Schriften,* 468–532. Berlin, 1966).

Ogilvie, R. M. *The Romans and Their Gods in the Age of Augustus.* New York, 1969.

Oltramare, André. *Étude sur l'épisode d'Aristée dans les* Géorgiques *de Virgile.* Geneva, 1892.

Otis, Brooks. "A New Study of the *Georgics." Phoenix* 26 (1972):40–62.

———. *Virgil: A Study in Civilized Poetry.* Oxford, 1964.

Page, T. C., ed. *P. Vergili Maronis:* Bucolica *et* Georgica. London 1898. Reprint. 1965.

Parry, Adam. "The Idea of Art in Virgil's *Georgics." Arethusa* 5 (1972): 35–52.

Perkell, C. G. "Vergil's Theodicy Reconsidered." In *Vergil at 2000: Commemorative Essays on the Poet and His Influence,* edited by John D. Bernard, 67–83. New York, 1986.

———. "On the Corycian Gardener in Virgil's Fourth *Georgic." TAPA* 111 (1981):167–77.

———. "A Reading of Virgil's Fourth *Georgic." Phoenix* 32 (1978): 211–21.

Perret, J. *Virgile: L'homme et l'oeuvre.* Paris, 1952. 2d ed. 1965.

Pucci, Pietro. *The Violence of Pity in Euripides' Medea.* Ithaca, N.Y., 1980.

———. *Hesiod and the Language of Poetry.* Baltimore, 1977.

Putnam, M. C. J. "Daedalus, Virgil, and the End of Art." *AJP* 108 (1987):173–89.

———. *Virgil's Poem of the Earth: Studies in the* Georgics. Princeton, 1979.

———. "Italian Virgil and the Idea of Rome." In *Janus: Essays in*

Ancient and Modern Studies, edited by Louis L. Orlin, 171–200. Ann Arbor, Mich., 1975.

———. "The Virgilian Achievement." *Arethusa* 5 (1972):53–70.

Quinn, Kenneth. *Virgil's* Aeneid: *A Critical Description.* London, 1968.

Redfield, James M. *Nature and Culture in the* Iliad: *The Tragedy of Hektor.* Chicago, 1975.

Richter, Will, ed. *Vergil:* Georgica. Munich, 1957.

Ross, David. *Virgil's Elements: Physics and Poetry in the* Georgics. Princeton, 1987.

———. *Catullus and the Traditions of Ancient Poetry.* Cambridge, 1969.

Sedley, David. "On Signs." In *Science and Speculation: Studies in Hellenistic Theory and Practice,* edited by J. Barnes, J. Brunschwig, M. Burnyeat, and M. Schofield, 239–72. Cambridge, 1982.

Segal, C. P. "Ancient Texts and Modern Literary Criticism." *Arethusa* 1 (1968):1–25.

———. "Virgil's *Caelatum Opus:* An Interpretation of the Third *Eclogue.*" *AJP* 88 (1967):279–308.

———. "Orpheus and the Fourth *Georgic:* Vergil on Nature and Civilization." *AJP* 87 (1966):307–25.

———. "*Tamen Cantabitis, Arcades:* Exile and Arcadia in *Eclogues* One and Nine." *Arion* 4 (1965):237–66.

Segre, Dan Vittorio. *Memoirs of a Fortunate Jew: An Italian Story.* New York, 1987.

Smith, Barbara Herrnstein. *Poetic Closure: A Study of How Poems End.* Chicago, 1968.

Solodow, J. B. "*Poeta Impotens:* The Last Three *Eclogues.*" *Latomus* 36 (1977):757–71.

Spofford, Edward W. *The Social Poetry of the* Georgics. Salem, N.H., 1981.

Spurr, M. S. "Agriculture and the *Georgics.*" *G & R* 33 (1986):164–87.

Stehle, Eva M. "Virgil's *Georgics:* The Threat of Sloth." *TAPA* 104 (1974):347–69.

Steidle, W. "Die Anordnung der Arbeiten im ersten Buch von Vergils *Georgica.*" *RhM* 109 (1966):135–64.

Strauss, Leo. *Liberalism Ancient and Modern.* New York, 1968.

Syme, R. *The Roman Revolution.* Oxford, 1939. Reprint. 1971.

Thomas, Richard, ed. *Virgil:* Georgics. 2 vols. Cambridge, 1988.

Van Sickle, John. *The Design of Virgil's* Bucolics. Rome, 1978.

Vernant, J. P. "Le mythe hésiodique des races: Essai d'analyse structurale." *RHR* 157 (1960):21–54.

Wagenvoort, H. "The Crime of Fratricide." In *Studies in Roman Literature, Culture, and Religion,* 169–83. Leiden, 1956.

Wender, Dorothea S. "Resurrection in the Fourth *Georgic.*" *AJP* 90 (1969):424–36.

White, K. D. *Roman Farming*. Ithaca, N.Y., 1970.
Whitfield, B. G. "Virgil and the Bees: A Study in Ancient Apicultural Lore." *G & R* 3 (1956):99–117.
Wilkinson, L. P. *The* Georgics *of Virgil*. Cambridge, 1969.
————. "Virgil's Theodicy." *CQ* 13 (1963):75–84.
Williams, Gordon. *Technique and Ideas in the* Aeneid. New Haven, 1983.
————. *Tradition and Originality in Roman Poetry*. Oxford, 1968.
Williams, R. D., ed. *Virgil: The* Eclogues *and* Georgics. New York, 1979.
————., ed. *The* Aeneid *of Virgil: Books 7–12*. New York, 1973. Reprint. 1977.
————. "Changing Attitudes to Virgil." In *Virgil*, edited by D. R. Dudley, 119–38. London, 1969.
Williams, Raymond. *The Country and the City*. New York, 1973.
Winnington-Ingram, R. P. *Sophocles: An Interpretation*. Cambridge, 1980.
Wormell, D. E. W. "*Apibus quanta experientia parcis:* Virgil, *Georgics* 4.1–227." In *Vergiliana: Recherches sur Virgile*, edited by H. Bardon and R. Verdière, 429–35. Leiden, 1971.
Wuilleumier, P. "Virgile et le vieillard de Tarente." *REL* 3 (1930):325–40.
Ziegler, K. "Orpheus." *RE* 17.1 (1939):1200–1316.

Index Locorum

General Index

Compositor: Interactive Composition Corporation
Text: 10/12 Sabon
Display: Sabon
Printer: Braun-Brumfield, Inc.
Binder: Braun-Brumfield, Inc.